Children's Friendships

D1119852

Understanding Children's Worlds
Series Editor: Judy Dunn

The study of children's development can have a profound influence on how children are brought up, cared for and educated. Many psychologists argue that, even if our knowledge is incomplete, we have a responsibility to attempt to help those concerned with the care, education and study of children by making what we know available to them. The central aim of this series is to encourage developmental psychologists to set out the findings and the implications of their research for others – teachers, doctors, social workers, students and fellow researchers – whose work involves the care, education and study of young children and their families. The information and the ideas that have grown from recent research form an important resource which should be available to them. This series provides an opportunity for psychologists to present their work in a way that is interesting, intelligible and substantial, and to discuss what its consequences may be for those who care for, and teach children: not to offer simple prescriptive advice to other professionals, but to make important and innovative research accessible to them.

Children Doing Mathematics
Terezhina Nunes and Peter Bryant

Children and Emotion
Paul L. Harris

Bullying at School
Dan Olweus

How Children Think and Learn (second edition)
David Wood

Making Decisions about Children (second edition)
H. Rudolph Schaffer

Children's Talk in Communities and Classrooms
Lynne Vernon-Feagans

Children and Political Violence
Ed Cairns

The Work of the Imagination
Paul Harris

Children in Changing Families
Jan Pryor and Bryan Rodgers

Young Children Learning
Barbara Tizard and Martin Hughes

Children's Friendships
Judy Dunn

Children's Friendships
The beginnings
of intimacy

Judy Dunn

With a foreword by Jerome S. Bruner

Blackwell
Publishing

© 2004 by Judy Dunn

BLACKWELL PUBLISHING
350 Main Street, Malden, MA 02148-5020, USA
9600 Garsington Road, Oxford OX4 2DQ, UK
550 Swanston Street, Carlton, Victoria 3053, Australia

The right of Judy Dunn to be identified as the Author of this Work has been asserted in accordance with the UK Copyright, Designs, and Patents Act 1988.

All rights reserved. No part of this publication may be reproduced, stored in a retrieval system, or transmitted, in any form or by any means, electronic, mechanical, photocopying, recording or otherwise, except as permitted by the UK Copyright, Designs, and Patents Act 1988, without the prior permission of the publisher.

First published 2004 by Blackwell Publishing Ltd

2   2006

Library of Congress Cataloging-in-Publication Data

Dunn, Judy, 1939–
Children's friendships : the beginnings of intimacy / Judy Dunn.
p. cm. — (Understanding children's worlds)
Includes bibliographical references and index.
ISBN 1-4051-1447-9 (hb) — ISBN 1-4051-1448-7 (pbk)
1. Friendship in children. 2. Social interaction in children. 3. Interpersonal relations in children. I. Title. II. Series.

HQ784.F7D86 2004
302.3'4'083—dc22
2004009018

ISBN-13: 978-1-4051-1447-9 (hb) — ISBN-13: 978-1-4051-1448-6 (pbk)

A catalogue record for this title is available from the British Library.

Set in 10/121/2 pt Sabon
by Graphicraft Ltd, Hong Kong
Printed and bound in the United Kingdom
by TJ International Ltd, Padstow, Cornwall

The publisher's policy is to use permanent paper from mills that operate a sustainable forestry policy, and which has been manufactured from pulp processed using acid-free and elementary chlorine-free practices. Furthermore, the publisher ensures that the text paper and cover board used have met acceptable environmental accreditation standards.

For further information on
Blackwell Publishing, visit our website:
www.blackwellpublishing.com

Contents

Foreword

Jerome S. Bruner

The study of the developing mind in the young of our species has, until recently, been anomalously dedicated to the solo child and his or her developing cognitive powers and skill. What makes it so anomalous is that we now know beyond any reasonable doubt that human intelligence depends upon and is strikingly specialized to assist us in communal and interpersonal enterprises.

The human condition is par excellence dependent upon the forming and maintenance of community – not only institutionally, but at the intimate interpersonal level as well. Sociologists and anthropologists have for over a century been discussing learnedly the importance of primary and secondary groups, of *Gemeinschaft* and *Gesellschaft*, in the conduct of human affairs. The latter, of course, consist of institutional systems for the control and exchange of goods, services and respect. Thanks to the pioneering efforts of such figures as Durkheim, Weber, Malinowski, and others, we have benefited from a century of vigorous research inspired by them.

But what of the more intimate primary groups, how they are formed and sustained and made effective in shaping the more direct and private substrate of our institutionalized societies? In this domain, we human scientists have been curiously narrow in our efforts. Perhaps we have been too preoccupied with the evident pathologies of human interaction (like interpersonal aggression and conflict), or perhaps tempted to limit ourselves to the 'drama of the family' for, after all, it is the family that is crucial to reproduction, to the care of the young and, indeed, to the fomenting of many of our most urgent emotional problems.

But what of such less conspicuous, less flamboyant matters as personal friendship, being together for the pleasure of each other's company? What *is* friendship, and what do we mean when we say that, somehow, we feel committed to our friends? We know in countless indirect (and direct) ways that 'being friendless' is a form of lonely hell. We even have reason to believe now that being friendless is to be less effective in the practical world. But what is involved in *having* and *keeping* friends? And what do we *do* with friends to maintain friendship?

And perhaps most important of all, how and when and under what conditions does a talent for friendship begin to express itself? On what does early friendship grow, what functions does it serve? It is with these questions that Judy Dunn's searching book is concerned. Its scope is broad, yet its observations are detailed and movingly local. This is a book about how kids form friendship, about what is 'shared' among young friends, and about the joys and vicissitudes, the costs and benefits of early friendship.

I must resist the temptation to tell about what's in the book: that's the author's function. But I can't resist letting one cat out of the bag. What has she learned? The principal thing that kid friends share is pretending: pretend games, pretend stories, pretend actions, pretend heroes and villains. In a word, early friendships are the open sesame to possible worlds. And is that so different from us adults 'talking things over with a good friend', again exploring possibilities?

Figures

Acknowledgements

I have been extremely fortunate in having colleagues and students who have made great contributions to several of the studies on which I draw in this book – research we carried out in Cambridge, England, in Colorado, in Pennsylvania and in London. I would especially like to thank Jane Brown, Clare Stocker, Cheryl Slomkowski, Lise Youngblade and Carla Herrera in the US, and Alex Cutting, Claire Hughes, Penny Munn and Lisa Davies in the UK. Particular thanks are due to the children, families, teachers and schools who made the research possible – and fun. The research was funded by the NICHD in the US, and the ESRC and MRC in the UK.

Ross Thompson kindly read the entire manuscript and gave splendidly constructive and lucid advice; I am extremely grateful to him for his wise comments. And many thanks to Sarah Bird at Blackwell for her encouragement, and to Tara McKearney for help with manuscript preparation.

The book is dedicated to Sophie and Lucie, friends from four years to forty.

1

Friends matter

The scene is a small room in a nursery school – empty except for a table and a pile of dressing-up clothes and toys. Alone in the room, Harry and Joe, two four-year-olds who've been together at the nursery for the last year, begin investigating the dressing-up clothes, and a story of high adventure begins. First they are pirates sailing on a search for treasure, then their ship is wrecked, and they are attacked by sharks; they reach the safety of an island, and build a house (under the table). What to eat, and how to cook it are problems that are ingeniously solved. Their elaborate adventure, their quickly solved disputes (are they being attacked by sharks or by crocodiles?), their extended conversations about what happens next – all are captured by our video-camera in the corner of the room.[1]

The absorption of Harry and Joe in their joint adventure is striking, and so is the skill with which they tune into the shared narrative. Their discussion of whether and how they'll escape the sharks/crocodiles, their amusement at the scatological turns the conversation takes – all this is so unlike what happens with their parents, with the other children in the nursery, or with Harry's (for the most part despised) younger sister. Note three features of this exciting and complicated joint enterprise:

- The pirate adventure depends on *both* children – on the coordination of their ideas and imagination. It wouldn't happen unless they joined together in the story.
- Sharing ideas like this is a considerable intellectual feat for such young children – it is the beginning of intimacy.
- It is emotionally absorbing, and exciting for both children.

Joint adventures like this are key to the relationship between Harry and Joe. And it is a relationship that matters very much to both children; when Joe is away from nursery, Harry is distressed and clearly misses him –

and vice versa. Their relationship began over a year ago, and continues for the next three years that the boys take part in our research.

Is it appropriate to think of Harry and Joe's relationship as *friendship*?

The nature of young children's friendships

There's a long history to the debate about what constitutes friendship. Most people agree that a crucial feature of friendship is that it is a reciprocal relationship between two people with both affirming it.[2] Reciprocity or mutuality of affection is of particular significance: such reciprocity distinguishes friendship from one child's desire to be liked by another, when that other doesn't return the preference. It also distinguishes friendship from acceptance by a group of peers, or popularity. Acceptance describes the tendency of a group of children to like a particular child; how that child sees the others in the group is not relevant – so acceptance is a 'one-way' construct.[3] Friendship is a voluntary relationship, not one that is prescribed or obligatory (so it excludes those relationships where one child has been assigned to be the 'buddy' of a new child starting school, for instance). Those who study friendship in 'middle' childhood (say from 8 to 12 years old) commonly describe friendship as a relationship that includes *companionship, intimacy and affection*.[4] (*Loyalty* and *commitment* are also seen as key features of adult friendships, but are assumed to be achieved only at adolescence). When children are old enough to talk or write about their perceptions of their friendships, they do indeed refer to companionship, intimacy and affection, and they talk about these dimensions of friendship in describing their satisfaction (or otherwise) with the friendship.[5]

The relationship between Harry and Joe is certainly one of companionship and affection, mutually expressed. And the first glimmerings of intimacy are evident in their sharing of their imaginative world. When do such relationships between young children begin? And when does *support* and *concern* for a friend's feelings and well-being develop? If we watch and listen carefully to children, what can we learn about the growth of intimacy between them?

The first theme of this book is that important relationships with other children begin very early. With the evidence from the recent studies of toddlers and young preschoolers, the first challenge we tackle is to understand what kind of friendships very young children have with each other, and how these change with development. Of course, children don't leap into full-blown intense friendships that are loyal and committed relationships, during the preschool and early school years. It is with the development of the features of sharing feelings and ideas, of mutual affection and attachment, of concern for the other, which lead eventually to commitment and loyalty, that this book is concerned. Is the developmental story that emerges simply an account of growing social skills? No. There is an important distinction between social skills, and friendship as an intimate bond. Social skills can be used for self-promotion and gaining self-interested goals, *or* to cooperate with, care for, and support another; they can be used to win arguments and get your own way, or to solve disagreements in the interests of the other, or of both. Friendship is indeed a forum for developing social skills and understanding of another person, but it is much more.

Why is it important to study friendship?

First, it is important because friends *matter* to children. We are missing a major piece of what excites, pleases, and upsets children, what is central to their lives even in the years before school, if we don't attend to what happens between children and their friends. The pleasures, but also the betrayals, the jealousies and tangled intrigues, make friendships key to the quality of children's lives. The focus of most research on children's social development until relatively recently, though, has been either on their relationships with their parents, or on their relations with the group of classmates at school – their popularity or isolation in the classroom or playground – as the major players in children's development.[6] Less attention has been paid to the close relationships within individual pairs or triads of friends. Yet friends are very often, as parents know, far more exciting companions than parents; they are figures who can make or break children's pleasure and happiness. Harry and Joe's shared imaginative world was one of particular excitement – not a feature of their other relationships. The experiences of rejection by other children, or of acceptance and popularity, are undoubtedly important for children's later development and adjustment, but what happens between friends is different – and *also* important for children's development and adjustment.

Second, it is important to study friends because young friends can also be important as *emotional supports*. At key turning points in children's lives, we now know, having a close friend can make a real difference to how children manage those transitions. Take the transition to 'real' school faced by five- and six-year-olds – often a stressful experience for children, even if they have been at day care or preschool. How children cope with the demands of that new world of school is closely linked to the kind of relationships that they have with friends when they first start school. For even younger children, there is a striking example of the support that friends can provide, at which we will look in detail in Chapter 5. This is the evidence that a close friendship may well buffer a child from the stress of the family upheaval when a new sibling is born. The ways in which friends provide support are likely to change as children grow up, of course, and those patterns of change will be examined in the chapters that follow.

And there's a third reason why it is important to describe and understand the early relationships between young children today. Many small children spend major parts of their days outside the family in day care or nurseries, in the company of other children. The issue of what kind of social relationships they have with these others is of increasing social significance – reflected in a recent surge of research on children in childcare settings. If we are to understand the full impact of these experiences we need to know what kinds of relationships children form with other children, and what these relationships imply developmentally.

But a close look at children in the context of their friendships does more than illuminate the early stages of an important relationship. It gives us a new window on children's cognitive and social development – their understanding of their social world – and on how their friendship experiences influence the development of that understanding, and vice versa.

Friends and the development of understanding others

Here are two incidents described by Lawrence Blum, a philosopher who watched the development of his own daughter Sarah's understanding of her friends.[7] Sarah was only two years old in the first incident, and three in the second:

Sarah, 2 years 3 months, is riding in the car with her cousin Ali, who is 4. Ali is upset because she does not have her teddy bear, and there is a fairly extended discussion about how the bear is probably in the trunk and can be retrieved when they arrive at the house. About ten minutes pass and as the car approaches the house Sarah says to Ali, 'Now you can get your bear' . . .

Sarah, 3, gives Clara 3 (her friend), her own Donald Duck cap (to keep 'forever') saying that she has done so because Clara has (recently, but not at the moment) lost her (Boston) Celtics cap.

Sarah is not just sensitive to her friend's immediate needs; she draws on her memory and her understanding of what her cousin and friend like, she wants to make them both happier. In this concern about their happiness and feelings we see the beginnings of children's moral understanding. The second theme of this book is that careful study of young friends gives us a different view of children than the perspective we gain from studying children with adults. It presents distinctive evidence on the nature of children's grasp of what other people feel, think and believe, and the connections between people's beliefs and thoughts and the way they act. This ability to 'mind-read' is an absolutely core feature of being human, and a major milestone in children's development. The evidence from young friends gives us a fresh perspective on children's developing understanding of self and of others – their family as well as their friends, a window on what they understand about the social world more broadly, and on their sensibility and views on moral issues.

Why should a focus on children with their friends be so revealing? The argument here is that it is because of the distinctive features of young children's friendships that we gain this window on what children know and understand about the social world. A friendship is usually a child's first close relationship outside the family, and it can be very different in nature from family relationships with parents or with brothers and sisters. Consider the adventure of Harry and Joe with which we began. The distinctive features of young friends' relationships include the *emotional* quality of the relationship, closely linked to the nature of the *particular games and conversations* which friends share.

First, the emotions – the affection, the excitement, the jealousy, the interest children have in their friends. Children care about their friends, and they are often highly motivated to stay friends, in spite of disagreements and tensions. They *want* to sort out quarrels with their friends – whereas with their siblings they often don't bother or don't care (or even enjoy the power play, if they win). A friendship is often the first relationship in which children begin to care about and try to understand someone else, and to respond to the feelings, needs and troubles of another. Talk to a seven-year-old about his friend and you will be surprised by the depth of his grasp of how this friend sees the world. He can tell you what his friend is upset about, and what would cheer and amuse him. You may well be surprised by the subtlety of his understanding and by how much he cares about his friend.

Here are some examples from a study by Inge Bretherton and her colleagues,[8] which illustrate the subtlety of six- and seven-year-old children's emotional understanding in the context of their friendships:

[1] A 7-year-old explains to his mother about an incident at school where he accidentally hit another boy:

'And I tried to go up to Jim to play with him again, but he won't come near me. And he's not . . . when a kid isn't really your friend yet, they don't know you didn't mean to do it to them'.

[2] Another 7-year-old explains to a friend why another child did not respond to friend's efforts to comfort her:

'Well that's all right. Sometimes when I hit you and then I want to comfort you, you push me away because you're still angry.'

You see a very different side of a child in the context of his friendships: Empathy, concern and understanding of the other person can be evident in very young children talking to and about their friends. If we eavesdrop on friends talking (as we will throughout this book) we get glimpses of that private, different world outside the family that is so important to them, and of how they function in it.

How soon does this understanding of the feelings and needs of another begin? Is it among children in the middle school years, and in adolescence that it is evident? We will see in the next two chapters that the evidence points much earlier – to the preschool years. And why is it the interaction between *friends* that is revealing? The argument of this book is that particular features of what happens between young friends – such as the sharing of fantasy play, and the discussion of why people behave the way they do that this play involves – are closely implicated in the early stages of children's understanding of others. More generally, we find that the experience of cooperating with a friend or sibling – child-to-child interaction – has a special role in the development of social understanding.

Friends and moral understanding

The emotional quality of friendship is also implicated in children's growing moral sensibility. In a centrally important sense friendship is the crucible in which moral sensibility is formed. Because children care about their friends, they think about their needs and rights in a way that is quite different from their views on moral issues when they are asked about hypothetical situations – and quite differently from how they think about morals when their siblings are involved. 'It's fine to take a toy from her, 'cause she's only my sister!' says a five-year-old, who was adamant that he'd not take a toy from his friend.[9] So what we learn from listening to children talking with their friends is very different from the messages about moral development we gain from 'testing' children in other situation.

As well as the emotional quality of friendships, the power relations between friends are also implicated in their growing moral sensibility. The power politics of parent–child and brother–sister relationships are quite different from those of friendships: children are usually much closer to their friends in status and dominance than they are with their siblings or parents. And this may be important in explaining why friendships can foster moral understanding – a point made many decades ago by Jean Piaget.[10] He suggested that arguments *between children* were of special significance in the growth of children's understanding of moral issues. With adults, he argued, children face a disparity in status that makes it hard for them to argue back, or see the other person's point of view. We may feel that nowadays the power differentials between child and adult are very far from those of Piaget's day – that parents are no longer held in respect as authority figures as they were in Piaget's Geneva of 80 years ago – but the story of the recent research bears out Piaget's view that between peers, disputes and conversations about the social world carry special developmental significance.

The other feature of friendship that is a key contributor to children's growing understanding of the social world is that it marks the beginning of a new independence from parents. Children throughout our evolutionary history, and currently in many cultures other than those of North America and Europe, grow up not in isolated nuclear families, but within a wider world of others, including children – sisters, brothers, playmates, loose-knit gangs of children. This world of other children means opportunities for friendship, enmities, gang life, leaders and followers. It means opportunities for working out the intricate balance of power and status between people, for sharing imaginative experiences, for understanding and manipulating the feelings and ideas of others, for a range of relationships that differ greatly from those of parents-with-children. The psychologist and psychoanalyst Susan Isaacs who documented young children's early friendships and group relations in her famous nursery school in Cambridge in the 1930s, saw the key role of friendships in children's increasing independence from their parents like this:[11] 'Under the shelter of this alliance with others of his own age that child wins his first real independence of his parents and teachers, and begins to see them more nearly as they are. They cease to be the gods, the giants and the ogres that they were . . .'

Individual differences and the impact of friends on children's development

The third theme of the book concerns individual differences. Eavesdropping on children talking, as we do in this book, also teaches us not to be sentimental about children's friendships. The birth of intimate relationships outside the family can mean the growth of jealousy and insecurity, and new experiences of rejection and loss. Understanding someone well is no guarantee of kindness and support. It can also mean a new dimension to teasing and bullying. One group of psychologists, struck by the viciousness of some of the behaviour they recorded in a careful observational study of young children at school, described the classroom as more the source of criminal behaviour than a nursery of morality.

What is clear is that the quality of children's friendships varies tremendously. Harry and Joe, with whom we began, shared an imaginative world of joint pretence that ran through their friendship for years. Other friends are less engaged in a world of make-believe. Some share intimacies, problems, secrets, and talk endlessly about the network of relationships among their peers. Others are good companions in the world of sports, but rarely discuss their feelings or problems. Some draw each other into deviancy. Some children move in a group of loose-knit connections between a number of others, some have just one very close friend. Some children enjoy and flourish in solitude – we certainly should not assume that children are *only* happy with friends. We will look in this book at what we know about why these differences develop, and what they imply for children's relationships and adjustment as they grow towards adolescence and adulthood. It is crucial to appreciate these individual differences in children's friendships, if we are to understand how friends affect children's development. There is not just one kind of friendship, and we have learned that it is the kind of friendship children experience, and who their friends are, that matter in terms of developmental impact.

Differences between boys and girls in the kinds of friendship they form are often evident, in the school years. For instance, girls, some studies suggest, are more intimate with their friends, sharing secrets, and disclosing their own feelings more than boys do, but there are also special tensions and traumas in girls' cliques, and in the making and breaking of friendships. What do these gender differences in patterns of friendships within and outside cliques imply for later in life, and what influences their development? What about those all-too-rare cross-gender friendships which can flourish 'underground', away from the critical eyes of the other kids at school? Are they, in fact, so rare? And do they differ from the friendships of boys with boys, and girls with girls? We look in Chapter 7 at these matters of gender.

Family and friends

Individual differences in the quality of children's friendships are indisputably clear. A key issue is the question of whether and how children's relationships with their friends are, or are not, linked to their family relationships. What connections are there between difficulties with friends – loneliness, trouble in making friends – and children's relationships with parents and siblings? What about that issue that can loom so large for parents – how to protect their children from those *unsuitable* friends: to interfere or not to interfere in their friendships? There is a long history to parental concern with the dangers of children's involvement with other children, illustrated in documentation from the early years of immigrant life in the urban centres of the US.[12] Life on the streets with other children could be a liberating experience for the children, but their parents were concerned that these experiences with other children meant growing away from the values and traditions of their immigrant parents. In the 1920s and 1930s parental fears about urban gangs and the pernicious influence of other children led to advice from psychologists for parents to supervise friendships, to monitor their children's relations with other children and to become involved themselves in the children's networks of friends. 'Parents as pals' became the catchword. Fathers especially were exhorted to be 'a boy yourself', to 'travel the road with your son'.

The idea of parental management of children's relations with other children is still with us now. Social forces in the last decade certainly have not decreased parental anxieties about their children's lives outside the family. On the one hand, there are concerns about the very real risks and dangers of deviance and drugs – introduced often by other school-aged children. On the other hand, the suggestion from experts that the quality of parents' relations with their young children is central to the children's adjustment and their ability to form and keep good friendships is still prominent, and leads to a real pressure on parents. In Chapter 8 these ideas are examined critically.

The book is firmly based in the real world of children. I draw on studies of children growing up in the US, in the UK, Italy, Israel. All the quotations of children talking to their friends, or about their experiences are real children speaking.[13] The pleasures and conflicts, excitements and difficulties that their conversations reveal illustrate the arguments of the book, which are based on systematic, quantitative studies of children with their friends and families. In summary:

- The first theme concerns the nature of children's developing relationships with other children, and what has been learned from a close look at what happens between children. This attention to early friendships shows us how much friends can matter to young children, that young children's friendships are in an important sense real relationships, not just the sum of two individuals' acts, and that their relationships differ from those of parents-and-children or siblings.

- The second theme is that our understanding of the nature of children's cognitive and emotional development can be illuminated by studying them within these relationships: the first intimate relationships outside the family. A close look at young friends shows us the link between caring about someone, and understanding them – a two-way connection that underlies all our important relationships, as adults as well as children. It is this combination of emotion and understanding that makes friendship a relationship of great potential influence on children's development – influence for good or for problems in adjustment. Friends can foster each other's development or get them in deep trouble. The intensity of what children can feel about their friends, coupled with their familiarity and intimacy, means that this can be a relationship of great power in influencing the development of their social understanding, their self-confidence, and their later relationships.

- The third theme, then, is that the nature of this developmental influence depends on the quality of the friendship, and that individual differences in the various dimensions of friendship are key. To assess developmental impact we need to understand how friendships differ in terms of affection and support, of intimacy and sharing secrets, of the 'meeting of minds' evident in connectedness of communication and play, of power dynamics and control.

The book is based on the recent research interest in young friends, but its argument is illustrated also by drawing on the biographies and auto-biographies of writers who have illuminated for us the part that friends played in their childhood experiences and their imaginative growth, and the power of the emotional quality of friendships in early childhood (so hard for psychologists to capture).

Friendships are formed in a particular time and place, a particular social world. Differences in time, place and culture mean that children have different opportunities to make friends; the forms and culture of friendships may well differ too. For children in the inner city ghettos, in the rural Appalachians, and in the prep schools of middle England, the opportunities for developing close relations with other children differ. What friends do together will differ in some ways too. The significance of friendships for children's development and their wellbeing will differ too, with time and place. In the extreme case of the children growing up in the concentration camps of the holocaust, or the homeless children of bombed cities in the Second World War, close friendships were a crucial source of emotional support and security. For children growing up today in ordinary families, friends are less likely to be such key security figures, at least in the early years of childhood; yet the increasing number of children spending much of their early years in day care or preschool, in a world of other children rather than their close families, raises the question of what kinds of close relationships they have with these others, and what developmental impact such child–child relations may have. For children enduring the horrors of boarding schools in the nineteenth and early twentieth centuries, friends – or the loss of friends – could make or break their spirits. Again, for children who are not subjected to such boarding school experiences, friends could well play a less central role in children's wellbeing. Yet the vulnerability of children to the betrayals and pain of broken friendship is not tied to time or place – a point that is brought home to us by comparing Margaret Atwood's poignant account of bullying and suffering in a quartet of nine-year-old friends in Toronto in the 1950s in her novel *Cat's Eye*, with the autobiographical accounts of being bullied by some of the writers from earlier times. A searing account is given by the nineteenth century novelist Anthony Trollope in his *Autobiography* of the bullying he received at school, while Graham Greene in his autobiography *A Sort of Life* describes the life-long impact of being bullied and tormented by two 'friends'.

The excitement, the pleasures, problems and humour, the compelling intensity of these relationships with friends (and enemies) in writers' early lives and their fiction are interwoven in the book with the present-day examples from the children in our research and that of others. The message is that the excitement and dramas of children's changing worlds of friends can not only amuse and move us, but greatly enlighten us about ourselves, our families and friends.

2

Beginnings

Reggie (18–20 months) and Jeffrey (15–17 months) had become great friends. They always played with each other and hardly ever took notice of another child. This friendship had lasted for about two months when Reggie went home. Jeffrey missed him very much; he hardly played during the following days and sucked his thumb more than usual. (Burlingham and Freud, 1944)

Do very young children have friends? Reggie and Jeffrey were children in the Hampstead Nursery, a residential nursery for children orphaned, or made homeless or destitute, in the Second World War. Anna Freud and Dorothy Burlingham, both psychoanalysts, were interested in how these experiences affected the children's emotional relationships; they carefully observed and recorded the children's behaviour and relationships in the nursery.[1] Friendships like that of Jeffrey and Reggie were, in the view of Freud and Burlingham, real attachments, and not uncommon among the children in the nursery. 'We observe many instances of friendship among infants which last days, weeks, or even months. Playmates are certainly not chosen indiscriminately; in playing together the partner often seems no less important than the game', Freud and Burlingham commented. In the circumstances of the nursery, they argued, the children developed a surprising range of responses to one another: 'love, hate, jealousy, rivalry, competition, protectiveness, pity, generosity, sympathy, and even understanding'.[2]

But the view that such very young children can form friendships is one that is at odds with what many people would expect. Until quite recently, many psychologists would have said that it is not until six or seven years old that children usually begin to form friendships outside the family, in the sense of stable, reciprocal, affectionate relationships with other children, and that intimacy and loyalty in such friendships are even later developments.

If we take friendship to include understanding and sharing the other person's interests and ideas, as well as mutual affection and support, then friendship between toddlers and very young preschoolers appears at first sight to be ruled out, on the grounds that toddlers lack much capacity to understand others' feelings or to read their intentions with sophistication. But how does the idea that children under four or five cannot or do not form friendships square with the account of Reggie and Jeffrey with which we began? They were after all not yet 20 months old. And how does it fit with the observations of the other pairs of friends that Dorothy Burlingham and Anna Freud described in their Hampstead Nursery? In this chapter we look at the evidence on the kind of close relationships that some toddlers form and how these develop over the second and third years; we also look at their understanding of others' feelings and intentions over this period, as it is reflected in their close relationships.

What the observations of Burlingham and Freud show is that under some circumstances, some pairs of children *even before they are two years old* seek out each other as companions, prefer to be together rather than with others, try to comfort each other in distress, express shared happiness together, and are unhappy if they are separated. The affection these little children in the Hampstead Nursery expressed was often striking. Here for instance is an incident between Paul, aged two, and Sophie, a 19-month-old:

> The nurse who entered the rest room during the children's afternoon nap found Paul (2 years) and Sophie (19 months) standing at one end of their cots kissing each other. She was amused and laughed. Paul turned around and smiled at her for a moment, then again held Sophie's head between both his hands and kissed her over and over again. Sophie smiled and was obviously pleased.[3]

It is of course possible that the attachments these very young children showed one another were the result of their unusual experiences in the war, without their families. Anna Freud herself did not think that such relationships would be found in children who were brought up in families. Within ordinary families, she suggested, relationships with other children develop 'only after the child–mother relationship has been firmly established.' Yet the way that Reggie, Jeffrey and the other nursery children behaved shows us that children have the *capacity* to express affection and concern, and to be attached to other children – even before they are two years old.

Evidence from sibling relationships

There is a second, powerful line of evidence that echoes the observations of the young children in the Hampstead Nursery. We don't have to look outside ordinary families to see that some very young children can and do form close relationships with other children. This evidence comes from what we see brothers and sisters doing together. What we can learn from watching siblings is relevant to the issue of friendship because the evidence is key to the issue of what capacities very young children have for sharing affection and support, and for their understanding other people. So we will briefly summarize what's been learned from sisters and brothers, before turning to the evidence on children's understanding that comes directly from watching and listening to young children with their friends.

In the first of our longitudinal studies of siblings, we included observations during the infancy of second-born children. We studied these babies and toddlers with their older brothers and sisters by watching the children together at home, tape-recording their conversations and play, talking to their mothers, and repeatedly visiting the families as the children grew up.[4] Many of the mothers commented vividly on how much they thought their baby missed the older sibling when the two children were apart, even when the babies were only eight or fourteen months old. Here are some typical comments by mothers in the study, describing their eight-month-old babies' interest in their older siblings:

> She thinks he's marvellous. Hero-worships him. If he plays with her foot, she kills herself laughing. She doesn't cry till he goes out of the room.

> She misses him a great deal if he isn't there. Shouts till she hears him in the morning. Fusses till she can see him. I'm not enough.

Many of the firstborn siblings in this study even before they were three years old showed real concern, and practical attempts to comfort, if their baby sibling was distressed. The children's affection and delight in each other's company and their attempts to support and comfort each other were clear to both their parents and to observers. At 14 months old, over half of the second-born babies we studied, when they were distressed, went to their older siblings for comfort; half of the sample were described as missing their older sibling if he or she was not there, and over a third of these were reported to miss the older sibling very much indeed. In the context of this affectionate relationship, they showed increasingly appropriate attempts to comfort their older siblings, and increasing concern over their distress – signs of appreciation of the other child's feelings.

Note that evidence of the negative side of siblings' relationships can also inform us about their understanding of each other. Siblings can be famously aggressive and hostile to one another, and many children show a powerful mixture of both friendliness and hostility to their brothers and sisters, depending on the circumstances. And this too provides key evidence on the nature of young children's understanding of other children. Teasing, for example, reflects some understanding of what will annoy or upset a particular person. The toddlers that we studied in two further studies in Cambridge began to tease both their mothers and *especially* their older siblings with increasing frequency between 15 months and the end of their second year.[5] The teasing actions were often finely adjusted to upset the feelings of their older siblings.

Here are some actions by toddlers between 15 and 23 months old that we observed, each neatly 'tuned' to what would upset their older sibling:

- removing the sibling's comfort object in the course of a fight;
- leaving a fight in order to go and destroy an object cherished by the older sibling;
- pulling the sibling's thumb (sucked in moments of stress) out of his mouth;
- fetching a toy spider and pushing it in the face of a sibling who was afraid of spiders.

The incidents of teasing observed in this study became both more frequent and more elaborate during the course of the second year. Ruth, aged 24 months, teased her older sister in an especially remarkable way. Her four-year-old sister had three imaginary friends, named Lily, Allelujah, and Peepee – these were very important figures in her sister's life. When the sisters were in conflict, Ruth taunted her older sister by announcing that *she* (Ruth) was Allelujah. It was an act that reliably infuriated her sister; it was also an act of considerable intellectual virtuosity for a 24-month-old child – to take on the identity of an imaginary friend of her sister!

Teasing mothers was also quite frequent in our observations (though it did not usually reach the elaboration of the teasing inflicted on siblings). Of 45 children in this study, 36 were observed to tease other family members by 24 months old. Mother-teasing was closely tuned to what might upset the mothers, just as teasing the sibling was tuned to annoy the sibling. The triumphant announcement that 'I don't love you, Mommy!'

was a technique already developed by 24 months by two of the children
in our study.

Evidence for attachment between siblings

The pleasure, affection and understanding that children in their second
and third year can on occasion show towards their siblings are key to the
matter of whether very young children do indeed have the capacity to form
close relationships with other children. The evidence from siblings is that
without doubt some children are very attached to their older siblings from
early in their second year, and sometimes from even earlier.[6] It is their
sibling that they want to play with, more than any other family members;
they show a delight in their games together, concern when the other is
upset, and distress when the sibling leaves, and by three years a degree of
cooperation in games that reflects a sharing of interests and attention.

Evidence for attachment between siblings has also been gathered
in experimental settings – in the classic 'Strange Situation' developed for
investigating the security of the attachment bond between child and
parent.[7] In this procedure, children are observed in a sequence of situations in which they are first separated from their parent figure and then
reunited with them. The children's emotional and behavioural responses
to this stressful sequence are used to characterize the security or insecurity
of their relationship with their attachment figure. When one-year-olds
and toddlers were studied in a sequence of separations from their mothers,
in the presence of their older siblings, the evidence showed that some
infants directed attachment behaviour towards their older siblings, and
that children of four years old can and do act as sources of security
for infant siblings. Over half of a group of older siblings aged 30 to
58 months were observed to provide care-giving and nurturance to their
younger siblings when they were distressed when their mothers left. And
the babies showed attachment behaviour by approaching and keeping
close to the older sibling when their mothers were away, but not when
they were present.[8]

So the evidence from children in residential nurseries and from siblings
shows us that very young children can show considerable understanding
of what will upset or comfort other children with whom they share a
familiar world; their cooperation in play, too, often reveals understanding of what the other child has in mind. They also demonstrate some
attachment behaviours towards their siblings, as toddlers, and can use
them as sources of security. Do children who grow up in families in fact

also develop close relationships – in terms of reciprocal, affectionate companionship – with other children outside the family, when they are very young? And if they do become close, what kind of relationships develop between very young friends, and how do these relationships change as children grow up?

The answer to the first question is yes. If children have an opportunity to spend time with other children and get to know each other well (in day care or at preschool, for instance) some develop preferences for particular companions, even as two-year-olds. Carollee Howes in Los Angeles has carried out a series of masterly studies of toddlers and preschool children in various day care settings, including family day care (child minders), and including children from early in their second year, followed through toddlerhood and the preschool years.[9] Her careful observations and detailed coding of the children's play – who they choose to play with, *how* and *what* they play together – has shown unequivocally that many form mutual, close relationships with other children. And there are three striking features of these early relationships – features that are a real surprise to us if we assume these very young children are unable to form friendships. The first is the stability of the relationships between these very young children, the second is the reciprocal quality of their relationships, and the third is the developing sophistication of their social understanding.

Evidence on stability

These early friendships between toddlers and preschoolers can last over several years – they can be quite stable relationships. In the Los Angeles studies of Carollee Howes, between 50 and 70 per cent of the friendships were maintained from one year to the next. In our own Pennsylvanian project a similar pattern of stable relationships emerged.[10] On average, the 50 children we studied as 47-month-olds with their friends had been friends for *two years previously*. And in our London study of friendship, the children – again seen before they were four years old – had on average been friends for about two years. But how does the evidence for the stability of some of these early friendships fit with the well-known taunts heard among preschoolers like 'I won't be your friend', and the widespread impression people have that friendships in the preschool or nursery are fleeting, and the children all-too fickle?

If you listen to three- and four-year-olds playing in day care, you may well witness incidents like the next exchange – which support that reputation of preschoolers for fickleness. It comes from Bill Corsaro's work on preschoolers.[11] Preschooler Barbara's comment is that she and Nancy do not like Linda today.

BARBARA TO LINDA:	You can't play.
LINDA TO BARBARA:	Yes I can . . .
BARBARA TO LINDA:	No you can't. We don't like you today.
NANCY TO LINDA:	You are not our friend.

It is certainly the case that three- and four-year-olds use references to friendship as a weapon in their armoury, especially to exclude others when they do not for the moment want them to intrude in a game. Here is another typical incident drawn from a group of three-year-olds in Corsaro's study. Denny and Leah are running around pretending to be lions, roaring. Glen, who had been playing with Denny earlier, approaches the two lions, who both roar aggressively at him.

DENNY TO GLEN:	Grr-grr. We don't like you.
LEAH TO GLEN:	Grr-grr.
GLEN TO DENNY:	You were my friend a minute ago.
DENNY TO GLEN:	Yeah.
GLEN TO DENNY:	Well, if you keep going 'grr' you can't be my friend anymore.
DENNY TO GLEN:	Well then I'm not your friend.

Denny uses denial of friendship to 'protect' his game (tête-à-tête) with Leah, while Glen uses the threat of denial of friendship as a strategy to overcome Denny's resistance. The children's idea of friendship and the way that they talk about it is clearly very different from our own. However this does not mean that no children of this age range have close or stable relationships with other children. It does remind us of how much the close relationships between young children may be affected by the group situations in which they find themselves – an issue that becomes even more important when they start elementary/primary school, as we will see in the next chapter.

Evidence on reciprocal relationships in toddlers

A friendship by definition involves two children, and reciprocity between the two. Hildy Ross and her colleagues have carefully studied toddlers playing and in conflict together to see whether we can really consider their interactions as reciprocal, whether they are influenced over time by *who* the child is interacting with and by what the previous exchanges between these particular children were like.[12] Their observational research showed that toddlers can and do develop such reciprocal relationships – in terms of both their friendly interactions and their conflicts. They studied 32 children of 20 or 30 months old grouped in same-age pairs, with each pair of children observed for 18 play sessions of 40 minutes which alternated between the children's homes. Hildy Ross and Susan Lollis make the case for considering the interactions between particular pairs of the toddlers they studied as *relationships* on the grounds of the marked contrast between the behaviour shown by each child when playing with a particular child (the friend), and behaviour shown by the same child in a different social context. That is, they distinguished a *relationship* effect from the individual effects of behaviour shown by each child towards peers in general. Moreover, they showed that children made friendly initiations specifically towards those who had been friendly towards them earlier: reciprocal exchanges of friendly overtures characterized particular pairs, and these relationship effects increased in prominence over the times that the children spent together.

Interestingly, in research on toddlers from kibbutzim (who were especially familiar with one another as they had spent much time together from early infancy) Hildy Ross and her colleagues also observed reciprocal patterns of conflict, in which children displayed antagonistic behaviour towards particular other toddlers – *who had previously shown similar levels of antagonistic action.*[13] That is, the children picked out particular children with whom they were most often in conflict, but as Ross points out, these were typically the same children with whom they also most frequently played in a friendly way. These were 'fighting friends', and their conflict arose in the course of their play. In the preschool years, it has been shown, children also have more conflict with friends than with other children:[14] these conflicts are less hostile than conflicts with other children who are *not* friends, and less likely to end with one child 'winning'. In the context of friendship, young children seem more able to resolve disagreements.

Evidence on cooperation and sophistication of understanding

Not only are these early reciprocal relationships frequently quite stable – they are also surprisingly sophisticated. Pairs of children who are friends often play together in a particularly grown up, mature way, in the sense that they manage to *cooperate* in games, to understand something of what the other child intends, and to share an imaginary world. By two- and three-year-old standards, they are the sophisticates. These issues of cooperation and especially of sharing in an imaginary world are key. They are central to understanding why, as children reach four years old, they find it easier than they did as two-year-olds to make and keep friends. They are also key to understanding why playing with a friend is a wonderful context for learning.

To see the changes in how children cooperate, as they grow up, com-pare these two incidents, drawn from a study in Cambridge.[15]

1   Jamey, 20 months old, looks at Tommy, 18 months. When Jamey bangs on a box, shouting 'waaaa!' Tommy laughs, joins him, bangs on another box, also shouting 'waaa!'
2   Jonny, 24 months, joins his friend three-year-old Kevin who is pre-tending to go on a picnic. Jonny, on instruction from Kevin, fills the car with petrol, 'drives' the car, then gets the 'food' out, pretends to eat it, says he doesn't like it! Both boys pretend to spit out the food, saying 'yuk!' laughing.

Both Tommy and Jonny are excited and happy, playing with their friends. But clearly there's a big change, even over the short six months difference in age of the two boys, between how Tommy plays 'with' his companion at 18 months, and the relative sophistication of Jonny's elaborate game as a 24-month old. This matter of *how* children cooperate, and what they cooperate over, is one of the keys to the beginnings of friendship. At 18 months, many children, like Tommy in the first example, will watch their companion, imitate, and join together to do the same thing – often with giggling, and excitement.[16] There does seem to be a particular thrill *at doing the same thing together* (premonition of the pleasures of football crowds, raves and pop concerts?). But over the next few months, children begin to do something much more complicated: They manage to contribute new ideas to the play, as Jonny did when he pretended to dislike the food, and express disgust (always a great source of amusement to preschoolers and toddlers). Suddenly the possibilities for cooperation and joint pretend play expand dramatically.

Most children make a 'great leap forward' in the way they play and cooperate with others, between about 18 months and two and a half years.[17] The developments during the second year include the increasing frequency of mutual imitation, in which both children are aware of being imitated, and sequences of turn-taking that become longer and more elaborate as the children reach two years old. One way of investigating whether children can cooperate is by giving them problems that can only be solved if the children work together. Here, the job the children confront is usually much harder than cooperating in play. In a game, yes, children do have to fit their own behaviour into an overall goal shared with the other kids, but there is still plenty of opportunity to take the 'theme' of the game in a new anarchic direction. For instance, if you are trying to play catch, and the ball rolls away from you, you can pretend it is now an animal that you are chasing, and simply change the nature of the game – as long as your companion doesn't go wild with fury. But if you are faced with a cooperation-problem task set by a psychologist, – the cunning scientist has usually designed the problem so that there is only one solution, which depends on you both cooperating in a particular way. There is simply no leeway for other ways of solving it. When very young children are given these kinds of task, we see the same developmental changes in children's ability to cooperate that is clear in their play with other children. They simply fail these tasks as 18-month-olds, and are increasingly successful as they reach two years old.

So there are big changes in children's ability to think and plan, to coordinate their actions with those of another child as they reach two years old. These changes are key to their success in solving joint problems, but they are also crucial in being able to cooperate in elaborate play with another child who may not be prepared to make all the allowances that devoted parents do to keep the play going with a toddler.

Here, changes in how well children can manage their frustration and anger are also important. There are bound to be disputes and conflict as children play together, and as every parent knows, toddlers do not yet have much skill at holding back their own emotional outbursts or their impulsive actions. This 'emotion regulation' turns out to be important in maintaining children's play on an even keel. There are striking developmental changes between 18 months and two and a half years in most children's self-control – there are also notable individual differences in this self-control,[18] and as we will see these are important influences on the kind of friendship that develops between children.

Evidence on developments in shared pretend: a key to early friendship

Planning, holding back on one's own impulsive actions, monitoring what the other kid is trying to do – all these are clearly key to managing to play with another child. But there is surely much more to being an exciting companion for a two-year-old than planning and holding your own wishes back (if only briefly). The key to these early relationships between children – and the domain that makes friendship so interesting and developmentally important – concerns the children's shared imaginative play.

Compare the children's joint play in the following three incidents, drawn from one of our Cambridge studies, in which we observed the children every three months during their second year.[19]

1 Dan (16 months) pretends to 'feed' himself, with a wooden spoon, from an empty saucepan, watching Ben (15 months) as he does so. Ben watches him, with a neutral expression.
2 Jane (18 months) pushes doll in toy pushchair, looks at Elly (18 months) who watches her. Elly puts her doll in second toy pushchair. Both walk round the room pushing their dolls.
3 Jane (21 months) puts doll to bed. Elly (21 months) brings teddy to put him in the bed too. Both pull the cover up, watch each other, smiling.

These incidents illustrate some of the developmental changes during the second year in children's joint pretend play, which Carollee Howes and her colleagues documented systematically in the pairs of toddlers that they studied. From these observations they developed a scale that reflected the increasing integration of the partners' pretend play.[20] In the first incident (1) above, Ben simply watches Dan's pretence actions without joining in or imitating, illustrating the lowest level on Howes's scale. Incident (2), Jane and Elly's doll-in-pushchair play, illustrates the essentially parallel social pretend that Howes categorized as level 2. Then the increasing integration of social pretend of the two children (level 3 on the scale) is illustrated by incident (3).

By 24 months the children Howes studied were beginning to engage actively together in a shared familiar theme (such as having tea) in which each partner took part in actions that were recognized by both as appropriate to the theme: between 24 and 30 months these actions became increasingly integrated between the partners, and between 30 and 36 months the children adopted *complementary* roles (mother–baby, doctor–patient), showing their growing ability to understand and expand on what their partner intended. So during the first months of the third year, children playing with their friends (or with their siblings) engaged together in an increasingly complicated way, each making independent contributions to a shared pretend theme.

Just look at happens in the following incident from one of our Cambridge studies: Annie is 30 months old when Carol, her five-year-old sister, instructs her to 'pretend you're a baby or my mummy.'[21] Annie picks up the idea with great enthusiasm, and as well as following her older sister's commands she makes lots of her own contributions to their imaginary domestic scene. For her role as Baby, she does the following – as her own contributions to the mother–baby play:

Makes babbling noises.
Crawls.
Says she can't put on slippers: 'I'm babby'.
Designates her 'baby bed'.
Asks for porridge.
Plays a guitar in a way she describes as 'a babby way . . . Me babby'.
Addresses Carol as 'Mummy'.
Acts naughty with the guitar.
Pretends to get lost.
Snores when 'asleep'
'Cries'.
In answer to Carol asking why she is 'crying' ('What's wrong, Babbu?')
    replies 'Me can't get to sleep.'
Instructs Carol what she should say, as Mummy.
Criticizes Carol's action in terms of her role: 'No you not a baby.'
Refuses to go on 'Mummy's' knee.

Annie is sharing an imaginary world with her sister – a considerable intellectual feat in itself. But Annie is not simply a docile, compliant underling who fits in with Carol's grand plan as mother-in-charge. In fact, she makes the mother-and-baby game far more interesting than it would have been if she had simply done what she was told by her bossy older sister. The drama takes off much more elaborately. Carol knows a lot about what babies do, and adds all this to the drama. She understands about babies being upset, and 'plays' with this; she knows how mothers 'should' behave and ticks off her sister for not being a proper mother. Yet she is only 30 months old. We know that such shared make-believe happens very early between siblings *who like each other* – the emotional quality of the relationship is key to the frequency with which toddlers and preschoolers can make this imaginative 'giant leap forward' with their siblings.[22]

The significance of the development of this capacity for sharing an imaginative world lies partly in what it tells us about children's capacity to recognize the intentions of another person, sharing their focus of attention, and coordinating their communications about these shared intentions (a capacity that's been termed 'intersubjectivity').[23] Artin Goncu has drawn attention to the ways in which children communicate about 'pretend' to adopt a shared focus with their playmates between 18 months and three years, initially by nonverbal exchanges (exaggerated movements, facial gestures and voice inflections); he argues that communication between friends that 'this is pretend' is evident much earlier than three years. Then at around three years, there's a change from nonverbal to increasingly verbal means by which children communicate with each other about pretend.[24] These have been precisely described by a linguist Catherine Garvey, who studied pairs of acquainted children playing together, and documented both the 'enactments' of pretend characters and the verbal means by which children signalled 'pretend'.[25]

> How do we know that a child has adopted the role of wicked witch or working woman? She is most likely to announce her new identity to the play mate, but further she is likely to signal the transformation by speaking in a modified voice, by performing some identifying action, or by moving or gesturing in a manner that contrasts with her normal behavior. Pretending tends to be redundantly marked, and the signs are especially clear at points of transition to and from the pretend state.[26]

Garvey notes that all of the 48 children she studied in pairs (who ranged from 2 years 10 months upwards) could make the distinction between 'real' and 'pretend', and its application to their interactions was a matter of real concern to them.

What is particularly interesting in the example of 30-month-old Annie playing with her sister (above) is that Annie *pretends to be upset*, as part of the drama of the make-believe with her sister. And this is not an exceptional case. Many children of rising three are adept at playing with feelings – in the right circumstances – that is, playing with someone they know well, who has similar interests, and who can take a guiding role. Think for a moment what being able to play with feelings means. Children are riveted with interest by emotions shown by other people: Once they get the hang of *pretending* to be angry, happy, sad, disgusted, there is no stopping them, in make-believe. With their new skills of understanding what another child also has in mind for make-believe, this means a new world of shared fantasy opens up for three-year-old children. Quite simply, it means that play with a child you know well has suddenly new and thrilling possibilities.

It is not surprising, then, that once children have grasped how to join in constructing a make-believe story together, and 'play' with emotions, that their play with other children takes off dramatically, and the possibilities of forming friendships with other children rapidly increase. At this stage, other children become far more exciting companions than parents or other adults. There is a sharp change in *who* children choose to play with and *what* they choose to do, at around three to four years old. If children have any choice in the matter, by three and a half or four years old it is other children who are far more sought out as companions than boring old parents, as long as these other children are individuals who they know and like.

And it is the special significance of other children's way of pretending that plays a great part in their new preference. We compared the way mothers and children joined in pretend with young children (two-year-olds), in a study in Cambridge.[27] Quite simply, most adults who became involved in pretend did so in a rather boring, conventional way. Listen to a mother pretending to go shopping at the supermarket with her child. Inevitably she'll want to do it 'properly': 'You're the person who takes the cash, so you take it from me . . . now you take my change . . . here's the way out to the car . . .'.

In our studies in Cambridge we found that two differences in children's pretend play with their mothers and with their older siblings (aged on average four years) were marked, and were particularly interesting. First, there were differences in the way the joint pretend play was set up, and in the way objects were used as props. Of the bouts of joint pretend play with the mother, 97 per cent were focused on object props as a vital part of the game, and the objects provided a focal topic for mothers' instructions. In contrast, 27 per cent of bouts with the older siblings did not involve objects at all, but were sustained through talk and or nonverbal actions; moreover, one kind of play, in which children 'took on' a different role identity, or psychological state, occurred *only with siblings, not with mothers*.

Second, there were striking differences in the ways in which mothers and siblings participated in the joint pretend play. Mothers usually entered the play as interested spectators, offering relevant comments and suggestions, but very rarely adopting a pretend identity or role. In 85 per cent of joint pretend play bouts with mothers, in our Cambridge study, the mothers took on 'spectator' roles. Siblings, in contrast, often joined in the play as complementary actors, and their play involved close meshing of each partner's verbal and nonverbal actions. In 60 per cent of the bouts observed with child-and-sibling playing, the sibling and child took complementary roles.

Just as the pretend of siblings is less tied to the re-telling of conventional domestic practices than that of mother and child, what happens when two friends of three- or four-years-old 'go shopping' together can be far more anarchic than the pretend shopping expeditions of mother and child. The trip can turn into a Cinderella story, or can involve the latest favourite Disney person or Harry Potter character; they can even end up going to the moon. Children invent marvellous adventures with their friends, and in the stunning dramas of superheroes and of life-and-death adventures, and the anarchic versions of the narratives of domestic life that develop when friends play together, we see an extraordinary capacity to be *with* their friends in imagination. Children of four cannot usually tell you in a coherent way why they like being with their friend; they cannot give you a disquisition on the nature of friendship. But they have extraordinary skills of sharing a pretend world with that friend. Here is how John Gottman, who has conducted key research into young friends, sees the skills that are involved when two young friends are playing pretend together:[28] 'Friends can create a world of great involvement and high adventure, and they can do it at the tender age of 3 or 4. They must coordinate their efforts with all the virtuosity of a jazz quartet, and they must manage the amount of conflict between them. These things require enormous social skill.' In fact, we do children a real disservice by assuming that because they cannot tell us about what the friendship means to them, that it is a relatively trivial matter to them.

The beginnings of intimacy

There is a particularly close link between shared pretend play and friendship. It is worth considering for a moment what has recently been learned about the nature and significance of pretence in children's development, and why it is a domain that deserves our attention. Why do children typically spend hours pretending? Why are children of 18 to 20 months old drawn – as by a magnet – to the pretend games of older siblings and their friends? Why should people have evolved to spend so much time in fantasy worlds – how could this be adaptive? And does the view that young children have difficulty distinguishing between reality and pretence stand up to the scrutiny it has received over the last decade?

Twenty years of careful research have been summed up recently in a clear account by Paul Harris, and the message from his research and scholarship clarifies at least some of these questions.[29] First he shows that even two- and three-year-olds are adept at distinguishing pretence from reality. They *know* that they are pretending. Parallel evidence that children with imaginary friends are aware that these friends really are imaginary (though much loved) has been provided by Marjorie Taylor.[30] Children can reason and draw causal inferences within a pretend narrative. In the experiments Harris describes, three-year-olds can explain that if an imaginary teddy had not spilled the ink, his hands would not be dirty. Two-year-olds predict that imaginary tea spilled on an imaginary teddy will make the teddy wet and angry. These studies of pretence have, as Alison Gopnik has noted,[31] completely reversed the traditional idea of the fantasy-ridden preschooler, irrational and illogical. And there is striking evidence from other research that in the context of pretend, children of three are able to identify *intention* as the mental cause of action, and that they can reason correctly about counterfactual mental representation in the context of pretend before they can do so when faced with non-pretend tasks.[32]

But there is still the puzzle about what the excitement and draw of pretence should be, about why children should spend so much time in these fantasy worlds, and about why this capacity evolved – why it should be adaptive to spend time in an unreal world.

Here, Harris draws attention to the parallels with language. Children begin to pretend very much at the time they begin to talk – as many have noted. Harris argues that understanding a connected discourse with someone else is only possible for someone who can set current reality aside and construct a 'revisable situation model'. He argues that this same capacity underpins a child's understanding of an unfolding narrative sequence in a pretend game, and the ability to sustain a connected conversation that is not about only the here-and-now. To take advantage of information from others – in talk – we need to take their narrative perspective, even if their story is far from our own immediate experience. Harris suggests that the coincidence between the ways in which we as adults process narrative discourse and the ways in which children comprehend a make-believe narrative is in fact *no coincidence*. And here is where the developmental importance of joint pretend lies. The cognitive capacities that flourish and grow in shared pretend are those that underlie our ability to communicate verbally, to share ideas and understanding.

A powerful argument for the significance of narrative as a process through which understanding of mind and emotion are influenced has been developed by Jerome Bruner. He proposes that it is patterns of narrative that scaffold the kind of meta-cognition about intentions that lies at the core of children's understanding of the links between what people think or believe and how they act, and that narrative images are powerful in generating our ideas of ourselves within a particular culture. Stories, Bruner argues 'provide . . . a map of possible worlds in which actions, thought, and self-definition are permissible (and desirable)'.[33] In children's enthusiasm for pretend play narratives with their close friends we see their eagerness to explore and understand the social world. And it is particularly interesting that experimental studies have now provided evidence for the significance of narratives in children's understanding of other minds. Charlie Lewis and his colleagues showed that children who were being tested on their understanding of other minds succeeded best when they were given the opportunity to link the events involved in the task *in a coherent narrative*.[34]

Harris also draws attention to a crucial feature of pretend narratives – they are emotionally absorbing. He suggests that children's pretence is like theatre is for adults – and points out how easily we put ourselves in the shoes of characters we hear about in stories. With clever experiments he has shown that absorption in fiction leads to genuine emotions. As Alison Gopnik sums it up 'Becoming caught up in a story, it seems, is not just a rarefied experience of Shakespeare-lovers, but a deep part of our human cognitive experience.'[35] So the contexts in which children can explore and enjoy pretend narratives take on a particular developmental significance, and those contexts include, most importantly, their early friendships. Adding to that proposal – which highlights the cognitive significance of what Harris terms the 'work of the imagination', our argument here is that these experiences of shared pretend with a friend add an *emotional* significance, in that shared pretence opens up a new kind of human relationship for children, a relationship of shared emotion and ideas.

The connection between pretence and friendship is likely to go both ways. On the one hand children may select each other as friends if they both enjoy the same kinds of imaginary worlds: they may both have a passion for being policemen, or pirates. And on the other hand the experience of sharing fantasies together is important in the way their friendship grows. Sharing that pretend world can be a key setting for the growth of intimacy, and sharing the excitement generated by the fantasy; it may also perhaps be an important context for sharing what is worrying, as well as exciting. Children of three and four rarely have elaborate conversations about what they feel or fear. But they do explore the issues that make them afraid or excited, when they are playing pretend with their close friends. When Kitty, a four-year-old in one of our studies, said 'Let's play that our Mommies have gone away and left us, and we're afraid', and her partner May retorted that only babies do that, a link between the two was lost. When Kitty suggested a similar game to Shelley, a few days later, Shelley agreed, and their play took off; they shared their fears and invented adventures that ended with excitement not terror. Such shared imaginative play is the beginning of trust and intimacy.

Is this a far-fetched idea? Look at the themes of friends' fantasy play together. Ruth Griffiths in the 1930s reported that the recurrent themes in the fantasy play of the friends she studied were the following: jealousy of siblings; power relations with parents and being *small*; abandonment, separation and loss; and birth.[36] Bill Corsaro more recently describes a list with similarities: lost-and-found, danger and rescue, death – and rebirth.[37] Of course, the 'self-disclosure' here is far less explicit than it will be later, when teenagers endlessly discuss their problems together. But it is far from trivial that children playing lost-and-found together are able, as Corsaro puts it '*to share* both the anxiety of being lost and the relief and joy of being found'. This way, they are able to confront their fear together and cope with their anxiety together, without facing the risks of being lost in the real world.

The close links between developing and sustaining a shared imaginary world and friendship are confirmed when the pretend play of pairs of friends is compared with that of children paired with an 'acquaintance'. The pretend play that develops with friends is more sustained, more complex and more harmonious.[38]

However, we should note that the evidence that particular emotions *lead to* certain pretend games – that emotion is the cause, steering the imagination is by no means systematic. (It's an idea to which we return in Chapters 4 and 5). More convincing is the evidence that pretence can *lead to* particular emotions – excitement, fear, amusement. And the pleasure of generating such emotions together with another child is very clear.

What about children who rarely engage in pretence? Being able to cooperate, plan, hold back till it is your turn, see the other child's goal – these are skills and achievements that are important for playing all sorts of *other* kinds of game with a friend, as well as pretending together. Indeed, some kids don't get into pretend play all that frequently, and nevertheless enjoy early friendships. We'll look in Chapter 4 at individual differences in how much children are drawn to pretend, and the relation of this interest and experience in joint pretend to their social understanding – in terms of standard formal assessments of their emotion understanding and 'theory of mind' abilities. Sometimes these non-pretenders are the children who love making huge constructions, digging up the stream, or are the precocious football players. These 'non-pretend' activities involve thinking ahead, planning and coordination with their friends – a different kind of cooperation from sharing an imaginary world.

Whatever may lie behind the individual differences in what friends do together, it is clear that the enjoyment of shared cooperative games and pretend are top of the list of key developments that make friendship possible among very young children. And these are activities in which *other children*, not adults, star. One researcher reports a conversation with a four-year-old, in which he asked (rather coyly trying to reverse roles) what kids should be teaching adults, instead of it always being the other way around. The reply was terse and without hesitation – that adults should learn how to play properly.

The potential of play with a friend

To children, play is clearly and simply the best thing to be doing. To psychologists, of course, nothing is that simple. They have looked in detail at the significance of play for children's well-being, their development, their growing understanding of themselves and other people, for their language development, their ability to resolve conflict, and (most recently) their acquisition of some of the gender stereotypes of their world, and their incorporation into the less acceptable aspects of our culture. Certainly any hard evidence for how play in itself contributes to many of these developments is not easy to provide. But if we stay at a common sense level, it is clear that children who have had not the opportunity to play with other children at all are likely to be deprived of a range of centrally important experiences. In fact children show an extraordinary capacity to play with other children in the most dreadful and deprived circumstances, and to form friendships with other children in these circumstances, as records from children from concentration camps have shown.[39]

So the story of very early friendships we have covered so far is this: children younger than two do show particular preferences for other children, if they have had the chance to get to know other children well, and there are very rapid developmental changes in the ways that they can share a pretend world and cooperate with such a friend. By three and four years old their passion for playing with other children, and with special friends in particular, has taken off in an astonishing trajectory. Between three and four years the ability to share imaginary worlds, to take on complementary imaginary roles within a rule-governed context, increases rapidly: the length of these sequences of shared pretend increases, and children are increasingly able to *agree* with each other on the roles and themes of their pretend narratives. Four-year-olds talk to each other more than three-year-olds and are more likely to 'tune' their behaviour according to their companion's level of understanding.[40] But all this has been about companionship and shared play-obviously important in a host of ways to children's development, including the development of communication skills, the management of conflict, and the capacity to share imaginative play. Yet this is hardly the whole of friendship. What about affection, caring for the other child, and the mutual understanding of close friends that is so obviously important in later life? Is play all that these friendships are about?

Changes in caring and affection

Paul and Sophie, the children in the Hampstead Nursery who we glimpsed on page 13, clearly enjoyed kissing and cuddling. One of the most striking features of the children who had spent so much time together in the nursery was the emotional security and support they provided for each other, and the concern they showed for one another. This was even more clear in another group of children that Anna Freud and her colleagues studied – children who were rescued from concentration camps after the Second World War (described in Chapter 5). Children who have had more 'orthodox' family experiences also show caring and concern for other children in distress well before they are two – even if it is an unknown child who is upset. Babies are in these respects benevolent. Concern for a companion who is upset is not unusual among two-year-olds, though expression of affection in terms of caresses is relatively rare between toddlers.[41] But both affectionate expressions and concern become more evident and more frequent as children grow up. As Nancy Eisenberg and Richard Fabes show in their overview of developments in expressive emotion and emotional understanding, four-year-olds show more direct approval and affection towards their friends than three-year-olds and increasingly practical responses to others' distress.[42]

Children show us their curiosity about what people are feeling, and why, in their determined questions. Here's Jay (not yet two and half years old) from one of our Cambridge studies, who overhears his mother talking about her fear of a mouse she saw, behind the settee.[43] He is persistent in trying to find out what she had seen, and whether she was frightened:

JAY: What's that frighten you, Mum?
MUM: Nothing.
JAY: What's that frighten you?
MUM: Nothing!
JAY: What is it? . . . What's that down there, Mummy? That frighten you.
MUM: Nothing.
JAY: That not frighten you?
MUM: No. Didn't frighten me.
JAY: What that there?

What has this to do with early friendships? In fact, there is a key link between understanding of others' feelings, and forming friendships. It is not just that the way you relate to someone else is profoundly affected by your understanding of the other person's feelings. The link goes the other way too. Friendships can, it seems, increase children's understanding of others' feelings – an issue we'll examine further in later chapters. In a classic book from the 1930s, based on her careful studies of the children in the nurseries that she ran, Lois Barclay Murphy tells the story of a four-year-old boy, Saul, who initially is not a particularly caring or sympathetic child.[44] Saul develops a friendship with another four-year-old, Gwen, and as their relationship grows his understanding and sympathy for the other children in the group develops. Lois Barclay Murphy's conclusion was that the quality of his friendship with Gwen increased his own sense of security, and he was increasingly able to relate to, understand, and show sympathy towards the other children in the nursery.

A real concern for others involves much more than the response to an immediate distress or an obvious need. And we can see in young children's concern about their friends something that goes beyond a recognition that *at this minute* he or she is upset or wants something. Recall the incidents described by Lawrence Blum, watching the development of his daughter Sarah's understanding of her friend (see pages 4–5).[45]

Conclusions

We began with the question of whether very young children have friends. The observations of children at home, at nursery and at preschool show that if they have the chance to make relationships with other children – through frequent opportunities to be with particular children – some children will form relationships that are mutually affectionate and warm, and these relationships can be stable over years. These young children show caring, supportive behaviour (which we examine in more detail in Chapter 4); they play together in a way that is relatively intellectually sophisticated, sharing an imaginative world of pretend. This play involves a meeting of minds that is a key first step in understanding what another person feels and thinks, and it reflects a kind of intimacy and trust. This engagement in pretend is closely related to other aspects of children's social understanding. As we will see with the evidence from longitudinal studies described in Chapter 4, the experience of shared pretend with a friend is likely both to foster and to reflect that understanding. Through a focus on children's conversations and play with their friends, we gain a new view of what they understand about other people, and what influences that understanding.

Even as three-year-olds their friendships have different dimensions that teachers, for example, can distinguish. A study of teachers' reports on the mutual friendships of preschoolers within their classes showed the teachers reliably differentiated the extent of *support, conflict, exclusivity, intimacy* and *asymmetry* in the relationships of the different pairs of friends.[46] These are just the same features that are agreed to characterize older children's friendships.

Not all toddlers and preschoolers develop such relationships, of course; many are happy and sociable with a big circle of companions, but do not yet have a close friendship. Their capacities and their opportunities for making such a friend increase when they make a transition from home or nursery to school settings – the world we turn to next.

3

Friends within a social world:
the early school years

Kevin and Jeff, five-year-olds in our study in Pennsylvania, are discussing the other children at school, while they play at Kevin's house:[1]

> KEVIN: Remember old Wilbur at school? Remember him? I hate him, do you?
> JEFF: I hate him, don't you?
> KEVIN: Yes, everybody hates him at school!
> JEFF: Well Wilbur loves me, and I hate him!

Friendship in a social world

For many children, the beginning of preschool or school means a sudden increase in the possibilities of friendship. It can also mean new chances of rejection, and of loneliness. Once school begins, the issue of being liked, being chosen, or being excluded often looms large. All the children, after all, now have choice in who they play with or talk to. The new question is, will they choose me? In this chapter we look at the friendships of children after the toddler and early preschool years in the years between four and six.

This social world of preschool and the first years of school, together with the increasing sophistication of four-, five- and six-year-olds about other people's relationships, means that many children become both fascinated by and astonishingly worldly-wise about the network of relationships within their classroom. Ask a six-year-old about who wants to sit with whom, in their classroom. You are likely to get a detailed account that covers the choices of everyone in the class. Whatever the accuracy of the account may be (and in fact the children in a class usually give pretty similar accounts), it is fascinating that already children have such strong opinions and beliefs about the network of relationships in the group. And for some friends, this web of relationships between the others is a constant source of shared interest and amusement.

It begins quite early. Eavesdrop on three- and four-year-old friends talking, and you will hear occasional, scattered 'gossipy' remarks, usually brief comments about things 'we' don't like about X. The comments are frequently couched in terms of 'us' versus 'them', and appear to be bolstering the solidarity of the pair against others – and usually very particular others, as in this snatch of talk between four-year-olds Kirsty and Tess:[2]

KIRSTY: We don't want Jay in here.
TESS: We don't like her one bit.
KIRSTY: Not one bit!

A critical, derisory note to the comments about a particular other child is frequently heard. Here are comments from a four-year-old and a five-year-old from Gottman's (1986) study:[3]

B: Danny and Jeff did that. They did. They're dumb, aren't they?
S: Yeah.
B: Aren't they?
S: Yeah.

In a further exchange, the agreement between the children about 'we' sharing feelings about another child, was explicit:

S: Go! We want her to go away.
B: We don't want Allison here to bother us again.
S: We're very mad at her.
B: We are very mad.

Sharing dislike, anger against someone else, or jokes about another's shortcomings are hardly very attractive features of these young friendships. They are, however, aspects that become more and more prominent over the next few years. Exchanges like Kirsty and Tess's comments on Jay, or Kevin and Jeff's on Wilbur, are not uncommon. Interestingly, these conversations between preschoolers about *disliking* X often lead to the earliest instances of self-disclosure: the times when a child first tells another about what she feels, and shares her anxieties or fears. 'I hate it when . . .' 'I'm scared that . . .' These disclosures often also involve enquiries about what the other child feels: 'Do you like it when . . . ?' And these first discussions of feelings frequently include attempts to get confirmation that the child's feelings are shared: 'That makes us mad, right?' In these brief exchanges, we see the beginnings of what can be the core of many friendships later – gossip, self-disclosure and intimate sharing of feelings – often focused on others in the social group.[4]

Fully-fledged gossip and self-disclosure are of course rare in the early childhood years. But as children get more interested in and preoccupied with the larger group of children at school, or the gang with whom they hang around in the neighbourhood, the issues of 'you-and-me' versus the rest, and of who is friends with whom, become centrally important for many children. The elaboration and effectiveness of their character assassination of others grow notably, and their jokes about others become more psychological in nature. Other kids are mocked and disparaged not only for being *weird, mean, mad, cry-baby, dumb*, but for failing in a whole range of social norms: not helping, not sharing, telling tales. They are given nicknames that often hone in all too accurately on the features of a child's appearance or background that he or she would most like to forget: 'Goggle eyes', 'Snotty nose', 'Misery', 'Fleabag' – names that are hugely enjoyed by the mockers.

In the intimate cruelties of these conversations between friends that involve disparaging other children, we see some of the earliest signs of the children's growing understanding of others and of the social mores of their world. The other side of this same coin, of course, is that with their new powers of understanding their social world, children become increasingly effective in their support and reassurance for their friends. Most importantly, this knowledge is used to create solidarity between friends and to gain as well as provide support for wavering self-confidence. Disparaging someone else can be an important part of building up solidarity and support for each other.

A whole series of striking examples of these conversations that establish the closeness between two children through their shared dislike of a third, are included in a classic book from the 1937, *Social Development in Children*, in which the psychologist Susan Isaacs published the detailed records she had made of the young children in her Malting House School talking as they played.[5] Here is five-year-old Conrad, talking to Jane about another girl, Lena:

CONRAD: When Lena makes anything and says 'Isn't this nice?' I say, 'No, it's horrid', because I don't like Lena. I hate Lena, don't you?
JANE: Yes.

Susan Isaacs concluded that these gossiping conversations about disliking others were crucial to the development of friendships, commenting that many friendships are sustained as much by shared animosity towards others as by genuine intimacy and affection – a view that seems a little over-pessimistic, given what we know of the affection and caring that friends also show one another.

Changes in the nature of friendship

Conciliation and compromise

The growing articulateness and psychological understanding that is revealed in the gossip of five-, six-, and seven-year-old friends means that the quality of their close friendships changes in a host of other respects too, ways that are much more acceptable to adults. The increasing grasp of the needs, feelings and wishes of their friends means, for instance, that their skills at resolving conflict and disagreement are transformed. Instead of simply insisting on their own way, or wailing, grumbling, protesting or threatening the other child (behaviour in conflict that is all too common among young preschoolers), four- to five-year-olds often now offer compromises ('How about we both be queens, then?'), they bargain ('I'll give you He-man if you give me two Shredders') or they attempt outright conciliation ('OK I guess since I went first last time, you can go first this time').

What is especially clear is that children make these conciliatory moves and compromises more frequently in disputes with their friends than they do with their siblings, or with children about whom they do not much care. In the studies we carried out in Pennsylvania and London, we filmed and tape-recorded the same children in three situations – *alone with a friend, with a sibling*, and *talking to their mothers, in their families*.[6] In our analysis of how the children behaved in disputes with friends and family members, we made a distinction between whether the children used *reasoning* in their disputes, or simply protested, without offering any justification, reasoning or compromise. Then a further distinction was made between reasoning in terms of the other person's interests (*other-oriented reasoning*), or reasoning that was in terms of the child's own interests (*self-oriented reasoning*). Here is Sarah, aged 47 months, and Kay, her friend, aged 48 months. They are playing princesses, and both want to wear a particular crown.

SARAH: I should have the crown. Because it matches my dress. It looks ugly on you!

Sarah's attempts to argue for the crown are, for a child who is not yet a four-year-old, quite subtle. The issue of whether you look pretty or ugly was a big one for many of the girls in our studies by the time they were four, and it was a topic that recurred frequently in their conversations. The issue of matching clothes also mattered. So Sarah's grasp of what will carry weight with her friend is quite subtle. She uses these powers to get her own way in the dispute – successfully. It's an example of what we termed 'self-oriented reasoning'.

Now consider another exchange between other friends from the same study. Kerry, another 47-month-old, is also in conflict with her friend over who should have the prized crown:

KERRY: I know – we'll *both* be queens, because we both want to. Two queens in this palace, and you have the crown first, then it'll be my turn OK?

Here Kerry's compromise was coded as *other-oriented reasoning*, as she took account of what her friend wanted. And here is Sarah, at 33 months, arguing with her older sister Lynn about who should have a desired toy, 14 months before she was in the conflict with her friend Kay in the observation quoted above:

SARAH: Belt up Lynn, and give it to me!

Sarah's simple protest and demand directed at her older sister includes no reasoning or justification. We found that children usually behaved very differently in disputes with their friends, mothers and siblings.[7] In conflict with their friends, the children were significantly more likely to use reasoning that took account of the other person's point of view or feelings than they were when in conflict with their siblings (see Figure 1). This difference could reflect the greater equality of power between the friends as compared with the child–mother or child–older-sibling dyads. It could also reflect the emotional quality of the exchange: Children may well care more about managing to maintain continuous equable communication with their friends than they do with the family members – particularly their siblings.

Importantly, the probabilities that a child would take account of the perspective and desires of the other person and try to resolve the conflict with mother, with sibling, and with best friend were not correlated. For example, five-year-old Shirley (taking part in our London research) who dealt with disputes with her sister by simply screaming and reiterating

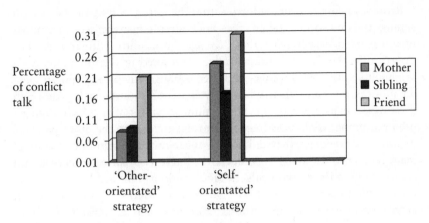

Figure 1 Children's conflict management strategies with friends, mothers and siblings
(From data in Dunn, Slomkowski, Donelan and Herrera, 1995)

what she wanted (and eventually pulling hair) went to some lengths to compromise or bargain when she was in conflict with her friend. 'Let's take it in turns – I'll go first then you can have two goes . . .' 'How about we both do it?'

What's important about this lack of correlation between children's behaviour in conflict with their mothers, their siblings and their friends is this. It shows us that even when children have the capacity to conciliate (through their understanding of the other person's needs or intentions), they don't *use* this ability in all their relationships, or all social situations. In fact the emotional dynamics of the relationship are key to how children use their new cognitive capacities, to sort out disagreements and disputes. It is usually of real importance to a child that relations with a friend don't founder on disagreements about how to play or what to do. And often their sense of what would work as a conciliatory move is surprisingly good. One five-year-old wanted to exchange her necklace for the one her friend had, when both were dressing up, in our Pennsylvanian study. After asking her friend directly for the necklace – a request which failed – she said 'I know, this would look really pretty on you, and it matches your dress.' (Again, an appeal to prettiness and matching clothes to her good friend – an appeal that worked.) These attempts at compromise and negotiation with friends increased in frequency between the ages of four and seven years – though in some friendships they remained pretty rare even when the children were eight or nine.[8]

It is interesting that in conflicts within the family, with mother or with sibling, the developmental changes in children's management of conflict were rather different from these changes in conflict with friends. For instance, in the Pennsylvanian study, we looked in detail at children's arguments with their mothers and their siblings when the children were 33 months old, and then when they were 47 months old.[9] Although there was an increase in the proportion of conflicts in which children used reasoning, references to social norms, appeals to the other person's intentions or feelings, they did not use this new understanding of conflict management to resolve the conflict in the interests of the other person, but rather, to gain their own goals. In fact, children were *less* likely to argue for conciliatory purposes at 47 than at 33 months in disputes which began with their own 'oppositional' moves – such as refusals. The new powers of reasoning were used in the interest of the child, rather than in the interest of family harmony.[10] Interestingly, the mothers and siblings also became less likely to compromise and conciliate with their increasingly argumentative children at 47 months than they had been with the same children at 33 months.

The general point established by these findings is that the relationship within which conflicts take place is crucial to the use children make of management strategies, and friendship is a context in which they show particular concern with resolution and conciliation. The lesson is that we should not regard social understanding as a 'within-child' trait or characteristic that is expressed uniformly across social relationships. Rather, how children use their social understanding depends on the nature and emotional quality of that relationship.

The growth of intimacy

Friends tell you their secrets, and you tell them yours.
(six-year-old in our London research)

Among three- and four-year-olds, there is a special kind of intimacy and shared understanding in the pretend play that they share, as we saw in the last chapter. They can explore together what frightens, excites or amuses them in the shared world of make-believe. By five, six or seven years, sharing thoughts and feelings becomes far more explicit, as children are better able to understand what their friends are thinking. There is a striking increase in children's talking about their feelings, memories and beliefs with their friends.[11] Here is Dee, a four-year-old, who is taking part in one of our studies in London, talking to her friend Jonny, when they are playing together in a room at school. No one else is present, but their conversation is recorded on a tape-recorder. Dee reports on a scary experience she has had on a trip to the ocean:

DEE: You know, when I was on holiday, I did go to the seaside ... and I cried ...

JONNY: Did you go in the sea?

DEE: Yeah, I was whinge- whinging [whining] ... I was ...

JONNY: Was there, was there a big waves?

DEE: That's why I cried.

JONNY: Was you scared?

DEE: Yeah, that's why I ...

JONNY: Did they take you out?

Talking about such scary times first begins with toddlers and young preschoolers – usually in their conversations with their mothers. They'll discuss scary TV programmes, or stories, as well as what has happened to *them*. And they'll show great curiosity about other people's emotions, especially when it is a family member or a friend. They can show lots of persistence in attempting to get to the bottom of what caused someone to feel sad, or frightened – as we saw in the last chapter, with 28-month-old Jay determinedly questioning his mother about what frightened her.

By 47 months old, the children in our study were talking about 'inner states'-including feelings – much more with their friends than with family members.[12] This discourse about feelings has real developmental significance for children's growing understanding of other people's emotions and the links between inner states and people's behaviour, as we'll see in the next chapter. And if you ask children who are a little older *who* they confide in about secrets or troubles, it is friends and mothers who come out top of the list. Between seven and ten years, the increase in confiding in friends is especially strong for girls; for boys it often happens a little later. Here is the novelist John Updike's marvellous account of the intimacy of one of his boyhood friendships:[13]

> Then comes intimacy: now we laugh before two words of the joke are out of the other's mouth, because we know what he will say. Our two beings seem marvellously joined, from our toes to our heads, along tingling lines of agreement; everything we venture is right, everything we put forth lodges in a corresponding socket in the frame of the other ... To be together is to enjoy a mounting excitement, a constant echo and amplification.

With adolescence, this capacity for intimacy takes a quantum leap upward in frequency, but even among nine- and ten-year-olds, it can be central to some friendships.

Intimacy shows up in unexpected ways within the classroom cliques that develop in the middle childhood years. Nicknames, for instance, are not exclusively employed to tease and upset: they reveal the strong friendships within a classroom as well mapping its hostilities. One group of psychologists studied the nicknames among the seven-year-olds in a classroom in England, as one way of documenting the network of relations between the children. One pair of friends, Lucy and Camilla, were known as Plum and Pudding. The explanation of the nicknames was simple, according to the other children: Lucy always goes with Camilla, and Plum always goes with Pudding (traditional English Christmas pudding!). In the same class, the strength of the bond between another pair of friends was reflected in the fact that they had the *same* nickname: they were both, simply, known as Puss. And the degree of intimacy between friends is also reflected in whether others actually *know* their nicknames. One triad consisted of Caz, Diz, and Saz, but most of the children in the class were quite unaware of the nicknames, which were only used within the trio of friends.

Moral issues

Because children care about their friends, they think about the needs and rights of their friends in a way that can be quite different from their views on moral issues as they apply to other people. In a centrally important sense, friendship between young children is a crucible in which moral understanding and sensitivity is formed.

Consider the comments of four-year-old Kevin, in our Pennsylvanian research, discussing with an interviewer whether it was OK for him to take a toy away from his sister, and then compare his response when it was a question of taking a toy away from his friend Jeff:

INTERVIEWER: What about if you took a toy from your sister? Would that be OK or not OK?
KEVIN: [Cheerfully] OK . . . because she's my sister and I hate her guts . . . well, I don't actually *hate* her, but . . .
INTERVIEWER: How about if you took a toy from Jeff?
KEVIN: [Solemnly] I would *never* do it. Because he's my friend. My best, best, best friend!

Increasingly, as children move through the school years, loyalty, self-disclosure and trust are seen as important in friendship. Friends 'don't drop you as soon as something goes wrong', an eight-year-old tells us. And children continue to consider moral issues quite differently, in relation to their friends, as compared with other people. Cheating, taking things that don't belong to you, making reparation for injuries to other people – all can be seen as serious breaches when it is a friend who would suffer from the action. We caught a glimpse, in talking to four-year-old Kevin, of a moral sensibility that he showed towards his friend Jeff that was certainly not evident in his relations with his sister. This heightened moral sense that is often apparent in young children's relations with their friends becomes clearer still as children grow up. Carol Gilligan suggested that children's relationships may provide critical evidence 'about both the promise of moral wisdom and the danger of lost moral insight':[14] it is in their friend-ships that the promise of moral wisdom is especially clear.

Take for instance the findings of our research on children growing up in central Pennsylvania, which focused on the development of social understanding, in particular on what connections there might be between children's early experiences in their families, their understanding of other people's feelings and thoughts and their close relationships as they grew up. In the study, we followed children from age two through their kinder-garten and first-grade years at school; we visited the children each year at home, watching them playing with friends and family, and talked to their parents and siblings as well as to the children themselves. When the children were five, six and seven years old, among the various assessments and procedures, we read them each a series of moral stories in which a child of the same age and gender cheated, accidentally hurt someone, or took something that didn't belong to them, a procedure developed by Grazina Kochanska.[15] The 'victim' in the stories was sometimes a close friend, sometimes a sibling. We asked the children how they would feel as the victim, but also as the transgressor, and asked them how the story would end – to see if the reparation mattered to them. There were strik-ing differences in the comments that the children made in relation to transgressions involving their friends, and those involving their siblings or children they did not consider to be their friends. For instance, in one story, the child cheated at a game of checkers, and as result of the cheat-ing won the game. When asked how they would feel in this situation if they had been the cheater and if the opponent was their friend, some of the children talked about feeling bad, and worried about their friend's feelings or state of mind. Here's how one seven-year-old commented: 'I'd feel happy but a little bit sad that she had to lose; I really shouldn't have moved the checkers.' When asked why she'd feel this way, she replied: 'Because if that was your best friend you'd feel really really bad that she lost and you changed checkers.' When asked to finish the story of cheating-at-checkers, the girl decided 'Maybe they play another game and she lets her friend win.' This kind of reparative comment was simply much less frequent if the other child in the story was a *sibling*. Mostly the children then said cheerfully that they'd feel happy that they had won!

A similar picture of heightened sensitivity to social and moral issues *when your friend is involved* emerged from our discussions with the children about recent conflicts, with both their friends and their siblings. For instance, when asked whether they felt they had learned anything from the outcome of a recent quarrel, they were quite likely to make comments, *in relation to conflict with a friend*, which suggested they had indeed learned something. Some typical examples were: 'Yeah, I learned that you can't always do your thing first' and 'Yes, I learned it's important to understand what my friend wants . . .'

If it is a recent fight with a sibling that is being discussed, children are far less likely to make these constructive inferences. 'Yeah, I learned I should have thumped him first!' was a typical response in relation to a sibling conflict. This seems more like a moment of 'lost moral insight' than one of 'moral wisdom' in Gilligan's terms – a depressingly frequent feature of children's comments on their fights with their siblings.

In contrast, there was growing evidence for friendship as a crucible for moral growth, through the caring and concern for the other child, the intimacy and the self-disclosure that are fostered. We return to this point in the next chapter when individual differences in friendship are considered: in our research both in Pennsylvania and in London we predicted that children whose friendships were particularly close, and characterized by high levels of shared pretend play, would show relatively mature levels of moral orientation. The grounds for this prediction were that shared pretence reflects an intimacy between the young children that is evident well before the verbal disclosures of later friendships, and that their understanding of emotion and their mind-reading skills, linked to the friendship quality, would also be linked to their moral understanding. We also predicted that mature levels of moral understanding would be correlated with relatively infrequent conflict between friends.

Pretend and the wider social world

The new and complex social world of school, we've seen in this chapter, increases the possibilities and nature of friendships. And over the preschool-to-school years, children's understanding of their various

different social worlds – family, school, neighbourhood – becomes increasingly clearly portrayed in their pretence with their friends. Pretence with
a friend provides a window on children's growing grasp of the roles, iden-
tities and characters of these worlds – their perspective on what happens
within families, within the playground, at parties, going shopping, on car
trips or in spaceships. In the explicit directions children give their friend-
partners in shared pretend, for instance, normative statements about
what's expected within particular roles or 'scripts' are frequent: 'Boys
don't drink coffee', 'Ladies use vacuum cleaners, not men', 'Daddies don't
have handbags'. Catherine Garvey, in documenting these expectations
and children's enactments of roles makes the point that:[16]

> Most enactments are clearly created from concepts of appropriate behavior
> and are most likely not direct imitations of models. For example, a boy
> who walks into the house announces *Okay, I'm all through with work,*
> *honey. I brought home a thousand dollars*, and hands over the money to
> his beaming Wife has probably not witnessed this scene in his own home.
> He has, however, generated certain characteristics typical of husbands.

The majority of enactments, Garvey argues, reflect 'information gained
and organized by the child as he learns more and more about the nature
of the social world and about himself as part of it'.

The roles and plans that are explored in friendship differ both with
age and across cultures and communities. Expansions of children's worlds
as they grew up were reflected in Garvey's research in the way family
role-choice was greatly influenced by age. Only the younger children
were Babies (adult roles were the most favoured at all ages – they could
do so much more), and Baby was replaced by Child with the increasing
age of the pretending friends; older children represented Husband and
Wife roles. In the themes of averting threat that became increasingly
frequent with age (monsters, sharks, accidents, fires), the younger pairs
were more often victims and less often defended. Only the older children
called in defenders or reinforcements when they were victims, and they
succeeded in destroying most the threats they faced.

Cultural differences in the frequency and themes of shared pretend play
have also been described, even for toddlers: Goncu and his colleagues
describe more frequent engagement in shared pretend among toddlers
in a Turkish village and in Salt Lake City in the US than in the communities they studied in India and Guatemala.[17] Play themes apparently
differ among groups and tend to reflect activities important to the culture
studied.[18] In Hopi Indian settlements children conduct pretend rabbit

hunts, and pottery making; in South London we found children from families of west African origin playing at the rituals of their particular churches. There's disagreement among anthropologists however about the extent and nature of cultural differences in young children's pretence in different groups, and we simply don't know whether such differences are reflected in other aspects of children's friendships.

The end of pretend?

Does the sophistication of six- and seven-year-olds mean the end of shared make-believe as a core feature of children's relationships with one another? Not in the relationships between some close friends. Shared fantasy can be a central theme in the close friendships of eight- and nine-year-olds, but it is a *private* world, rarely accessible to outsiders. Even among five- and six-year-olds, the fantasy play of friends is very vulnerable to the presence of adults. Leave a tape-recorder on where friends of this age are playing, and you'll find that when a parent enters the room – the flourishing pretend play is suppressed, and simply dies (a point established in the studies by Gottman, for instance).[19] Over the years, make-believe becomes an increasingly private matter. But it can still be the major occupation of particular friends. Annie Dillard in *An American Childhood* recalls the Indian exploits of her friendship with a neighbouring child in Pittsburgh, and the contrast with the return to their mothers' world of the 1950s.[20]

> By day, Pin Ford and I played at being Indians straight out . . . As Indians, Pin and I explored the wooded grounds of the Presbyterian seminary at our backyards. We made bows and arrows; we peeled and straightened deadfall sticks for arrows, and cut, stealthily, green boughs to bend for bows. With string we rigged our mothers' Chesterfield cigarette cartons over our shoulders as quivers. We shot our bows. We threw knives at targets, and played knife-throwing games. We walked as the Indians had walked, stirring no leaves, snapping no twigs. We built an Indian village, Navajo style, under the seminary's low copper beech: we baked clay bricks on slate roofing tiles set on adobe walls around a twiggy fire. We named the trees. We searched the sky for omens, and inspected the ground for signs. We came home and found our mothers together in our side yard by the rose garden, tanning on chaises longues.

Making dens and camps, having close-knit gangs with fantasy names for each other, writing stories together, having adventurous expeditions in the style of Tom Sawyer and Huck Finn, all these have strong pretend themes, and all can be central to friendships in childhood. The form of shared pretend changes, but its significance for the friendship does not disappear.

So the nature of friendship changes over the preschool and early school years, in ways that are closely linked to children's growing understanding of other people. The new awareness of the relations between the other children at school, the growth of intimacy, of moral sensibility, of new ways of handling conflict and disputes, combine to mean changes in the close relationships between friends. These developmental changes are striking. But if we are thinking about what impact a particular friendship is likely to have on a child's development, we immediately face the importance of *individual differences* in the quality of friendship between children. How a friendship influences the two children involved will depend on the *kind* of relationship between the two, and this can differ very much. We look next at how children's friendships differ, and then at how these differences are linked to the influence the friendship may have on the children's development.

4

Differences in children's friendships: links with social understanding

Close relationships between children differ greatly. Even among the three-year-olds, we saw in Chapter 2, the differences between friendship pairs in the extent of support, conflict and exclusiveness (keeping out other children) were evident to teachers.[1] With Cathy and Mary, two friends in our Pennsylvanian project, fantasy flourished, and the two children played with matters of life, death, birth – as well as boyfriends, dinner dates and the crucial matter of what to wear for the ball. It was a relationship that was striking in its intimacy, and their shared imaginative games continued over the years; as seven-year-olds they were still joining in shared imaginative games. But by no means all friendships include this kind of intimacy. Tom and Dan, another pair of friends in the study, spent their time together in a cycle of soccer games, video games and bike riding. They were almost always cheerful companions, and inseparable during the long summer weeks. But when as seven-year-olds they were asked about whether they share secrets or discuss problems, their reaction was an immediate 'No!' Kay and Shelley were different again: They had a tempestuous up-and-down relationship, full of drama, quarrels and intense emotions. Their friendship was on one week, off the next.

These differences are obvious, at an anecdotal level. And systematic research adds to the picture, by showing us some general patterns that apply across lots of children. In our Pennsylvanian study, for example, two clear and separate aspects to the children's friendships were evident when they were six and seven.[2] One was the emotional quality of the friendship – the expression of friendly affection, caring and happiness between both of the two children. The second dimension was the quality of the coordinated, complex play that the two children built up together. The key point here is that these two aspects were relatively independent of one another. Some children were very affectionate and positive together, but did not necessarily build up elaborate games together. Others were strikingly effective at coordinating and constructing sophisticated play together – but they did not necessarily show much affection to one another or much positive excitement. Some, of course, were both affectionate *and* great playmates. Other studies distinguish different dimensions of friendship, including the extent of conflict in the relationship for instance, and as children grow up, differences in the dimensions of loyalty and commitment can become evident.[3]

A moment's reflection on the children you know will highlight the point that there is not simply one kind of 'friendship', and it is not the case that children either have or do not have a best friend. Indeed the same child often has a number of relationships with other children that differ. Cathy, in our Pennsylvanian study of friends, was as a four- and five-year-old particularly in tune intellectually with Mary – a friend for close talk and pretend – but on lots of other occasions she also enjoyed a wild relationship with a neighbouring kid Jerry, which was more focused on shared mischief than on talk and make-believe. As adults we enjoy very different kinds of relationships with our different friends; we certainly should not be surprised that our children do the same.

There are differences, too, within relationships. Mutual interest, co-operation and sharing may be the hallmarks of friendship, but that does not mean that a particular friendship is experienced in the same way by both children within the relationship. Often, one child is the leader, the dominant one, and the other tends to follow. Differences in power within the friendship can be a source of tension in the relationship, or can be easily accepted by the 'follower', as in the case of Carl, a six-year-old in our Pennsylvanian study. His mother described his friendship like this: 'He gets on very well with Jake; he lets him boss him around, but he's so easy going, he doesn't seem to mind . . . it's almost as if he likes all the decisions made for him!'

Friendships between children of different ages are often a bit 'uneven' in power terms, as in the case of some of the children in a study of seven-year-olds in Nottingham, an industrial town in the north of England.[4] This was a large-scale study in which around 700 families were followed from when the children were one-year-olds to their adolescence. The mothers in the study were interviewed in detail about their children at several time points. In the example that follows, a mother is commenting on the imbalance in her seven-year-old daughter's friendship with an older girl of 12 years, and muses on a number of possible explanations for the success of this imbalance:

> She plays an awful lot with a girl across the way, and she's 12 or 13. Whether she likes-er-older company, you know; whether she finds that a child of her own age is not sufficiently intelligent enough to tell her what to do; whether she's the type of child that *likes* being told what to do – she likes being told what to do, and she's quite willing to do it.

In the Nottingham study, about 17 per cent of the children were happily in a 'follower' role in their friendships, and a larger 29 per cent were described by their mothers' as the 'boss' in a close friendship. Roughly half of the children enjoyed friendships in which there was 'give-and-take' about power issues – with no noticeable domination by either child, or with amicable alternations in who was in control.

Who makes friends with whom?

'Like me' attracts. As adults we are likely to make friends with individuals whom we recognize as 'like me'; the research on friends in childhood suggests this process begins pretty early. Children do tend to make friends with children who are similar to them, not only in gender (as we'll see in Chapter 7) but also along dimensions that are important in terms of 'reputation' in the local peer group. For instance, several studies have shown that friends are more similar to one another than children who are not friends, in several characteristics: in shyness, in cooperativeness and kindness, and in antisocial behaviour, in depression, popularity with peers, and achievement, for instance.[5] In our London research, the four-year-old friends were also similar to each other in their understanding of other people's feelings and thoughts, in their verbal ability and their general intelligence.[6] Children who enjoy breaking the rules, skipping school, taking things from shops without paying, often form friendships with others who share these same 'tastes'. The principle of 'like me' attracts appears to work in the formation of networks and gangs, too, and this drifting together of children with similar characteristics and interests makes the formation of close friendships between similar individuals even more likely. Children are more likely to actively *dislike* children who are different from themselves, and to end friendships with children who are different rather than similar.

Friends also become *more alike* over time – probably in part because of their shared activities and conversations. We don't know much about how children sort themselves out into friendship pairs. It seems it is not a matter of carefully weighted decisions, but through processes that some researchers have called 'shopping expeditions' – social choices about what 'feels right', that frequently get made within looser networks of friends.[7]

Networks of friends

Children differ not only in the quality of their friendships, but also in the extensiveness of their network of friends, in the early school years as well as later. Some have a range of easy, casual social contacts, some are part of a loose-knit gang, some have several close friends, while others have only one or two. Here is how one mother from John and Elizabeth Newson's study of Nottingham seven-year-olds describes her son's friends:[8]

> He has about three boys he's very pally with, but they vary from day to day as to which is the special one; and he also has a special girl who he's particularly friendly with, but he goes off her as well from day to day. I should think he's got about half-a-dozen close-knit friends, and he calls them the gang.

Another mother from the same study saw her son's relations this way: 'Well, he plays very well with strange children, but particular friends he doesn't seem to make – anyone special. He'll play with any child quite happily, but no one in particular.'

What leads to these differences?
Patterns over time

The question of what lies behind such differences in the quality of children's friendships is one which we explore throughout this book. In later chapters we will look in particular at what are the key influences on *problems* in friendships, and at the role of family relationships as an influence on the ways in which friendships develop. Here we focus on the significance of children's personal characteristics – such as their intelligence, especially their social understanding, and personality – for the kind of friendships they form.

The social setting

But first there are some obvious aspects of children's lives that can influence patterns of friendships, especially in the early school years, when children are inevitably less independent than they become as adolescents. The kind of cultural group they grow up in, for instance, can make a difference. If a child is growing up in an isolated rural community he may simply have little opportunity to meet a range of different children. If he lives in a close-knit group of families with children who all grow up together, he'll grow up with a familiar, stable group of children – which probably gives him the best opportunity to form a close friendship.

Another factor can be the school to which children go. When a child first starts school, she may be sent to a different school from that to which her neighbourhood friend is sent. Immediately, a hugely important part of her life is inaccessible to the friend. They cannot share, joke or gossip about that school world; they cannot provide each other with close support in the face of the trials and demands of the new social world of school. Conversely, a child whose close friends at school live in a different neighbourhood may not be able to keep up the friendship over the long vacation breaks.

The neighbourhood in which children live can be important. If there's a place where kids can 'hang out' together safely, or somewhere that during the long summer recess they can congregate – a pool, or gym, or somewhere where activities are organized, where the local streets are not too hazardous, or the suburban houses are not too far apart and isolated for the kids to run to and fro – all these can make a difference. And parents' involvement in their children's relations with other children may also be important (Chapter 8). But the major influences on the kind of friendships children enjoy with others are likely to be differences in their personalities and temperamental characteristics, their self-confidence with other children, their social understanding and their gender (discussed in Chapter 7). Clearly some children are much more outgoing than others, and these children find it easy to approach others and suggest joint games. Differences in social intelligence also turn out to be important from surprisingly early in childhood – as our studies in Pennsylvania and London have shown.

Social understanding

In our research we have followed the same children from the toddler years through their kindergarten and early school years, with studies both in the UK and in the US. We visited the children each year, and when they were three years old, we gave them a series of 'games' to play which were designed to tap the extent to which they were able to understand other people's feelings, and to 'read their minds' – the first signs of under-standing what someone else was thinking, intending, believing, and of the links between these inner states and how the person behaved.[9] In the last two decades there has been a great surge of research to clarify *when* and *what* children understand about other people's thoughts, feelings, beliefs and intentions, and how young children's understanding of why people behave the way they do develops.[10]

One way of studying this is to give a child a story in which someone mistakenly thinks an object is in a particular place – that, for instance, some chocolate has been put in the fridge – when the child hearing the story knows that the chocolate *has been moved somewhere else*. The child is then asked to explain why the person in the story looks for the chocolate in the fridge, rather than in the place *where the child knows it really is now*, or to predict where the story person will look for the chocolate. These kinds of stories are used to chart the changes in children's grasp of the ways in which people's beliefs (which the child knows to be mistaken) govern how they act. They can show us whether children can predict how puppets or story characters will behave, if the puppet does not know something of which the child is already aware. So, for instance, a puppet who has a sore thumb is looking for a Band-Aid: he sees a box marked Band-Aids, *however the child knows that this box is empty, and the Band-Aids are really in a plain unmarked box*. The child is asked where the puppet will look for a Band-Aid. If the child promptly says 'He'll look in the Band-Aid box 'cos he thinks the Band-Aids are in there', he or she has grasped the idea that people can have mistaken beliefs and that these beliefs will influence what they do.

Another way of tracing what children understand about other people's beliefs and ideas is to study their powers of tricking or deceiving people.[11] If you try to deceive someone – to get your mother to think your brother was to blame for the spilt juice when it was really your fault, for instance, you clearly have got the idea that your mother's beliefs can be mani-pulated. Mistaken beliefs, trickery and deception have been studied with groups of children aged three, four, five and six years old, to see how these abilities to 'read minds' develop. There is plenty of controversy about how to interpret the results of the tasks, especially when children don't succeed on the tasks, but it is generally agreed that by four to five years old, children's ability to understand the links between people's mental states and their actions is well in place.[12]

In the Pennsylvanian and London research we used a range of these 'false-belief' tasks, and other games that focused on the child's understand-ing of feelings.[13] These involved a set of puppet games and scenarios in which the puppet star was faced with incidents which were all likely to rouse feelings: meeting a big dog who jumps up, being taken on an exciting expedition, having his favourite – or his most disliked food for dinner, having a nightmare, and so on. In some of these scenarios, the puppet expresses the same feelings that the child would show. In others, the puppet expresses the *opposite* emotion to the child's own typical reaction to that scene (we established first with the mothers, what the child's usual reaction to these particular incidents was). For example, a child who loved big dogs was shown a puppet scenario in which the puppet was scared of the dog, and the child was asked what the puppet was feeling. In addition to these games – the standard way in which psychologists assess young children's mind-reading skills and under-standing of emotions – we assessed the children's verbal intelligence and language development, and the mothers filled in questionnaires for us that described the children's temperamental make-up.

What we found in the Pennsylvanian study was that the children, as 40-month-olds, differed markedly in the sophistication and maturity with which they could understand others' feelings, and 'read' others' minds. Some were already, at 40 months old, far more grown-up in these respects, and more successful in these tasks than others. Other children were not yet able to make judgements about how other people felt or thought. These differences were associated with, but not fully explained by differ-ences in the children's verbal ability and articulateness.[14]

The big surprise came when we looked at the pattern of differences in these children's relationships with their friends four years later. We had not really expected to find a close connection between how the children had behaved in these 'games' when they were only 40 months old, and the nature of their relations with friends in the sophisticated world of the five-, six- and seven-year olds. Yet the results showed clear links between the quality of their friendships and these early differences in understand-ing.[15] The children who had been particularly mature at understanding others' feelings, thoughts and beliefs as 40-month-olds were the ones who were engaging in particularly elaborate coordinated play with their friends in the early school years; their conversations were long and the children 'connected' smoothly with what their friend was talking about.

These children who had been early 'stars' at understanding other minds as 40-month-olds also behaved differently in conflict with their friends, as six- and seven-year-olds. We focused on the strategies used by the children in their disputes with their friends during the observations of the children playing with their friends, and their attempts at resolving the disagreements. The children who had been especially successful at the early social understanding tasks, four years later made more attempts to negotiate and resolve conflicts in ways that took account of their friends' views and needs than the children who had not been so mature as three-year-olds in the social understanding tasks. They managed to resolve their conflicts through compromise, and took account of what their friend wanted in sorting out difficulties. Interestingly, the *frequency* of conflict between the friends was not related to the measures of early understanding. It was not how often children disagreed and quarrelled with their friends that was associated with their early mind-reading and emotion understanding, but how they worked towards resolution. In fact, different aspects of early understanding predicted different features of how children handled their conflicts with their friends as six-year-olds. Attempts to distract your friend (with suggestions for a different game, or by drawing attention to something interesting), as a move to end the conflict, were more common among children who were skilled at mind-reading as preschoolers, while *submission* to the friend at age six was linked to an early concern with feelings and moral issues – not to the early mind-reading abilities.

The children who had been successful at the social understanding tasks were as six-year-olds, in these various ways, more 'tuned in' to what their friends were wanting and thinking than most of the other children. Although some of these differences were linked to the children's language abilities, how articulate and fluent they were in talking did not explain the key differences in their relationships with their friends.

This pattern over time was striking. Could it be a pattern that reflected the particular sample of children we studied in Pennsylvania – children growing up in small-town and rural communities in the US – or did it reflect a more general feature of children's early development? To examine this question, we then carried out a much larger study in a very different social setting: children growing up in the deprived inner-city world of south London, mostly in families facing considerable social and economic adversities, from different ethnic communities (families of African-Caribbean or West African origin, and mixed-race families as well as Caucasian).

Young friends in London: the story over time

In this research,[16] we used a broad range of assessments of social understanding, including tests of children's understanding of deception and of feelings, as well as the standard 'theory of mind' tests. As in the

Pennsylvanian study, we followed the young children in London from when they were nearly four years old until they were seven, investigating both their social understanding and their social relationships (with mothers, siblings and friends) at each time point that we visited them. And the results were notably similar to the findings of the American study: they demonstrated the significance of early social understanding for the children's friendships – both as four-year-olds and as they grew up.

The observations of the children playing with their friends as four-year-olds, each pair alone in a room without an observer present, but a video camera recording what they got up to, showed marked differences in how the pairs of friends played and talked together. Many engaged in a shared imaginary world with great skill and enjoyment. Alone in the confines of a small room at nursery or school, where we filmed them, they created worlds of emotional drama, medical emergencies, parties, high romances, crimes, births and deaths, as well as quieter domestic stories. The children who most frequently played shared pretend games were less likely to quarrel or to fail in communicating smoothly with each other than the other children in the study.

Other pairs of friends enjoyed talking about shared wickedness and rule-breaking, cooperated in boisterous games, worked out how toys functioned, but their shared pretend play was less elaborate and sustained. They were particularly likely to join in shared jokes, laughter or riotous clowning together.

Were these different kinds of friendship linked to the children's abilities to read others' minds and understand emotions? Yes: Our prediction that these social understanding abilities would be related to a high frequency of children's engagement in shared pretend play (as in the Pennsylvanian research) – rather than to a high frequency of shared riotous running around, or shared delight in rule-breaking – was supported. And differences in social understanding were also linked to a low frequency of conflict between friends, and to the smoothness and success of the children's conversational communication. Of course, other variables were important too – for instance their mothers' educational level, as we'll discuss in Chapter 8, and the children's temperamental characteristics such as their sociability. Importantly, the *social understanding of the friend* was also a key feature too – reminding us that friendship is a relationship to which both children contribute. So, for instance, as much as 10 per cent of the variation in children's pretend suggestions and actions was explained by the social understanding skills of their *friend*, independent of the child's own social cognitive abilities.

The transition to school

What happened when these friends made the transition from nursery or preschool to 'real' school, a year or so later? The issue of whether children have friendships in their first year at school is key in terms of their adjustment to school. Gary Ladd and his colleagues have shown that in this first year, children's friendships are key predictors of their later enjoyment of and adjustment to school.[17] In their studies, friendship uniquely predicted changes in children's school attitudes, school avoidance and academic performance. If children started school with a friend from preschool, they were more positive about school, and if they formed a close friendship in the first year at school, this helped their adjustment. So the question of what factors are linked to children forming or maintaining their friendships in their first year at school is one of interest and practical importance.

We focused on three questions about the children's friendships in their first year at school, in the London research:

- First, were the earlier differences in their social understanding as four-year-olds important in the kind of friendships they formed later, at school? In particular, were the emotion understanding, and theory-of-mind abilities that the children showed as preschoolers related to their school friendships?
- Second, were the characteristics of the friends with whom the children had been close in the preschool period linked to the quality of their friendships at school? As four-year-olds, the quality of the children's friendships was influenced, as we've seen, by the characteristics of both children involved. Our prediction was that children whose preschool friends had shown relatively high levels of social understanding, who had been caring and helpful, would as schoolchildren show more insight and liking for their friends in their *later* friendships.
- Third, we asked whether the social experiences central to the *preschool* friendships – the shared imaginative play, the connected communication, the extent of conflict – were linked to the quality of the later friendships the children enjoyed at *school.*

Some of the children in the study made the transition to school with their preschool friend – they both went to the same primary school. Other children were 'parted' from their friends at the transition to school, because they were sent to different schools. With this latter group of children, it was possible for us to investigate whether children's preschool friendship

experiences would show systematic links to the quality of the new friendships that they formed in their first year at school. Thus we could begin
to test the idea that in their early friendships preschoolers might form
representations of friendship relationships on which they then draw when
developing subsequent friendships.[18]

Our prediction was that (a) children whose preschool friendships had
been characterized by smooth effective communication, high levels of
shared imaginative play and relatively low levels of conflict, and (b)
those whose understanding of emotion and of 'other minds' in the preschool years had been especially well-developed, as had those of their
preschool friends, would as children at school enjoy particularly good
friendships. We predicted that these children would show insight into
their friends, and much liking for them, even when the friendship was
formed *after* the children had made the transition to school.

At the school stage, then, we interviewed the children informally, asking
them a series of questions about their friend and what they did together
as a pair. The children's comments throughout the interview were then
rated to give us three scales: one of *liking* for the friend, one of *insight*
into the friend and one of *conflict* in the relationship. We analysed how far
these measures of school-age children's friendship and insight into their
friends could be predicted from their preschool experiences with their
friends, and from their early understanding of emotions and others' mental
states. How did our key hypotheses about the importance of early social
understanding, characteristics of the preschool friend and shared friendship
experiences in the preschool period, stand up in light of the findings?

The five- to six-year-old children talked freely to us about their *current*
friends at school – about what upset them, what they liked and disliked
about them, and about the conflict in their friendships. And there were
indeed links between the children's expressed liking for their best friend
at school, and their insights into this friend, and their earlier friendship
experiences and social understanding. Thus, preschool social understanding was clearly related to the children's expressed liking of their friends
at school. For children who had made the transition to school with
their preschool friend, their preschool experience of smooth successful
communication with their friends contributed to how much liking
they expressed for their friends at school, independently of their social
understanding at the school stage.

The evidence from the children who had formed *new* friendships was
particularly interesting here. These children had formed new friendships
in most cases because they had been sent to different schools than their
preschool friends, not because their preschool friendship had broken down.

First, for these children, their experience of shared cooperative play with their *old* preschool friends was linked to later differences in their liking for their new friends at school. Those who had enjoyed frequent shared pretend play with their (old) preschool friend expressed more liking for their new friends than the children who hadn't experienced such frequent shared imaginative play. This evidence supports the argument that sharing and negotiating an imaginary world in pretend play provides a potent context for talking and learning about why other people behave the way they do; relevant here is the evidence that talk about inner states is especially prominent in pretend.[19]

An example from our Pennsylvanian study made this last point clear. We found that children who had taken part in conversations about thinking and mental states – in which they commented on or discussed what someone *knows, feels, thinks, believes, remembers* – as part of their play were more mature later in development in their understanding of others' inner states – their ability to 'mind read', in terms of our standard assessments of how well the children managed the deception tasks, and the 'false belief' tasks. By four years old, children were much more likely to have these conversations with their friends than with their mothers; see Figure 2.[20]

When do these conversations take place? They are especially likely to be during shared pretend play, when the two children have to work out together what the characters in their pretend narrative are doing, feeling

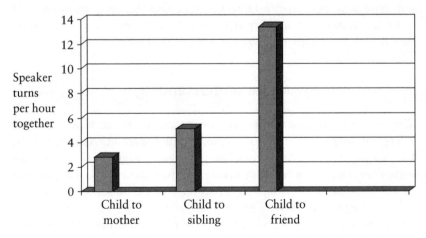

Figure 2 Children's talk about mental states with friends, mothers and siblings
(From data in Brown et al., 1996)

and thinking, as a number of different research projects have made clear.[21] These findings give us a strong indication of what the processes are that underlie the development of individual differences in children's understanding of other people. Earlier work on family experiences has shown that children who grow up in families in which feelings are discussed, and in which they participate in talk about *why people behave the way they do* are likely to perform particularly successfully on tests of social understanding.[22] The friendship studies show that these conversations are especially likely between young friends, and that this is part of the developmental story linking early shared pretend to later sophistication in social understanding.

The second point concerning the patterns over time in the London study for the children who had formed new friendships was that *who* the child's *preschool* friend had been – specifically whether the preschool friend had been a caring, helpful, 'pro-social' child – was related to the liking and insight children showed towards their *new* friend at school. The importance of the identity of a child's friends has been emphasized for older children and adolescents.[23] These results on the young London friends show that the developmental significance of *who you are friends with* begins in the preschool years.

So this evidence for these links between children's preschool experiences with their (old) friends – especially shared pretend – the social understanding of both child and friend as three- to four-year-olds and their insights and liking for their (new) friends at school supports the important argument of Carollee Howes – that children may form internal 'representations' of friendship relationships in the preschool years upon which they then draw in later friendships at school.[24]

Moral understanding

The question of how individual differences in friendships might be related to differences in children's moral understanding was raised in the last chapter. William Arsenio and his colleagues suggested that children's early friendships may be of particular significance in the development of moral sensitivity, following Piaget's emphasis on the significance of what happens between children.[25] Moral understanding may, in addition, contribute to the quality of friendship: there is evidence that children with friends are better at seeing the world as others see it, and more altruistic than those without friends.[26] In the London studies, as well as observing the children interacting with their friends, and testing them on emotion understanding, mind-reading abilities and language, we interviewed them about hypothetical transgressions – name-calling, taking a toy from a friend and excluding a friend from play, with each transgression presented as involving the child and his or her close friend. The children were asked for their views on these transgressions *if they themselves were the victim of the transgression*, and also *if they themselves were the transgressor*.[27] So we obtained their views on the permissibility of the transgression ('If [friend's name] won't let you play with him, is that okay or not okay?') and then for each question, we asked them for a justification for this view ('Why is that okay/not okay?'). We coded their answers on a system that distinguished between *reference to external punishment, references to social/conventional rules* and *references to feelings, psychological issues and interpersonal issues*.

The results of the study showed that those children with particularly close, intimate friendships gave more interpersonally oriented justifications concerning moral issues that involved friends – our initial prediction was supported. The children whose friendships were characterized by shared imaginative worlds and infrequent conflict were more likely to talk about what was acceptable behaviour between friends (and what was not acceptable) in terms of the feelings, welfare and relationships of the children in the incidents. Importantly, the findings also showed that children's understanding of inner states was related to the moral orientation in which reference to feelings, interpersonal relationships and welfare was reflected.

We can't draw conclusions about causal influence from these correlations. It could be that the quality of the friendship interactions actually contributed to the children's developing moral understanding and sensitivity; it could also be that their friendships flourished particularly and deepened in intimacy if the children themselves were sensitive to the moral concerns of their friends. But one general conclusion from the pattern of results is that individual differences in mind-reading and emotion understanding carry wide implications for children's social and moral lives. And friendship, we have seen, may well have a special place in the development of this understanding.

Are there also 'social costs' to social understanding?

It is clear that individual differences in children's understanding of other minds and of other people's feelings have meaningful links with children's everyday lives. They are linked to the differences in the quantity and quality of children's pretend play with their friends, to their social skills and to their moral sensitivity.[28] And the Pennsylvanian and London research shows that these early individual differences are not only related to children's *current* social relationships but also have sequelae in children's later social lives – in their school-age friendships, as we've just seen. Evidence is also accumulating on how problems in social understanding are associated with current problems in children's relationships with other children.[29] But before we assume that a more advanced or mature 'theory of mind' is an advantage with no disadvantages – consider this possibility. A child who is sensitive to the thoughts and feelings of others may well find it easier to make friends, to get along with other children, or explain her own point of view. However, having a well-developed understanding of other people's thoughts and emotional responses could possibly be a disadvantage in some situations. An early sensitivity to other people's disparaging remarks and expressions of dislike could be damaging to a child's sense of self, and self-confidence, which are just developing in children in the early school years.

Two lines of evidence support this view. First, in our Pennsylvanian study, we interviewed the children in their first year at school about their experiences. To our initial surprise, we found that the children who had earlier been 'stars' at reading minds and feelings, were reporting more negative experiences with other children at school – in the sense that they commented that some other children did not like them, or did not want to play with them, and that they sometimes had no one to play with. In contrast some of the children who years before had done poorly on the tests of social understanding gave very sunny accounts of how everyone liked them, and how they had no problems with other children. Second, the children who had been especially mature on the tests of social understanding as three-year-olds were also more sensitive to criticism from teachers, in that they were more likely to take account of such criticism when rating the quality of their own work.

Would this pattern of connections also be found in the London research, with a much larger, inner-city sample of children, and a more comprehensive set of assessments of social understanding? The results supported the Pennsylvanian study findings on school-age sensitivity to failure and teacher criticism. The five-year-old London children who were most sensitive to teacher criticism were those who had had more advanced social understanding as preschoolers.[30] We don't know what the implications of this pattern are for children's experience of other kinds of criticism or failure – including what happens within friendships but the evidence that low self-esteem and self-confidence may have wide implications for children's well-being implies that the suggestion that there is a 'downside' to early social sensitivity deserves study.

Social understanding, temperament, friendship quality and genetics

Early differences between children in their understanding of other people are, we've seen, linked to some features of their friendships in the school years. Does genetics play a part in these differences? On common-sense grounds it seems likely that children who are temperamentally sociable and gregarious will have more opportunity to make friends. Given that personality characteristics like sociability and shyness are influenced by genetics, this reminds us that some of the differences in how easy children find it to make friends, and indeed who they choose as their friends, are likely to be attributable to their genetic make-up.[31]

There has been surprisingly little research into the extent to which differences in friendship are related to genetic differences between individuals. In one of the few studies that investigated this issue, through a comparison of identical (monozygotic) twins (who are identical genetically) and fraternal (dizygotic) twins, who are 50 per cent similar genetically, Alison Pike and her colleagues studied friendship and sibling relationships in adolescent twins.[32] She found that one aspect of the adolescent friendships – a dimension of validation and caring for the friend – was genetically influenced. Similar findings were reported by Beth Manke and her colleagues, from a study of 701 adolescents, in which twins, full siblings and stepsiblings were compared. Again, it was the positive aspects of best friendships (warmth and support) that were found to be genetically influenced; neither study found evidence of genetic influence on the negative features of friendship.

Were these differences related to temperament? Pike found that the positive aspects of friendships were indeed related to sociability and activity, paralleling the findings reported for children in middle childhood by Clare Stocker: this study found that the more sociable children were rated as having more positive relationships with their friends, and more closeness and less hostility in their closest friendships.[33] Pike's results also showed that the temperamental trait of emotionality (being hot blooded and quick tempered) was related to relationship negativity with both friends and siblings – however this was only moderately influenced by genetic factors.

So there is still not a clear story on the links between genetics, temperament and friendship in childhood. What about the possibility that individual differences in social understanding – which we've seen are related to some aspects of friendship quality – are influenced by genetics? The evidence is mixed. One small twin study found that individual differences in theory-of-mind skills were related to genetics;[34] however this finding was not replicated in a larger twin study. A third, large-scale twin study which focused on behaviour, rather than on the false-belief assessment of theory of mind, reports moderate heritability. So the findings are inconsistent, and of course this evidence does not directly inform us about possible genetic influence on *friendship*. On that important topic, we remain in need of more research.

The developmental influence of friendships in early childhood

The evidence for just how different children's friendships can be means that the impact of a particular friendship on a child's development will depend on the *kind* of friendship the children enjoy together, on *who* the friend is, as well as the kind of broader social group and neighbourhood in which they are growing up. Parental support or disapproval of the friendship will also, of course, play a part (Chapter 8). What aspects of children's development are likely to be linked to the quality of their early friendships? Four stand out, from the research on children over time. First, the quality of children's later friendships; second, their understanding of other people, and the solving of social problems; third, children's feelings of self worth and their emotional well-being; fourth, the development of antisocial or deviant behaviour.

Early and later friendships

Both the studies of toddlers by Carollee Howes[35] and our studies in Pennsylvania and London highlight the over-time associations between children's very early friendships and those of their early school years (see also Ladd's studies).[36] We don't yet have evidence to draw causal conclusions about these associations: the processes underlying the connections over time remain unclear. It could be that individual characteristics of children that are continuous over time are key (their sociability, their understanding of others, their own self-confidence in social situations, their capacity for playing exciting games), or that children do indeed in the school years draw on their 'internal representations' of friendship experiences formed earlier, as we argued on the basis of our London friendship study findings. Given the importance to children of their friendships in the school years, these connections deserve our attention.

Understanding other people

The patterns over time that we found in both the Pennsylvanian and the London studies highlight the links between early understanding of other people's feelings, and other minds, and the quality of children's later friendships. The Pennsylvanian children who were early 'stars' at mind-reading and understanding feelings were particularly likely to develop friendships in which they shared exciting and elaborate pretend play, and long, connected conversations. The London research replicated and extended these findings. But the connections between understanding and friendship are very likely to go the other way as well. As we found in the London research, friendship can be a context in which children's understanding of other people is fostered. Once a friendship begins to develop, the opportunities for the children involved to learn about what this other person feels and thinks increases markedly. It is through their creation of joint imaginary worlds, their extended conversations and their management of problems and disagreements that these opportunities arise. The discussion of inner states, especially prominent in friends' pretend play, is a strong candidate for the social processes which underlie these developments.

And studies by educationalists have shown that children faced with logical, mathematical or scientific problems can make particularly good progress in solving these if they tackle them with a close friend. In fact, they make much better progress in finding solutions to these problems with a friend than if they are paired with a child who is not so close.[37] As a final example, children who were faced with a problem involving social ethics with a friend discussed the problems in quite a different way than they did when they were with a child who was not a friend. They gave more explanations, criticized and disagreed more freely, and changed to more mature solutions. The friends took more time to work out differences of opinion, and were more prepared to take account of what the other person wants.

Well-being and self-esteem

There is no question about the connections between children having friends, and feeling relatively happy about themselves, and self-confident. Having companions to share interests, having fun with other kids, feeling part of the larger group are part of the story here, but as well as the companionship – clearly important in the school years – the more intimate aspects of friendship are important for well-being. Feeling that another kid *likes* you and values your friendship is rewarding. Children without friends are much more likely to describe loneliness and isolation from others; they are also more vulnerable to feeling depressed sometimes. Of course, the direction of influence is likely to be two-way here: having a close friend can lead to less unhappiness and loneliness, but being depressed and lonely can also make it harder to form and keep friendships. We look at these issues in detail in Chapters 5 and 6.

Predicting trouble

Friends are likely to influence each other not only through conversations, but in other ways, too. Children are particularly likely to imitate and emulate their friends – from the earliest stages of toddlerhood.[38] Friends are, as a result, especially powerful *models* for either good or evil! What does this mean for the impact of friendships on children's being drawn into trouble? If you talk to children about their friendships, they sometimes tell you, quite clearly, that they get into trouble partly because of their friends. Here is Guy (eight years old, from our London study) who is talking to us about how different he is from his brother, in terms of his preferred friends – who do indeed get him into trouble. The interviewer has asked him about the differences between him and his brother Sam in terms of their being in trouble at school:

GUY: I am worse than he [Sam] is, because the friends I am around, they screw off all the time in class. I am kind of like them sometimes . . .
INTERVIEWER: And how do you think you and Sam became different [about getting into trouble] – what do you think caused the differences?
GUY: Probably like I said – the people I hang around with . . . I don't know how it happens . . . I just got tired of being quiet . . . once I am around my friends, I just change . . .

If you are trying to predict which children are likely to become deviant and get into trouble, it is pretty important to know who their friends are. There is evidence that children with deviant friends increase in their own antisocial behaviour, and that they talk together about deviant activities even when they are being videotaped by psychologists! In our research in London, the observations of pairs of four-year-old children playing together in a room at school, with no observer present, but a video recorder running, were strikingly revealing. Sometimes the children joined together in plotting to break rules, in shared swearing sessions and in games of pretend that were focused on violence, stealing and robbing, escaping from prison.[39]

But this evidence for the *fun* of shared deviance between friends brings us to a paradox, in terms of the impact of the friendship on the children's development. We might chose to emphasize that having a close, supportive and intimate friend is very good for children's well-being, their sense of self-esteem, their understanding of each other and their social confidence. But what these children are doing together may well be deviant, antisocial activities, which are in fact *fostered* by the friendship (shades of Oliver Twist being initiated into picking pockets by his friend the Artful Dodger). The significance of a particular friendship for how a child develops in terms of trouble will depend crucially on *who* that friend is.

Friendships do often form between children who share some particular experiences, as well as being similar in personality characteristics and gender. Children from single parent families, and those with divorced parents tend to make friends with others who have been through similar family upheavals or transitions. This may in part be the result of spending time with similar families (single mothers often become friends, and then their children get to know each other well, for example). It could also be the result of the attraction of being with someone who has had similar experiences. The sharing of background and experience may well mean that such friendships can provide support in the face of family difficulties – though as we will see in the next chapter, the story is not yet fully clear on *how* or even the extent to which these friendships are supportive.

Conclusions

The answer to the question with which we began this chapter – what lies behind differences in friendship quality – is a complicated one. In the early school years differences in the nature of children's friendships are clear, as are differences in the extensiveness of their networks of friends. Opportunities for making friends differ for children growing up in different social worlds, opportunities for keeping friends over the years also differ, for instance with transitions between schools. Parents play a role in fostering and influencing friendships, as we will see in Chapter 8, however differences in children's personalities and their social intelligence assessed early in childhood give us particularly strong clues on the kind of friendships they are likely to form later on.

Importantly, the London study showed that it was the social understanding of *both* children in the preschool friendships, and their shared experiences in those preschool relationships, particularly their shared pretend experiences, that were associated with the quality of the children's later friendships. It was not just a question of the individual characteristics of the two individual friends, but the importance of the relationship they created together.

Friendship provides a marvellous context for children to learn about how others see the world, and what makes them happy or upset. Individual differences in friendship quality are also related to moral understanding; positive aspects of friendship are related to temperamental characteristics, and genetics is likely to contribute to the positive features of friendship, though there is still little investigation of these issues in young children. The significance of these friendships as support for children in stressful situations we turn to next.

5

With a little help from my friends

When we're sad, Laurie and me talk ... we both like the same things, and we hate the same things ... I was scared sort of, when I started school, and then when Laurie was my friend – well I wasn't any more.

Ray, six years old (Pennsylvanian study)

In the novel *Jane Eyre*, Jane Eyre is sent away as a little girl, to a school in which she suffers terrible humiliations and unkindness. It is chiefly her friendship with another girl, Helen, that sustains her through these dreadful experiences. In describing both the horrors of the school and the supportive friendship so vividly, Charlotte Brontë drew directly on her own childhood experiences – her recollections of the school to which she was sent as an eight-year-old. The Superintendent of the school confirmed the significance of the friendship, recalling that Charlotte's friend was a great ally, 'ever ready to protect her from tyranny'.[1]

That friends can be enormously important as supports in extremely stressful situations we know from the story of the holocaust children studied by Anna Freud and Sophie Dann.[2] This was a group of pre-schoolers who at the end of the Second World War were found living without parents in a concentration camp. Their parents had been killed in the gas chambers when they were babies, and while they had had some care and attention from other inmates of the camp, they had for two years before liberation stuck together very closely as a group. When they were rescued after the war they were very wild and destructive, and hostile to all adults. Towards each other they were intensely attached, and caring. These children, according to Anna Freud and Sophie Dann:

> Had no wish other than to be together and became upset when they were separated ... No child would remain upstairs when the others were downstairs ... If anything of the kind happened, the single child would constantly ask for the other children, while the group would fret for the missing child ... there was no occasion to urge the children to 'take turns'; they did it spontaneously. They were extremely considerate of each other's feelings ... At mealtimes, handing the food to the neighbor was of greater importance than eating oneself.

The emotional security of these children was completely dependent on the presence of the others. When they grew up they were able to develop good relationships with other adults – and it appears that this small group of other children had provided the emotional resources and support for each other that is usually supplied by parents. The extent to which friendships can buffer children from the impact of more everyday stressful situations is still not very clear. However for children undergoing family stress and change, there's some evidence that friends can make a real difference to children's emotional well-being.

Family stress and friendship

A 15-year-old girl who was taking part in our research on children growing up in different family situations[3] looked back on the time that her parents had separated, five years earlier, and commented to us that it was that week when all her friends became so important to her. 'I was glad I had spent the last 8 years of my life with these people because they understood what to do and how to do it, to make me happy. I felt such a sensation of sticking together.' She went on to recall how they had done everything they could think of to cheer her up, including giving her 'piles of Easter eggs'.

One Californian study of divorce suggests that this picture is not uncommon.[4] Friendships helped the children in that research through the stressful period of their parents' conflict and separation. The pattern of effects was clearer for the boys than the girls: the boys especially turned to their friends, and appeared to distance themselves from their families at this time of trouble. However, a study of children whose parents' marriages were in difficulty in England tells a slightly different story.[5] Here, the children who had good friends were indeed showing less disturbed behaviour than those without a close friend, but it was not clear whether the friendship was a *cause* of the well-being of the children, or whether the friendship itself was a sign of the children being well-adjusted initially. That is, the good friendships may have been a consequence of the children's resilience. It could be that having a good friend is indeed a real support for children, but it is also possible that the children who were less upset by their parents' troubled relationship were better able to make and maintain friendship. It is very likely that both were important.

Another study of parental separation and remarriage highlights a further point: the characteristics of the child's friend are also important. Mavis Hetherington and her colleagues showed that having socially well-adjusted friends with few behaviour problems promoted the resilience of children whose parents separated or remarried, whereas having immature friends with behaviour problems did not.[6] Again, we see that *who* your friend is may be crucial to the kind of support the friendship provides.

Where an association between friendship and children's coping with difficult situations is found, we do not always know *how* the friendships are helpful. As adults, we know that the presence of a friend in whom we can confide and talk through our problems can be very helpful. Indeed it is one of the key protective factors buffering adults against the negative impact of stressful events. For young adolescents, it seems likely that friendships can work in the same kind of way to protect against depression or anxiety.[7] But for children who have not yet reached adolescence, the evidence that they confide in friends about family problems or serious anxieties is inconsistent. In our research on family changes, in which children who had experienced parental separation were studied over several years, we talked to the children about what had happened at the time of their parents' separation, and in the weeks that followed.[8] We asked them who they had talked to about concerns they had about the family situation. The children were on average about 10 years old, but ranged from 8 to16 years. Top of the list of people in whom they had confided in the weeks following their parents' separation were their friends, followed in frequency by their grandparents. So, at least for the children in this community study, friends were an important source of confiding.

The implications of this research are that for children going though family break-up, having a good friend was linked to being less troubled, and probably provided some protection against children being upset, and that friends can be a key source of confiding about problems, even for children who have not yet reached adolescence. However other studies report that relatively few children actually talk over their family problems in detail with their friends. We should perhaps not be surprised that the support that young friends provide for each other is not necessarily that of a counsellor; there are after all a host of other ways – direct and indirect – that having a friend can help when a child is having to cope with family conflict or separation. It could be that having a close friend helps by making a child feel better about himself, liked and appreciated, or by providing entertainment, distraction and companionship, a social world outside the distressed family circle. The 15-year-old who reported on her friends' support to her as a ten-year-old faced with her parents' separation made no mention of confiding, but described graphically the kinds of caring gestures her friends made. The evidence from young friends reminds us that we do not have to think of support as exclusively 'counselling' in nature.

The issue of *how* the support from friends changes as children grow up is not well understood, but one group of researchers investigated the question of how conversations with friends actually support children faced with distressing events. Several different possible sources of conversational support have been distinguished in research on support.[9] Talking with a friend may help by (a) *emotional support* (expressing sympathy or understanding, (b) *giving advice*, (c) *distraction* (discussing a more pleasant topic), (d) *providing excuses* (for instance, blaming others, minimizing the nasty event) or (e) *accepting an excuse* (and thus enhancing the validity of an excuse). We know that as children grow older, they increasingly view friends as providers of emotional support,[10] and that they become increasingly sophisticated about excuses.[11]

We also know that children report that they themselves use distraction as a means of coping with distress. Paul Harris studied children's own accounts of how they coped with distressing experiences, such as being in hospital, or sent away to boarding school.[12] In one study, when children were asked whether, when they were sad, there was anything they could do to make themselves happy, they focused on distraction strategies: 'then you should call up your friends and play with them'. The older children recommended changing the mental processes that were caused by the situation: 'You mustn't think of it any more, otherwise you'll get sad again.' The most popular strategy of the youngest children, six-year-olds, in the study was to engage in some activity or game, as in the next, typical exchange:

INTERVIEWER:	Say you were ill and you felt sad. Is there anything you could do to *change* the way you felt, to change that feeling of sadness?
CHILD:	Try and be happy.
INTERVIEWER:	How?
CHILD:	By playing about.
INTERVIEWER:	What would that do?
CHILD:	Get happy – make me feel happy.

The six-year-olds only occasionally talked about cognitive processes being important. One said 'You could go and play outside and try to forget about it.' The ten-year-olds more often talked about how activities could 'take your mind off' the sadness or negative feelings. Here's the response of a ten-year-old:

CHILD: Well I could stop thinking about the pain or what's
                  going to happen and get my favorite toy out or my
                  favorite thing.
INTERVIEWER: And what would that do?
CHILD: It would make me not think of being sad and it
                  would cheer me up.

In Harris's study of children in hospital, again distraction (by engaging in other activities, or thinking of happy things) was frequently the strategy mentioned – usually with no mention of mental processes by the six-year-olds. Here's what a six-year-old hospitalized with suspected appendicitis said:

CHILD: I could get someone to play with me.
INTERVIEWER: What would that do?
CHILD: Make me more cheerful . . .

We might predict then that distraction would be one aspect of support found in children's conversations with their peers when faced with stressful events. The study that focused on age differences in the use and effectiveness of support offered during conversations about negative events reported that talking to friends lessened distress across all the ages studied, that distraction was common among the younger children (ten-year-olds), and that support through the provision of excuses was more common among adolescents.[13] The researchers comment that distraction does not require intimacy and requires a lower level of social skill than other support strategies which involve more elaborate forms of psychological defence (excuses, and excuse validation).

How does this picture of support coming from the distraction offered by other children fit with the findings on children faced with parental conflict and separation? There are some clear, and quite general lessons from this research. The first is that on the whole, most children do not usually confide in their peers in detail about family troubles. They may get valuable support from them (as in the Easter eggs story), but this support is not usually through detailed sharing of narratives about what happens at home. There are exceptions, as in our family research just described.[14] But it is worth reflecting that some counsellors and therapists are now coming to see this 'distancing' from the source of distress provided by distractions as helpful. Indeed they question the idea that 'denial' of one's problems is necessarily a bad thing. The idea that to avoid thinking about your problem is a misguided way of coping is now being reconsidered and re-evaluated by some of those who counsel others.

A second lesson from the research on children whose parents are in conflict is that children often have a number of friends, from the different spheres of their lives, and what they confide to these different friends can vary. A child may well have friends, for instance, from the world of the sports that he plays, and different friends from his classroom at school, and other friends again from his neighbourhood world. He will talk about sports concerns – successes and failures – with the friend from his world of football, not with the classroom friends or the kid next door. And he'll talk about the dramas of school life with the friend from school, not with the others. Most likely he will not talk about family problems directly with any of his friends. We don't know how far this is because the family experiences are too painful, too embarrassing or too confusing to expose to his friends. But the lack of discussion of family issues does not mean that he's not helped and supported by his close friendships outside the family.

A third lesson is that having a very strong interest outside the family can in itself be a major help for children whose families are in stress. Kenny, a star football player in our research on family change, with a gang of friends linked to that world, weathered the storms at home with considerable calm. So too did Joanne, a ten-year-old who was already a fanatically serious ballet dancer, with a best friend who was also a dancer. But neither of these two talked about home difficulties very frequently with their friends.

Friends and the normal transitions of childhood

Do friends provide support during the more common stresses with which many children have to cope, such as the upheaval surrounding the birth of a brother or sister, or the normal transitions of childhood – starting or changing school, moving house, or changing neighbourhoods, which involve separation from friends?

Birth of a sibling

An intriguing example of support from friends very early in childhood comes from a study by Laurie Kramer of three-year-olds whose mothers were expecting a new baby.[15] The arrival of a sibling is an event that involves considerable upheaval in most first-born children's lives, and the majority show signs of upset, signs that are not usually trivial or of short duration.[16] The children in Kramer's study who had good friends before their new sibling was born, showed markedly less disturbance after the sibling birth than the other children who did not have close friends. Clearly the protective effect of friendship between the three-year-olds was unlikely to be mediated through heavy-duty discussions about the displaced first-born children's hurt or jealous feelings. However Laurie Kramer suspected that the experience of shared pretend play, which the friendships made possible, might be fulfilling a useful function. She found that it was the children who had friendships in which they frequently joined in shared pretend who were less hostile to the new baby sibling. And many of these children engaged in repetitive sibling-related fantasies. Perhaps these make-believe games helped the children both before and after the baby's arrival. In anticipation of the birth, playing at siblings could help the children to understand 'what it will be like to have a baby in the family and to gain support from their friend as they explore their feelings about becoming a sibling', Laurie Kramer commented. After the birth, again, pretend play with a friend could possibly provide opportunities for 'playing out' troubling concerns for the displaced older sibling.

A particularly vivid example of a child whose pretend play with his friends clearly reflected his preoccupation and upset at the arrival of his baby sibling is given in Vivian Paley's description of the children in her Chicago kindergarten, in her book *Bad Guys Don't Have Birthdays*.[17] Four-year-old Frederick's mother has just had a baby, and he is pretty upset, but won't discuss it with his teacher. Instead, he wants to be a baby in every game of pretend that starts with his friends at the nursery. Sometimes they let him be the baby; sometimes they refuse. Here is Frederick insisting on being the baby of two three-year-olds, Petey and Jonathan; he reiterates that both of them should be his mommy not his daddy:

'No daddies. Just two mommies. I'm both your baby cat. Meow, meow. I want my milk now.' Frederick lies down on the floor. Petey smiles.
'Mommy will come. Here, kitty, your bottle.'
'Call me new baby, okay? Meow, meow. Put me to bed, two mommies. Don't go away.'

On another day his attempt to get his two friends Mollie and Margaret to accept him as their baby is strongly resisted:

'Ma-ma, ma-ma.'
'We're not playing baby, Frederick,' Margaret tells him abruptly.
'Ma-ma.'
'Stop that, Frederick,' Mollie warns. 'No babies. We didn't *have* our babies yet.'

After many repetitions of being 'baby', Frederick transforms himself first into a mother, then a hunter: 'I'll be right back, mother, I have to hunt for a lion for our supper. The baby is hungry for lion meat.'

Gradually, Frederick returns to his position as leader of the little group of friends. The careful documentation of his pretend play over the weeks makes a plausible case that he was able to play out his concerns about his displacement by his baby sibling because of his pre-existing friendships with Mollie and the other children. It also shows that playing out his distress in this way was acceptable to his friends. If he had shown his upset by being aggressive (as many young children do) he might well have been spurned by the other children. But because he had this group of friends, he was able to express his distress through the play, *and* stay part of the group of friends. What is important here is not simply that Frederick had social contacts as any child in day care or preschool would have, but that he had friendships with Mollie and Margaret that provided the context of shared imaginative play in which he could express and explore distress and worries.

Playing with fears

Children return repeatedly to the themes that scare, upset or excite them, in their pretend play with close friends. Sometimes these include the fears that, as part of normal development, often show increases in the preschool years. Lots of children go through a phase of being frightened of the dark, in early childhood, for instance. And the psychologist John Gottman, who recorded the conversations of young friends playing alone together gives us an example of how children can play with this fear, and eventually lose it.[18] A little girl Naomi, great friends with a neighbouring child Eric, was afraid of the dark, and slept with a nightlight. When she and Eric played together, their pretend play often involved dolls who were afraid of the dark. The children would turn off the lights, and Naomi would pretend to be the doll and scream, then pretend to be the mommy and comfort the doll, with Eric comforting too. Then after a few months, Naomi told her parents she did not need the nightlight, and the theme of 'being afraid of the dark' disappeared from their joint pretend play. As Gottman notes, both Naomi and the doll were cured! Of course, we don't know that the pretend play in itself helped in the 'cure', but John Gottman's argument that repetition may provide the children with some sense of familiarity, control and mastery over the source of fear is a plausible one.

Another typical source of fear for young children is fear of separation from parents. This is also a theme that recurs again and again in some friends' play. Here are Eric and Naomi again:

ERIC: This is my house, remember?
NAOMI: Where are your parents, remember?
ERIC: My parents? I don't have any parents. My mommy and daddy went; they didn't like me anymore.
NAOMI: So they went some place else?

The solution the children work out for this fearful situation is also well rehearsed:

ERIC: I live here all alone. Hey, you can live with me.
NAOMI: Yes, and keep you company. I'll cook the food . . . and we can all go to bed too.

Friends and school transitions

The beginning of primary/elementary school is a major change for young children, even for those who are old hands at preschool or day care, one that can present particular stresses and new demands. And it is a transition in which friends can play a key supporting role. When we talked to the children in our Pennsylvanian research about how they had felt about starting school, the key importance of having a friend recurred in what they told us. Ray, for example, whose comments begin this chapter, was very clear on the importance of his friendship with Laurie. Another child, Lisa, decided to draw me a picture of what she remembered about starting school – and there was first a picture of an unhappy child (mother disappearing out of a door at the top of the picture, tears running down child's face). Then there was a triumphant picture of a smiling child with her new friend, both crowned with golden crowns to complete the happy ending. We asked the children in the study, who were at this point sophisticates who had been at school for a whole six weeks, what advice they would give to a younger child who was about to start kindergarten. 'Get a friend!' was one boy's terse reply. Advice on how to do this was also given. Five-year-old Emma gave remarkably astute guidance on how to make friends with the new children at the school in her comments about what school is like for a younger child:

I'd say it's really fun once you get used to it, and you'll start knowing the kids a lot, and they'll start being nice to you. Once you start knowing what, like, what they *like*, and you start talking about it, they'll be going, like, 'Oh that happened to me too!' and stuff like that.

The children were absolutely correct in their advice that making new friends is a key help. They also said – again quite correctly – that it would help to start school with a friend from preschool days. Research has now demonstrated what the children were so clear about – that having a friend when you start school is associated with a better adjustment to school. Studies by Gary Ladd[19] showed for instance, that children who started school with a friend and who maintained that friendship had a much more positive attitude to school over the subsequent year. They also increased their liking for school over the year more than those who started without a friend. Those who made new friends in the first year at school also made greater gains in school achievement than those who did not.

It is always a challenge to try to sort out what is cause, and what is effect in findings like these. Self-confident happy children may make friends more readily than less confident children, and they are also likely to find school transitions less problematic. But the nature of the particular friendship does seem to be key here. It is the quality of supportiveness within the friendship that seems to matter especially.

It is also possible that the protective effect of having a good friend when you are faced with a school transition – in comparison with not having a good friend – works chiefly for the more vulnerable children. That is, having friends may matter more for the children who are more vulnerable for some reason before the transition. It has been found, for instance, that the stresses linked to developmental transitions such as starting primary (elementary) school or junior school, accentuate differences among vulnerable children to a greater extent than among less vulnerable children. Those who find changes frightening and anxiety-provoking are more likely to find the transitions hard to take.

One source of vulnerability to the potential stresses of starting or changing school is shyness. Children who are extremely shy can have particular difficulty in the playground and classroom, facing groups of children, feeling intimidated and unable to join the others.[20] What they tend to do is 'wait and hover' around of the edge of the group of children. This is a 'low risk' strategy, in the sense that they are less likely to be rejected outright than if they made a direct attempt to join the other children. But what happens as a result of the 'hovering' is that they are usually ignored, and remain lonely outsiders. Unless, that is, they have a friend in the group. With a friend in the group, they are more likely to be noticed and permitted to join in the game or talk. The result is that shy children who have a friend are much less likely to be put through the humiliating experiences of being rejected. Friends are protective in this sense. And probably as a result, extremely shy children who have a friend are less likely to feel bad about themselves and suffer from low self-esteem than very shy children without a close friend.

Separation from friends

So friends can play a key role in children's happy adjustment to starting school, and a protective role for very shy children. The other side of the coin is that losing friends, through changing school or neighbourhood, also affects children's well-being in a nontrivial way. The impact of such losses can be seen even in the preschool years. In her Los Angeles studies of preschoolers at day care, Carollee Howes showed that children who lost a friend when the friend moved away from the day care showed a clear drop in the maturity and competence of their play after their friend left – and this was not just a brief effect for a day or two after the loss.[21] And a study by Tiffany Field of preschoolers whose friends left their day care amplifies the picture.[22] This research showed that the children behaved in a much more agitated way at preschool after their friends had gone, and their stress was measurable in terms of their physiology: their heart rates and skin conductivity reflected their anxiety. The children who knew that their friends were going to leave also showed marked signs of anxiety before the separation, with an increase in nightmares, for instance. Anticipating the separation from a friend was a real source of worry to these children, even before they were four years old.

Children's relative helplessness in the face of changes imposed on them by the adult world is poignant, and illustrates how important is the quality of the friendship before the separation. Two sets of comments by mothers of the seven-year-olds in the Newsons' study of families in Nottingham, England,[23] make the point:

Well, one little boy left – he was very good friends with him and his little sister, and then they left and went to Mapperly, and that seemed to upset him, and he closed in and didn't go out much at all – until *we* moved, he didn't seem to want to go out to play, and I told my husband, I think he was missing that little boy. He's not a child that makes a lot of new friends easily, but once they are, you know, he keeps them a long time.

Tania is that type of girl that she'd make a friend and it would be a lifetime friend if possible – she's not the sort for having a pal for a month and them dropping off and having another pal next month. No, 'cause when we left Nottingham she did miss a little girl – ooh every hour of the day they'd played with one another, you know, that was free for playing in – and she *did* miss her. And I think *that*, p'raps, was why she was a little slow at making friends at school . . . I didn't want to worry her into thinking that, you know, she'd *got* to make a friend. I know what she is – if she takes to someone . . . she'll be a real friend and stick by them, no matter what they do to her; she'll stick to them.

Tania's mother felt that Tania would be a real support to her friends. But not all friendships are source of support. We are back to the issue of individual differences in the nature of friendships. Even at preschool, the upset children show at being separated from a friend depends on how affectionate and closely coordinated their relations had been before the separation. This theme – the importance of the quality of particular friendships – recurs throughout childhood and into adolescence. Children who describe their friendship as supportive and intimate are also as individuals less likely to be depressed or low in self-esteem than those who describe their friendship as rivalrous and low in intimacy. They are also more likely to do well at school, to be strongly motivated to achieve, and likely to be popular in the group.

But which is cause and which effect? Are certain children more able to form supportive friendships, and also more sociable and successfully effective at school? Do close supportive friendships help children to feel good about themselves? One way of disentangling cause and effect is to study children over time. By following their progress at school and the quality of their friendships over the course of a school year, for instance, we can begin to see whether the nature of their friendship contributes to changes in their adjustment and progress. Research on young teenagers suggests that you can indeed predict changes in school adjustment from the quality of teenagers' close friendships at the start of the school year.[24] While good friendship and good school adjustment go hand in hand, students whose friendships were intimate and supportive at the start of the school year became increasingly positively involved with school as the year progressed. Here, then, the findings parallel the results of Ladd's studies of kindergarten-aged children. Intimate, affectionate and supportive friendships do apparently support children and help them to adjust to school.

Children who are emotionally troubled

Friendship quality can also be importantly linked to young people's recovery from depression or anxiety. One study followed a group of people for a year after the onset of their depression or anxiety.[25] Those who had good friendships had a much better chance of improving in mental health than those who had poor or only moderately good friendships. The association was particularly strong for depression. Again, it would be very hard to come to conclusions about cause and effect here. Did the children who were already feeling better, and 'on the mend' manage to form better relationships with their friends? Or did the quality of their friendships exert a specific helping effect on their states of mind? Happily it is relatively unusual for children to suffer from depression. Much more common are the troubles caused by the tangled intrigues of small groups of friends, or by bullying, and it is to these we turn next – and to the question of whether friendships can protect children from the impact of bullying.

6

Intrigues, bullying, rejection and loneliness

Anna (aged six years) has just been excluded for the fourth time from a game with her two friends, Sally and Lydia, during recess; she leaves them and sits with her head in her hands, alone by the fence of the school playground:

Anna (mutters to herself): 'I take it in turns for them, so they should take it in turns for me . . . [begins to cry] . . . I don't know why I even made friends with Sally . . . sometimes I'd be better without her . . . actually it's more horrid with Lydia . . . I don't know how *anyone* could be friends . . . [watches the others] . . . Now they've upset another person . . . they just don't have any care . . . [cries again].'[1]

In this chapter we focus on some of the stresses that accompany children's friendships in the world of primary/elementary school: the issue of betrayal by friends; teasing, bullying and victimization and the question of whether friendship can protect children from such torments; then the broader issue of rejection by a group of peers, and again the question of whether friendship can buffer or protect children is our primary concern. Finally, are the risks for children's well-being and later adjustment different for these various painful experiences with friends and peers?

Betrayal and friendship

Anna, crying at the side of the playground, was taking part in a study by Alison Tamplin in Cambridge; she was wearing a tiny radio microphone that recorded even her unhappy mutterings to herself. Her poignant distress reminds us that the world of friends can be for some children a world of betrayals, jealousies, and even cruelties. In Margaret Atwood's novel *Cat's Eye* these cruelties are particularly vividly portrayed.[2] In the book, eight-year-old Elaine, who hasn't until now had the opportunity to make friends, becomes part of a little group of girls – finding to her surprise that what's involved is sitting together, looking through magazines, talking about favourite film stars, grooming each other. Through such lessons in feminine conformity the group of friends develops close ties. Gradually the close-knit group becomes a context for teasing and relentless punishment for not conforming. Elaine becomes a victim of bullying, within a friendship group from which she cannot break away, in which the themes of conformity, standards and acceptability are woven into a horrific net around her. The bullying and teasing are linked to the friendship, inextricably it seems: the friends *know* what is right, they *know* her, and their approval and disapproval alternate capriciously.

How does this picture of cruelty born of the intimacy that is central to friendship, relate to children's experiences in the real world? Should we see it as part of a novelist's imaginative world, or does it reflect the relationships of children today? Evidence that shows children do indeed undergo such experiences comes from current research on bullying and victimization by groups of children, as well as from the accounts of writers looking back on their own childhoods. Particularly vivid examples from writers are the autobiographical accounts of their childhoods by the novelists Graham Greene and, from the nineteenth century, Anthony Trollope.[3] Such accounts make two points very clear.

First, it is not just girls who form such intense 'cliques', in which friendship, affection, understanding, teasing and cruelty are so tightly interwoven. Second, it is clear that these cruelties leave a trace that can last a very long time – well into adulthood (a key point of the Atwood novel). Both points are powerfully made by Graham Greene, looking back on his childhood in his autobiography *A Sort of Life*. He was the son of the headmaster at the school he attended; it was a position that made for painful clashes of loyalty, which were mercilessly exploited by his two 'friends', Watson and Carter. Greene commented that 'The sneering nicknames were inserted like splinters under the nails . . .' He saw the years of humiliation at school as having a very long shadow: 'For many years after leaving school, when I thought back to that period, I found the desire for revenge alive like a creature under a stone. The only change was that I looked under the stone less and less often . . .' The impact of those 'friendship' experiences was, he thought, important for his writing as an adult. Reflecting on an accidental meeting with Watson, 30 years after their schooldays, he commented: 'I wondered . . . if I would ever have written a book had it not been for Watson and the dead Carter, if those years of humiliation had not given me an excessive desire to prove I was good at something, however long the effort might prove.'

In the case of six-year-old Anna, sitting at the side of the playground in the Cambridge study, of Graham Greene, and of Elaine in Atwood's *Cat's Eye*, the pain came from what happened within a small group of friends. Repeatedly in our own studies we see the potential problem of triads – that two into three all too often does not go. A and B are friends, C becomes a friend of B, A feels excluded, resentful, jealous, betrayed. The very intensity of the friendship increases the powerful impact of the exclusion. 'Everyday' intrigues and changes of loyalty within small groups of friends are very common. At three or four years old, children often exclude other children briefly in the course of play as we saw in chapter 3; the preschoolers' comment 'We don't like you today' implies that tomorrow it may well be different. But by six or seven years, the impact of being excluded takes on a different quality, that reflects the greater intensity of the friendships, the new and increasing concern with the approval of the group, and the greater understanding of what the others think of you. Many of us as adults can recall those triangles or quartets of friendship cliques, and their powerful dynamics of jealousy and competition. Although victimization by peers has been primarily studied with group situations, it also occurs within dyadic friendships as research by Nicki Crick and David Nelson has documented.

Bullying and friendship

How common is it for children to experience being victimized by bully-ing, such as that described by Margaret Atwood and Graham Greene, and can friends *protect* children from such experiences?

It is notoriously hard to get accurate figures on how common it is for children today to be bullied, because most bullying goes on in settings that are not monitored by teachers (on the school bus, in the corner of the playground, on the sports pitch, in the lunch room), and because children who are being bullied by their 'friends' are usually very reluctant to talk about their experiences. They don't know who to trust among the adults, they are afraid of reprisals – and one of the effects of bullying is that children become stripped of their self-confidence. But the recent estimates of rates of bullying are disturbingly high. In the UK, recent reports present rather different estimates mainly because of different methodologies (for instance, self-report questionnaires versus face-to-face interviews).[4] But there is agreement that a substantial minority of children are involved, and there is evidence that victimization is stable over time. In a large-scale recent study by Dieter Wolke and his colleagues, in which 1,982 children between six and nine years old were individually interviewed, 4 per cent were direct bullies, 40 per cent victims, and 10 per cent both were bullies and were victimized frequently themselves (these children were referred to as 'bully-victims').[5] Information from the parents of these children about their adjustment showed that the highest rates of behaviour problems were found for the bully-victims and those involved in direct bullying. Some studies suggest that direct bullying (physical and verbal teasing) should be distinguished from 'relational' bullying (the hurtful manipulation of peer relationships/friendships that inflicts harm on others through 'malicious rumour spreading' or 'social exclusion'). In Wolke's large interview study, however, a substantial number of children were involved in both kinds of bullying, and these were also the children who had the most pronounced behaviour problems.

The research into bullying has given us a picture of the typical victims of bullying. They are usually sensitive, gentle and intelligent children; their relationships with their parents are generally good, and they are not accustomed to conflict, shouting and violence at home. They don't fight back when bullied, are manifestly anxious, use ineffectual persuasion techniques, and if they cry when tormented they become even better 'targets' for the bullies. The effects of the bullying on their self-confidence, happiness and well-being can increase the likelihood of more bullying – it is an unhappy cycle of suffering. Studies of children who are victimized over time report that 'internalizing' problems (worrying, anxious and depressed behaviour) contributes to increases in being victimized.[6] Some victimized children also react with disruptive behaviour, aggressiveness and argumentativeness, and it is thought that these responses irritate and provoke the bullying children further.[7]

Many of the children who frequently bully share some common features. They are quite likely to be victims of some kind of abuse, children who are not succeeding at school, who lack a sense of self-worth, and come from families in which there is already bullying. But other children who bully are rather different – they are confident children who expect to control others and to get their own way. And the view that children who bully are poor at understanding other children has had to be revised. Important research has shown that some bullies are, on the contrary, relatively *successful* on tests of understanding others' emotions and their minds.[8] And other children may occasionally bully after an upsetting event in their own lives – rejection by a friend, problems with a teacher or a parent, for example. The research into these bullying situations has led to some very practical interventions in schools, and advice to parents.[9]

Can friendship buffer children from the effects of being bullied?

The answer, for children in middle childhood at least, is a qualified yes. It depends on *who* the friend of the victimized child is, and how generally accepted the child is by the larger group of children. A group of researchers in Canada studied a group of 533 ten-year-old children over a year, with the children reporting on their experiences of loneliness and victimization, and their teachers reporting on their behaviour problems.[10] First, the results confirmed that children with either internalizing or externalizing problems (aggression, violence, delinquency) were more likely to be victims, and these behaviour problems *increased* the likelihood of their being bullied. But having a best friend did predict decreases in being victimized, over the year, regardless of whether the children had behaviour problems.

However, the quality of the children's friendship was importantly linked to whether there was a protective effect. Children whose friendship was described as being high in qualities of protection (e.g., 'he would stick up for me if another kid was causing me trouble') were at less risk for being victimized over time – but having a friend who was *low* in this protective aspect of friendship actually exacerbated the extent to which being victimized was linked to increase in internalizing problems. The finding reminds us that friendships may not always be helpful in terms of children's well-being.[11] If the victimized child's friend is also an anxious, worrying, child with internalizing problems, this increases the risk of victimization. And friends' strategies for protecting their friends may also be significant. Another study reports that the victimized children who were anxious, worrying and depressed – the 'non-aggressive' victims – had almost as many friends as other (non-bullied) children, but their friends tended to be weak, to have internalizing problems themselves, and also to be victims too. In contrast the 'provocative' aggressive victims were likely to have almost no friends at all.[12]

So, for victims who are not aggressive, having less-than-helpful friends may be part of the risks that contribute to the continuing victimization, but for aggressive provocative victims, it is being without friends that adds to the likelihood they will be bullied. Overall, the Canadian study showed that increases in behavioural problems over time for the victimized children were only found for children *without a best friend*. If children are also rejected by the larger peer group this adds to the risk that they will be victimized.

Popularity and rejection by the group

The experience of being unpopular with or disliked by the larger peer group[13] is one that is particularly powerful in its impact, and this too can inflict long-lasting pain. Again, what these experiences mean to children is vividly illustrated by the accounts of the 'victims', especially when those victims are writers who describe with particular sensitivity and insight their own childhood. The novelist Anthony Trollope, who as a schoolboy was isolated and rejected by his peers, looked back on that experience as a middle-aged man, in *An Autobiography*. He was humiliated at school because of his poverty: his clothes were poor and dirty, and his family was unable to pay his school bills. Trollope writes of 'the absolute isolation of my school position . . .' He was not able to participate in sports and the other activities of the boys, because of his poverty:

> I longed for these things with an exceeding longing. I coveted popularity
> with a coveting that was almost mean. It seemed to me that there was
> an Elysium in the intimacy of those very boys whom I was bound to hate
> because they hated me. Something of the disgrace of my school days has
> clung to me all my life.

Again, a lifetime's impact, from childhood rejection, is revealed.

The question of why some children become rejected by their peers has major social significance. For parents it raises many painful issues. Does this isolation from the group mean that these children are unable to form close friendships? What lies behind such rejection – could it be that the child has acquired a negative 'reputation' among his peers – the prejudiced expectations of the larger group of children? If so, would it help if he changed to a different school? Or is there a problem in his awkwardness in social situations, or something about his personality that makes him disliked – in which case, perhaps changing schools won't necessarily help? Will children who are rejected always be ostracized? Are they likely to have later problems in adjustment?

The evidence that some children who are rejected by their peers during the years between eight and twelve do have a range of difficulties later on has given these questions special importance. There has been a great burst of research that has attempted to answer them.[14] What have we learned?

Being alone

First, it is clear that children who tend to be on their own in the classroom or playground, who are rarely part of a group or gang, can be on their own for very different reasons. Some are quite comfortable on their own; they are not being rejected by others, but are particularly 'self-sufficient' and enjoy their solitary activities. Others (like Anthony Trollope) would desperately like to be part of a group but fail to be so. Their exclusion can be for very different reasons. Children who are not seen as popular by the others in their class include some who are actively disliked, some who are simply ignored or neglected (they may be very shy), some who happen not to be very well liked but are not really excluded from talk or games. Among those who are actively disliked and rejected, there are some who are very aggressive and assertive – attempting to boss and control, and others who are not aggressive, but are submissive, awkward, unhappy or withdrawn. The prognosis for these different groups of children is quite different, both in terms of the likelihood that they will form close friendships, and in terms of their later adjustment.

Friendship and popularity

One important lesson we've learned is that it is very important to distinguish between problems in popularity in the larger peer group on the one hand (how all the children in your class feel about you), and lack of a friend, or problems in close friendship between pairs of children.[15] In fact, many children who are not very popular with most of the children in their class do have a friend, and they are quite satisfied with these friendships. And not all popular children have close friendships – indeed many popular children don't have an intense, close relationship with one particular friend. We need to look separately at friendship and at children's social status in the group of children in their class or neighbourhood, if we are to understand their significance for children's well-being and adjustment.

Research that has focused on *both* the quality of children's friendships and their acceptance or rejection within the larger group of children has reported a range of findings (sometimes rather contradictory, an inconsistency that is probably linked to differences in how friendship was measured). In one study, children with friends – regardless of their popularity in the larger group, showed higher levels of altruism and understanding of others' point of view.[16] That is, *friendship* rather than *popularity* predicted the children's social sensitivity and moral understanding. Other research finds that low-accepted children with no friends received lower class-ratings of likeability than rejected or neglected children with friends.[17] Children without friends who were also low on the popularity ratings of other children were particularly likely to feel worthless and inadequate.[18]

In summary, children who are both low in popularity *and* without friends are at a definite disadvantage. At the same time, friendship may serve as a buffer against the negative effects of low acceptance by peers, or outright rejection by the group.[19]

An important further lesson, however, is that the friendships of not-very-popular children do tend to differ from the friendships of more popular children. The friendships of the less popular children are likely to be less stable over time, for instance. Whereas it is quite common for friendships between relatively popular children to last for several years, this is less likely to be so for children who are not regarded as popular. Their friendships are also likely to have more conflicts and disagreements, and to be less supportive, with less intimacy, caring, help and guidance.

Do unpopular children have special difficulties in understanding others?

A ball is tossed across the playground by Tim, intended for his friend to catch on the other side of the playground. But his aim is poor and the ball hits a third boy, Jake. The blow to Jake was not intended by Tim – he was just not very accurate in his toss. But Jake, who is not much liked by the other boys in the class, sees this as yet another hostile act directed at him – and hurls himself aggressively at Tim. Then the other boys, angry at what appears uncalled-for aggression, join in to thump Jake . . .

At one time, researchers placed great emphasis on the idea that children who were isolated or disliked by most of the children in their group were *unable* to relate well to the others because they were literally suffering from a lack of understanding of others. They were, it was held, less good at understanding other children's emotions and intentions, more ready to attribute hostile actions when none was intended, less effective at cooperating and sharing, less good at 'reading' the social signals of

others, and all this led to their social awkwardness – and to the subsequent rejection or isolation. What we have learned from the great
increase in research into children's understanding and children's relations with the peer group over the last decades has changed the picture
here in key respects.

First, there are some situations in which children who are rejected
by other children (especially those who are aggressive themselves) are
indeed more likely than popular children to interpret other children's
behaviour as hostile or aggressive, when it was ambiguous to others.
Some rejected children then react aggressively themselves, to behaviour
that more popular children would not see as aggressive – just as Jake
reacted to Tim's poor ball throwing.

But it is of course not clear whether this tendency to read ambiguous
behaviour as hostile is a *cause* of children being rejected, or indeed a
consequence of their experiences. It is easy to see how there can be a
spiral of influences in which increasing rejection leads children to interpret other children as hostile with increasing frequency, which leads in
turn to more frequent rejection. All this sounds very familiar and all too
like the way some adults interact.

A second lesson from the research is that it is unfair and unhelpful to
see children who are rejected by their peer groups as having 'deficits' in
understanding others. They are not on average less able intellectually.
Their problems in understanding others, and their biases towards seeing
others as hostile, appear to be related to specific social situations, those
that present especial stresses for them.

Are children unpopular because of their personalities?

Todd, a seven-year-old in our London study, has been extremely popular
with the other children at school from his first days at kindergarten. He
is an attractive, easy-going and friendly boy, cheerful and full of ideas
for games. His temperament and social style fit a common pattern for
popular children, who are very likely to be outgoing, friendly and good
at leading in play without being aggressive or unduly bossy.

In contrast, Roy is having much more trouble with his classmates. Our
playground observations show that he is a bit wild, often starts fights
and manages to rub other children up the wrong way. Somehow he
always causes problems in games, and rarely seems to cooperate smoothly.
He teases and annoys the other children, and all too often he turns a

pleasant game into an aggressive exchange in which the other children get hurt. Children who are actively disliked and rejected by the group are often disruptive and aggressive like Roy.[20] In contrast, those who are neglected by the other children – rather than actively disliked and spurned – tend to be shy, withdrawn and unassertive.

It is easy to see how these characteristics might contribute to children's unpopularity – that they might be the *cause* of the exclusion from the group. We've seen earlier that there is some genetic contribution to shyness and withdrawal in children, and genetics also contributes to differences among children in the likelihood that they'll show disruptive, hyperactive behaviour – the annoying, restless behaviour that drives both teachers and classmates to despair.[21] But it is also likely that these characteristics will be influenced by the children's experiences with the other children in the group. Roy is often unkind and aggressive – no wonder the other kids don't want him to play – but if Roy is continually excluded, he simply won't have the opportunities to become adept at sharing, cooperating, making suggestions that help the joint play. If a child tends to be shy, being teased and excluded will only increase the likelihood that he will avoid contact and withdraw.

To try to tease apart what is cause and what is effect, psychologist Ken Dodge devised an ingenious study.[22] He set up groups of children who did not know each other and organized regular sessions in which they came together to play, over several weeks. Importantly, he assessed the children's personalities before they joined the groups. Then he and his team watched the children interacting with each other, over several weeks, focusing on the details of their interactions and their popularity or unpopularity as it gradually emerged in each group. It was clear that the personalities of the children *before* they had joined the groups did influence how they got on with the others, and whether they were excluded. But of course it is quite possible that these personality characteristics were partly the result of previous experiences with other children, experiences not monitored in the study. And there were also increases in 'disliked' children's negative behaviour that came right *after* the other children had begun to label them as unpopular. Clearly we cannot exclude the possibility that social experiences with children influence shyness, aggression or clumsiness in social interactions.

If being unpopular is both cause and consequence of children's difficult or aggressive behaviour, in this way, we would expect that children's relative popularity would be pretty stable over time. And this is so, for the actively rejected children at least. Even when they change school, they tend to remain rejected. In contrast, children who are simply neglected by their peers, rather than rejected, can become accepted if they change schools, or manage to join groups of children who haven't been involved in the labelling or 'reputation' (as a nerd, as no fun, as disliked by all the cool kids) they acquired in the classroom. It seems that their 'reputation' can be important in influencing the other children's lack of interest in them. Those gossipy conversations between the others, when children are labelled and 'put down' as being a geek, pathetic, can have a real significance for children's place in the group. If neglected children get a 'second chance', and move to a group of children who haven't been part of the gossiping circle, they may well become accepted.

We certainly shouldn't dismiss the importance of reputation, both for popularity and also for friendship. Even in the early school years, a child's prior reputation among the larger group of peers colours the way in which his behaviour is interpreted. Roy has a reputation for being aggressive, for instance, and he is more often perceived by the other children in the class as being *hostile in intent*. What seems so hard, for the unpopular children, is that *the same behaviour* that leads to them being rejected when they attempt to join a group of other kids, is responded to quite differently when it is shown by more popular children. And disliked children are held to be more accountable for unpleasant or negative behaviour than are the liked children in a class – who tend to be given the 'benefit of the doubt', and whose responsibility for bad behaviour is minimized.

Shelley Hymel, a psychologist who has pioneered the study of reputation among children, points out that because of this 'double standard', popular children will continue to be viewed positively, and disliked children will continue to be viewed negatively *regardless of their actual behaviour*.[23] It is, as Hymel emphasizes, not only what you do, but who you are that counts. Your reputation as aggressive or dislikeable will act as a self-fulfilling prophecy. And these effects are not only evident among children from five or six years on – they increase in strength with age. The older children at school are even more influenced by reputation than the younger.

One encouraging note comes from the research on children's reputation as popular, or rejected. Patricia East and Karen Rook studied children in southern California who were either isolated 'loners' at school, or disliked because they were seen as aggressive, and found that these children were just as likely as the popular children in their classes to form and maintain friendships *outside* the school.[24] East and Rook comment that if children are given the opportunity to rid themselves of a reputation as either a loner or aggressive at school, they can form good friendships outside school, *and receive support comparable to other children* in these non-school friendships.

Who is at risk for later adjustment problems?

Which children are at risk for being unhappy and disturbed – the children who are without a close friend or who have problems in their friendships, or those who are rejected by the peer group, or those who are neglected? Is Roy, with his disruptive aggressive behaviour, more at risk for later problems than his classmate Kevin, a shy and isolated child whose single friendship with another boy is far from being supportive?

Most of the careful research into how children's adjustment is linked to their relations with the other children at school has focused on the children who are actively rejected.[25] We know much less about the children who have troubles in their close friendships. The story is not a cheerful one for the rejected children who are particularly aggressive, like Roy. They are at considerable risk for a range of later problems. They are more likely than other children to perform poorly at school in terms of their academic work, to be truants, to drop out from school, to engage in delinquent and antisocial actions both within and outside school. One study which followed children for seven years, found that the very unpopular kids were, over the years, three times more likely to have come into contact with the police. In contrast, the neglected children in that study – those whom the other children tended to ignore and not go out of their way to include – did not get into later trouble, or do poorly at school. In general research suggests that neglected children are not at risk for later adjustment problems, in part because unlike other groups, their relations with the larger peer group are not very stable, and depend more on the particular group of which they happen to be a member at the time.

A convincing story of how the experience of rejection might be linked to the later antisocial and delinquent problems could go something like this: if an aggressive kid is repeatedly rejected by the other children in his class or neighbourhood, he is more likely to gravitate to a group of boys who accept and reciprocate his aggression. These boys join together in antisocial and deviant actions, and reinforce the boy's tendency to react aggressively to others. The path towards delinquency becomes clear. For children who are rejected by the other kids, but who are withdrawn rather than aggressive, the story is quite different, and they are less likely to develop such deviant behaviour over time. If they do develop difficulties over time, these are likely to be problems of fearfulness, anxiety and depressive mood, and loneliness.

Loneliness

Here is a poem by Katy, a six-year-old quoted in Alison Tamplin's study of friendship in Cambridge, in which Anna (with whom this chapter began) took part.[26] Katy describes what playtime is like for her:

> Bell's gone
> All out
> I'm lonely in the playground
> No one to play with
> People come and pull you about
> I tell the teacher but she says ignore them
> I stand near the wall
> People staring at me
> I feel sad
> I hate people staring at me
> Whistle goes
> All in
> I'm happy now

Until quite recently, some doctors and psychologists believed that children were not vulnerable to loneliness – that it was not until adolescence that individuals were intensely lonely.[27] Children, it was held, did not form really intimate relationships, and as a result, they did not suffer from the lack of such intimacy in the same way as adolescents and adults.

The picture is, we now know, rather different.[28] Children – even those as young as five or six – make it clear in their accounts of their experiences at school that they can be bitterly lonely. They talk about two aspects of loneliness. First, there are the feelings of sadness: 'it feels like no one likes me', 'I just feel sad about being left out.' Their metaphors are vivid: they talk about feeling that they are 'kept in a cage or something', 'always in the dark', 'the only one on the moon'. Then there are the feelings of lack of support: 'no one to turn to', 'without anyone to love me'; and lack of companionship: 'no one to talk to or be with'.

The picture of loneliness drawn by young children is strikingly like the accounts that adults give, which often include the themes of emotional loneliness (no one knows or cares about me) and social loneliness (I'm not part of any group). The measures of loneliness that have been developed show that children's responses to questions about loneliness and their self-reports on loneliness are stable over time from one assessment to another,[29] and the recent measures are methodologically sound.[30]

Feeling lonely can be the result of problems in friendship or it can arise through being rejected by the group; both can contribute independently to children's feelings of loneliness. Children who are rejected by other children are more likely to report experiencing greater loneliness – whether loneliness is assessed in classroom, playground, lunch room, or physical education situations.[31] The link between rejection and loneliness holds across age – it is found with children ranging from five to middle childhood, and in many different countries, and it is equally common with boys and girls. Those that are not just rejected but also victimized are especially likely to feel intensely lonely.[32]

Children without friends, unsurprisingly, report experiencing more loneliness than those with friends.[33] But the number of friends – beyond one – does not seem to be linked to loneliness. Rather, it is the quality of friendship that is important. Children whose friendships are high in qualities of intimacy, support, companionship, and in which conflicts can be resolved easily, experience less loneliness than other children – regardless of whether the children are accepted by the group. An aspect of friendship importantly linked to loneliness is how children behave towards their friends when in conflict with them: If they ignore their friends, or threaten to end the friendship – their friends are more likely to experience loneliness.[34] Of course, the question of cause-and-effect is difficult to answer, in the associations between loneliness and friendship quality. It may be that children's particular characteristics, and expectations about friendship contribute to both difficulties in maintaining close, rewarding friendships and the propensity to experience loneliness.

In summary, loneliness is not simply related to how well accepted children are by other children, or to whether they have friends. Some children have several friends, and still feel lonely. Cherry, an eight-year-old in one of our studies, was quite well accepted in her class; the other children described her in quite positive ways: 'she's pretty nice', 'she's good at sharing', 'she has cool clothes.' Yet she did not have a close friend and she described herself to us as very lonely. In contrast Michelle, who was accepted in a similar way in the class ('she's OK – not really someone I hang out with'), but had a good friend in a classmate Kelly, was rarely lonely. Loneliness in itself, Steve Asher points out, is not pathological – most people feel lonely at some point

during their lives, and short-term experiences of loneliness are sometimes the response to separations from friends, and are hardly a matter
for concern.[35] But at least 10 per cent of children in elementary school
report feeling lonely either always or most of the time, and this is clearly
a matter of concern.[36]

Being rejected by the group *and* being friendless or having very few
friends is a combination that is particularly likely to lead to feelings of
loneliness. But whether children who are relatively unpopular feel lonely
or not depends on *why* they are unpopular – there are big differences
within the category of 'low status' unpopular children in their emotional
experiences. Aggressive, bossy, destructive children are less likely than
other unpopular children to say they feel lonely, even though the other
children in the class tend not to like them. This could be because they do
in fact have a few friends (likely to be other aggressive and rather wild
children). But it is also possible that these children say they don't miss
having few friends, and don't feel lonely partly out of bravado – or
denial. Indeed, the real bullies in classrooms often have high self-esteem,
and paint quite unrealistic pictures of their own abilities (both social
and intellectual) and their social success. When asked about how often
the other kids want to play with them, they'll say 'lots' or 'most of the
time'; when asked whether they are like children in stories who are
very popular, they will say that yes, they are. They will also describe
themselves as doing fine at the academic side of school, and as having
few problems in schoolwork. In marked contrast to these children who
are very unlikely to say that they are lonely, unpopular children who
are anxious, submissive or withdrawing are extremely likely to describe
themselves as very lonely.

One encouraging note: while being friendless is linked to loneliness,
poor school achievement and unhappiness at school, this can often be a
temporary situation. A change of class, a new student joining the group,
can change children's opportunities for forming friendships.

Friendship, depression and anxiety

For some children, being without a friend is *not* a risk for loneliness
or problems. Some children do not need friends for healthy adjustment
– they are self-sufficient, and much enjoy their own company, or the
company of the larger group. But this contentment without friends is
relatively unusual. And even when children do have a friend, the quality
of that friendship can be linked to emotional problems. The caring and

concern, commitment, and the extent of loyalty and affection between friends of seven or eight and older can differ very much, and these differences are important for providing support to children who are unhappy or troubled. A study of young people who were clinically anxious or depressed, carried out by Ian Goodyer, a psychiatrist in Cambridge, found that 48 per cent of these troubled teenagers had, over the previous 12 months, experienced friendships that were not close, caring or supportive, or only moderately so. In contrast, only 16 per cent of children without such emotional disorders had experienced such poor friendships.[37]

If there is a causal link between depression and the quality of children's friendships, it is not clear what processes might be involved. There could be a 'direct' effect of the children's social behaviour: Depressed children may behave in a way that 'turns off' and discourages their friends from trying to keep the friendship going. They may be negative and unenthusiastic about doing things together, lethargic and always complaining or seeing the gloomy aspects – just not much fun to be around. It is possible, too, that children's perceptions and interpretations of their social interactions are implicated. Depressed children may be more likely to interpret their friends' behaviour as hostile, uninterested or neglectful.

Conclusions

From the wide set of issues covered in this chapter, the following points summarize key general findings:

- The intensity and intimacy of the relationships between dyads and triads of friends can be a source of painful experiences of jealousy and hurt, remembered by individuals over long periods of time. Unkind teasing can reflect these intimacies and be particularly painful.
- Bullying is disturbingly common in the early school years, and children can be both bullies and victims. Friendship can protect children to some degree from the impact of bullying, but this depends on the quality of the friendship and the characteristics of the friend.
- Social understanding is key to friendship quality, yet there is not a simple relation between social understanding and bullying. Some bullies are skilled manipulators of their victims, while other children have problems reading intentions, in the sense that they are likely to interpret ambiguous acts as hostile.

- The distinction between friendship (a relationship between two people) and popularity/rejection by the group is an important one – the causes, consequences and developmental impact of the two differ. From the friendship literature we have learned that friendless children are at risk – one or more good-quality friendships are important; from the peer-popularity literature we have learned that popularity and gregariousness are not essential, it is rather *why* a child is rejected or neglected that is important. The children who are most at risk for current and later problems are those who are both rejected by their peer group *and* friendless. It is important to distinguish rejection by peers from neglect by peers: it is the former that carries the most risk for later difficulties. Children who are rejected and aggressive are likely to continue to be so over time; in contrast some neglected children can become accepted with a change of school.
- The friendships of rejected children do differ in quality and stability from those of more popular children.
- Loneliness is reported by many children; it can result from problems in friendship, or from rejection by peers.
- Causal links between peer problems, lack of friendship and later adjustment problems are difficult to establish: they may be direct or indirect, as the results on depression and poor friendship in young people demonstrate.

7

Girls, boys and friendship

Are there differences in the friendships of girls-with-girls, and those of boys-with-boys? What about friendships of girl-and-boy? The idea that there are important differences in women's and men's styles of communication and the nature of their friendships is a familiar one. It is held that women (in the US and Europe at least) are, on average, more likely to have close friends than men, and to value those friendships very highly. Intimacy and self-disclosure play a central part in their friendships.[1]

Where and when do these differences begin? If they reflect deep differences in the nature of close relationships for women and men, then do we see their beginnings in children's friendships? Just as in the last chapter we saw how important it is to think separately about children's *group* relations (their popularity, acceptance or rejection by the group) and their *intimate friendships* (the relationship between two individuals), so too this distinction is very important in thinking about gender differences in children's relationships. In this chapter we begin with a brief look at boys and girls in *group* situations, where the evidence for gender segregation (the separation of boys and girls) and differences in how boys and girls play and interact can be striking; but second, we also look at evidence against a simple view that boys and girls form 'two cultures' in the early years. And then third, we look at *friendship*, where the evidence for gender differences is very much less clear.

Girls and boys at school: the group scene

Watch and listen to four- or five-year-old children in preschool or kindergarten. The most obvious differences you see are probably in the rough-and-tumble play of the groups of boys, rarely seen in girls, and the differences in the play patterns and fantasies of the girls and boys, which can be dramatic indeed. Superheroes, swords in hand, and cops-and-robbers contrast with princesses, pretty in pink, brides and babies. Raucous, rambunctious – these are fair enough descriptions of the roaming gangs of boys in their first and second years at school – much less accurate as descriptions of the girls. Boys are ingenious at inventing guns and swords for their group fantasies, sometimes from the most unlikely props; one study found that at four years, boys' pretend aggression occurred at twice the rate it was seen in girls, and at five and six-to-eight years, the differences had increased to over six to one.[2] Girls' pretend play often involves family roles, and these make-believe themes more often involve reciprocal roles (mother-and-baby, teacher-and-pupil). It's been emphasized that such reciprocal role-play is cooperative in a way that is not so commonly found in the pretence of groups of boys. Vivian Paley, watching and listening to the Chicago kindergarten children she teaches, is in no doubt about the striking differences in the play patterns of the boys and girls – differences that turned out to be very resistant to her sensitive attempts to alter the balance of play into something less gender-stereotyped.[3]

Differences in the boys' and girls' ways of handling conflict, and their ways of talking are evident too, especially when boys are involved in dominance issues within the group of children. And differences in their activities and interests are clear in the playground, with boys' football involving large groups of boys, while smaller groups of girls cluster around the edge of the playground, talking together.

Separation of boys and girls

This segregation of girls and boys in the playground increases in the early years of preschool and school. While the toddlers that Carollee Howes studied between 12 and 24 months showed no particular preference for same-sex companions, between 30 and 36 months, children begin to choose to play with same-sex peers and these preferences increase over the next few years.[4] Eleanor Maccoby and Carol Jacklin showed in a longitudinal study that in the preschool setting, children spent nearly three times as much time playing with same-versus other-sex partners, and this ratio increased to 11 times as much time by the point that the children were six and a half years old.[5] It seems likely that the children's experiences within these sex-segregated groups could well have an impact on the way the children develop, by channelling their interests and activities. Playing within an all-boy group could well foster different ways of interacting with other children from the experiences of playing within an all-girl group; these experiences may contribute further to the preference for same-sex peers.

This possibility – that experience in all-boy or all-girl groups does influence the development of sex-stereotyped behaviour when children are in groups – was tested systematically by Carol Martin and Richard Fabes,[6] in a study in which 61 children aged on average 53 months, were watched in free play at preschool, at two time points six months apart. First, the researchers investigated how *stable* the children's preference for playing with same-sex peers was over the six months (using a variety of ways to assess the stability). The individual differences in the children's preference for same-sex groups of play partners were pretty stable over time (perhaps because of temperamental characteristics of the children, or because of their expectations about same-sex play). Next, Martin and Fabes investigated whether experience in these same-sex groups was related to these young children's subsequent behaviour. What they found was that the more time the boys had spent playing with other boys in the autumn, the greater the likelihood that they were observed to be rougher, more aggressive and more active in their play the following spring. Martin and Fabes point out that these play styles are consistent with the greater emphasis boys place on competition in the formation of hierarchical status within the peer group. Other research by Lisa Serbin and her colleagues showed that boys' attempts to influence others took the form of direct and power-assertive demands and that over time boys became less responsive to indirect, more polite forms of influence. It seems that play in boys' groups gave the opportunity to learn and develop ways of influencing the other boys in their groups. Interestingly, the boys over time also expressed greater pleasure and excitement at this type of boy-play.

For girls, there was also evidence that the time they spent in all-girl groups affected their behaviour over time. Girls who had spent more time in the girl-group showed a calmer style of interacting, and less aggression than girls who had less experience in the girl-groups – even when the girls' initial level of sex-typed behaviour was taken into account. Again, the researchers link this impact to ways in which girls influence other girls: such influence attempts are increasingly likely to take the form of polite suggestions as girls grow older, and their interactions increasingly involve reciprocity and collaboration.[7]

Vivian Paley's conclusion, from her years of experience as teacher and child-watcher is that this segregation of boys and girls is well in place in kindergarten: 'Kindergarten is a triumph of sexual self-stereotyping. No amount of adult subterfuge or propaganda deflects the 5-year-olds' passion for segregation by sex.'[8]

By the later school years, the boys often control as much as ten times more space in the playground than the girls, with their football, basketball, skateboarding. What is more, the all-female games of jump rope and hopscotch, usually to be found in confined spaces at the edge of the playground, or close to the school wall, are often invaded and disrupted by the boys. The geography of gender, as Barrie Thorne termed it from her inventories of the activities and groups of kids in the playgrounds of elementary school, is striking.[9]

So the story from research on young children in the playground at preschool or school is that on average, girls prefer to play with girls and boys with boys. It is a pattern that appears, strikingly, to be worldwide. Beatrice Whiting and Carolyn Pope-Edwards reported from their observations of children in six very different cultures (in India, Japan, Kenya, Mexico, the Philippines and the USA), that same-sex preferences emerge in all these cultures at similar ages – 'a cross-cultural universal and robust phenomenon'.[10] Sara Harkness and Charles Super, living in a village in Kenya, report that the gender divide began to emerge there after the children were six years old, and were given freedom to wander further afield, and develop their own peer groups.[11] Much of the early US and European research also emphasized that while boys have *extensive* networks of playmates, girls tend to have *intensive*, smaller-scale groups of companions or 'cliques'. It was said that many boys hang out in large, hierarchical groups of other boys at school, and their games are often competitive, and may be aggressively aimed at teasing or disrupting the girls.[12]

The development of two different cultures?

The striking differences in young girls' and boys' fantasy play at school, the separation by gender that is so evident in the playground, the rhetoric and insults of the children themselves, the differences in aggressive behaviour and power politics of the classroom – all these add up to a story about gender differences in group social relations that has been set out by Eleanor Maccoby.[13] Here is how it goes.

Even as preschoolers, boys and girls begin to play separately when they are in group situations. We don't know what first sets off this pattern. Some writers draw on parallels with the separation of groups of young male and female monkeys and apes, to argue that like-gender companions are preferred by both human and nonhuman primates because of more compatible styles of play. Rough-and-tumble play, for instance, is particularly enjoyed by males (boys and monkeys!), less so by females. Another suggestion is that initially the boys start to be less responsive to the overtures and initiatives of the girls ('Come and play doctors with us?' 'No!'), in part because there are differences between boys and girls in the ways that they regulate their emotions (such as anger), for physiological reasons. It is argued that this makes difficult the smooth coordination and meshing that is so important in shared play – it is less *fun* to play with children of the opposite sex, because of these styles-of-interaction differences.

The role of biological differences in influencing these interaction differences has been widely studied in nonhuman mammals, and in children who have experienced hormone disorders. The generalizations possible from this latter research have been summarized by Susan Golombok and Melissa Hines, who note that girls who have been exposed to high levels of androgens pre-natally do show more masculine toy preferences, gender identity and playmate preferences – suggesting that hormones can indeed influence girls' gender-related behaviour.[14] Other biological differences that may contribute to gender differences in interaction include the biological underpinnings of differences in language and communication, and of inhibitory processes. However, it is important to recognize that links between this evidence and gender segregation are far from established.

The evidence on gender differences in language acquisition is mixed; studies do however show girls apparently acquire vocabulary somewhat faster than boys between 14 months and 20 months, and use language more at an early age. And there are hints that there are male–female differences in brain organization in relation to language, a neural substrate that enables girls to progress faster than boys in language. On gender differences in inhibitory processes or emotional self-regulation, the evidence is mixed, and again, it does not yet take us very far in explaining the beginnings of gender segregation. Simon Baron-Cohen has argued that there are differences in 'female-type' brains – which contribute to women's strength in empathy and communication – and the 'male-type' brain – which lead to strength in building systems, including abstract systems such as politics and music.[15]

We don't have much 'hard evidence' for or against such accounts as explanations for gender segregation, or indeed for the other speculations about the early stages of gender-based preferences. Other suggestions are that children prefer same-sex companions because they appreciate *similarity to self*, and this makes same-gender children more attractive – an explanation in terms of *cognitive processes*; that adults reinforce the preference for same-gender play partners, or that the sex-role stereotypes held by the peer group foster gender-linked preferences – explanations in terms of *socialization processes*. All these suggestions are quite plausible, and all such processes may well contribute to the growing segregation between boys and girls at nursery, preschool and school.

In summary, whatever the initial impetus for separation, it is clear that boys and girls increasingly avoid each other at school during the school years. The suggestion is that this segregation leads to, maintains and indeed increases gender differences in styles of relating and communicating, ways of expressing intimacy and disagreement, and efforts to mark and maintain status and competition. According to this account, the initial differences in play styles, ways of handling conflict and emotional exchanges mean that boys on average prefer to play with boys, and girls with girls, and the differences in interactive style contribute to the increasing separation of the sexes in group settings. The different 'cultures' of boys and girls, it is argued, lead to the differences in adulthood between men and women in ways of relating and communicating, in the importance of intimacy and independence. Thus, the playground practices of girls – talking, playing turn-taking games, working things out together – are seen as key steps in the growth of *connectedness* and intimacy that will characterize their relations as women. In contrast the boys, with their competitive, overtly conflictual and hierarchical interactions are en route for a male culture of status, individual assertiveness and competition.

However, there is an important caveat to this story. We should recognize that some recent research calls into question whether the story of gender segregation is quite as simple as this. The picture, these studies suggest, is more complicated, and the boundaries between the genders are a good deal more blurred than these stories imply. Before we conclude that there are clearly different cultures for boys and girls, here are two other important considerations.

School or neighbourhood?

Our ideas about gender separation have chiefly been built up from looking at children in schools, not in families or neighbourhoods. When we watch children playing and talking *outside the school setting*, in their neighbourhoods or in their homes, the picture can be different. Barbara Rogoff and her colleagues, for instance, observed over 400 children aged between one and twelve years playing and talking on summer afternoons

– at home and out-of-doors in a middle-income neighbourhood of Salt Lake City.[16] The children tended to play in groups; 33 per cent of the groups of children were indeed same-gender, but a substantial 28 per cent of groups were mixed-gender (the remaining 39 per cent of groups included parents or other adults). When the researchers looked separately at the older children, those who were eight years or more, there was still a lot of mixing by gender. And it was notable that the mixed-gender groups were also likely to be mixed by age.

Outside school, this study suggests, girls and boys do play and talk together in mixed groups. A similar picture comes from a study of 12- to 16-year-olds in a poor neighbourhood in south London by Helena Wulff:[17] Girls and boys regularly hung out together at street corners, and their interactions crossed ethnic, age and gender divides. But at school, these very same children separated into groups along gender, age and ethnic lines.

Barrie Thorne, impressed by the differences between what happens in school and what happens outside school in terms of gender segregation, argues that several features of schools make gender segregation more likely there than in neighbourhoods.[18] She stresses that the *crowded and public* nature of schools, and the continual presence of *power and evaluation* throughout schools both combine to make separation of the genders more probable. These features also heighten the probability of the aggressive, competitive male style of interacting.

This argument echoes the views of the great playground watchers Iona and Peter Opie. The Opies spent their lifetimes carefully document-ing the games, songs and rhymes of children in street and playground, tracing the lineage of many of these games back to children's rituals and games played hundreds of years earlier.[19] They are forthright on the point that in school playgrounds, children's play is more aggressive, and more gender dominated than it is in the streets, neighbourhoods or wastelands where they also studied them:

We have noticed that when children are herded together in the playground, which is where the educationalists and the psychologists and the social scientists gather to observe them, their play is markedly more aggressive than when they are in the street or in the wild places. At school . . . they indulge in duels such as 'Slappies', 'Knuckles', and 'Stinging', in which the pleasure, if not the purpose, of the game is to dominate another player and inflict pain . . . Often, when we have asked children what games they played in the playground we have been told 'We just go around aggravat-ing people.'

The Opies believed strongly that the opportunities for *privacy* and *space* crucially affect the kind of games and interactions children have, and that the restricted world of the playground both encourages these aggressive games and severely limits the chances that children will join together in playing the more imaginative and free-ranging games that are, as the writer R. L. Stevenson said, 'the well-spring of romance'. The matter of *where* children and their friends meet and play is key to what they do together. Crowding, so common in the corridors and playgrounds of school, exacerbates the teasing, and much of this is gender based.

Even within schools, classes can differ, for instance, in how far the children divide up along gender lines. One study compared nine different kindergarten classrooms and found that in four of these, there was a 'bonded and disruptive' group of boys – and that in these four classrooms there was much less mutual exchange between the boys and girls, and less harmony in their interactions.[20]

Beyond the dichotomy of boys' and girls' culture

The second consideration that weighs against a simple view of two cultures – boys' and girls' – concerns not so much the separation of the sexes, but the individual differences within each sex in how they play, think and interact with their peers. Even when there are average differences between boys and girls, the variation within each gender group can be much greater. Take for instance rough-and-tumble play – the wild but playful pushing and rolling around that many excited preschoolers enjoy. This is thought of as quintessentially male. One widely cited study of preschool children reports that 15 to 20 per cent of boys scored higher than any of the girls on rough-and-tumble play. *But* in this very same study, the data show that *80 to 85 per cent of the boys remain indistinguishable from 80 to 85 per cent of the girls*, a point highlighted by Carol Jacklin.[21]

This picture is repeated every time we look at a 'well-established' difference between boys and girls. There can be an average difference between the gender groups, but there is a huge overlap between the boys and girls in their scores on whatever aspect of their talk or behaviour is being measured. If all we knew about a child was his or her gender, we would have very little power indeed to predict how aggressive, talkative or competitive he or she would be. We clearly have to move beyond thinking in terms of simple contrasts in *boys versus girls*, whether it is in personality, size of group, preferred activities, or style of arguing or organizing play.

By emphasizing the 'conventional' average differences between boys and girls we may seriously misrepresent what happens in children's lives and the quality of their relationships. For instance, Barrie Thorne reports that if she divides the data from her observations of boys and girls in the classroom into the conventional 'large hierarchical' and 'small' groups, 'I have to ignore or distort the experiences of more than half the boys . . .'[22]

We should now recognize both the multiple differences within the gender groups, and the overlap between the genders. The prescriptions of a cultural group – whether of children or adults – about gender are seen and responded to *differently* by individuals. So in turning to look at *friendship* in boys and girls, we have to be sensitive to these complexities, and recognize that the simple dualisms don't usually stand up to careful scrutiny.

Friendship and gender in the early years

Despite the dangers of stereotyping boys' and girls' behaviour, the predominance of boys choosing to play with boys, and girls with girls, the differences in their fantasy play as four-, five-, and six-year-olds, the differences in the ways they behave in conflict, and their increasing separation by gender all raise questions about how close *friendships* are affected by gender during these years. Are boy–boy and girl–girl friendships *different* from one another in important ways? Do boys and girls in fact make close relationships with each other, friendships characterized by affection, commitment, loyalty and intimacy as well as companionship in play? Just how likely are boy-and-girl friendships, given the differences between boys and girls in play style, handling of conflict, competitiveness, and so on?

A different quality of friendship?

For many children, the entry to preschool or school opens up their first opportunity for making close friends. And this is, as we've seen, a world that is increasingly gender-segregated. Just in terms of opportunity, then, it is probable that the friends children make at school are increasingly likely to be of the same gender. Although boys and girls do talk together in classrooms and at recess, such cross-gender contact is much less likely to develop into stable friendships or alliances than are the same-gender encounters. By the time children reach the later school years, many of the daily interactions between boys and girls are, according to

Janet Schofield, like contacts between 'familiar strangers' who recognize each other but have little understanding or knowledge of what the other is like.[23] Does this suggest that the nature of friendship differs for boys and girls?

We come back here to the distinction between on the one hand *average* differences between boys and girls, and on the other hand the very great overlap in how they behave. Taking first the research on young friends, between about three years and six years old, even in terms of average differences between boys and girls, there are few differences in observational measures of what the friends are doing together, if they are observed playing and talking alone, and very great individual differences within each gender. Let's consider conflict, pretend play, and conversations about feelings and inner states.

Conflict   At 47 months and at six years, no gender differences in the frequency of disputes was found in our research in Pennsylvania, or in the London studies; however there were differences in how the girls and the boys handled resolving their conflicts. Girls were more likely to take a *submissive* or *distracting* resolution strategy. Such findings support other research reporting girls' greater use of mitigation in disputes – results that are often interpreted as reflecting girls' greater concern with maintaining the relationship.[24]

Pretend play   Evidence for average gender differences in shared pretence between friends is not consistent across studies. When the children in our Pennsylvanian study were 47 months old, gender differences in engagement in shared pretence did not reach significance. Similarly, no gender differences were reported by Janet Astington and Jenny Jenkins in their study of pretend play.[25] By six years old, girls and their friends in our research engaged in marginally more shared pretence, and girls' play was on average more complex. Other studies report gender differences in the themes of friends' pretend play, and the elaboration of the stories they develop in make-believe play differ too, with the girls' pretend reaching especially sophisticated heights. Particularly intriguing are the differences in shared fantasy play between boys and girls that have been described by John Gottman. He suggests boys who are friends introduce danger and frightening adventure into their play, and they deal with these fearful themes with fantasy and with humour, using what Gottman calls a 'mastery approach'. Here are Billy (B) and Jonathan (J), aged four and three years old, engaged in an encounter with sharks, reported in his book with Jeffrey Parker, *Conversations of Friends:*[26]

B: And I hate sharks. But I love to eat sardines.

J: I love to eat sharks.

B: Yeah, but they're so big!

J: But we can cut their tail. . . .

B: Yeah, what happens if we cut them to two?

J: It would bite us, it would swim, and we would have to run. Run very fast, to our homes.

B: Yeah, but ummm . . .

J: By the trees. Mr. Shark bited the door down and we would have to run way in the forest.

B: Yeah, but . . . if he tied all the trees down . . .

J: And then we would have to shoot him. Yeah and the shark is poison.

B: Yeah, but people are too. What happened if the shark ate us?

J: We would have to bite him in, on his tongue.

B: Yeah, what happened if we bit him so far that we made his tongue metal?

J: Yeah.

B: Then he couldn't have breaked out of metal.

J: He can eat metal open. Sharks are so strong they can even bite metal.

B: Yes.

J: How about concrete? Concrete could make it.

The boys' solution to the shark problem is both elaborately logical *and* magical; Gottman contrasts this with the ways that the girl–girl friends he studied dealt with fear in their conversations – by using emotional support to soothe and comfort, and by building solidarity on the basis of their similarities. The fantasy themes of pairs of girls who are friends are more likely to be domestic, or rooted in stories of princesses, fairies, boyfriends. There is no way we could conclude the two children in the next example, from our Pennsylvanian study, are two *boys* playing together.

Sara (S) and Eleanor (E), both aged nearly five years, are playing with dressing-up clothes, alone in a bedroom at Sara's house. They are dressing up and planning to go to a party – where and what kind of a party is yet to be decided:

S: Ooh we better take our babies!

E: Oh yes.

S: You look wonderful!

E: Yeah.

S: Wonderful.

E: This is yours. This is yours [gives her a necklace].

S: Better put my glasses on so I look cool.

E: I look cool also.

S: You look pretty.

E: Yeah.

S: How do I look?

E: Pretty! You look like you're going to a sun-tan party!

S: [excitedly] We are! We are!

E: [without enthusiasm] Oh. I think I'm going to a hoola dance party.

The disagreement about what kind of a party they are going to becomes acrimonious, till Eleanor comes up with an idea:

E: I've got an idea so we can cooperate!

S: OK?

E: Umm, I'll tell you the idea. If we split up at the crossroads, then we'll be with each other for a little bit, and we won't for a little while. So that's cooperating. Cooperating. So please?

S: Yeah, but how will we carry the luggage because we'll have to change when we get there.

A further argument develops between the two girls about the problem of which clothes will be needed for particular parties, till, with a minor hiccup of further conflict, all gets resolved by a complete change of plans:

S: So let's just not go to a party.

E: OK let's call back because they think we're going.

S: OK

E: I'll call.

S: [fiercely] I'LL CALL!

E: Both of us will call. You call to your party and I'll call to mine. [Both girls simultaneously pretend to speak on their respective mobile phones]

S: Hello!

E: Hello we're not coming because we . . .

S: Yeah we're not coming because we all want to change our stuff and we have to go to a meeting and we got to leave the same clothing on.

E: Yeah so we can't go, OK?

The party-going, looking pretty, babies, *appropriate* clothes – all these themes mark the play as girl–girl. While there is plenty of conflict, the way in which the girls reach a resolution is typical of many girls who are friends (efforts at conciliation, submission, compromise).

So the small average differences in handling of conflicts, in self-disclosure, in themes of nurturance and relationships in fantasy games that are found between young boys and girls with their same-gender friends do parallel some of the differences described among adolescent friends and adults. Girls and boys may well differ in their solitary make-believe play, too, but much less is known about such private fantasies in early childhood. If we look beyond dyads to include the triads and quartets of alliances that are often formed between girls, then another difference becomes apparent. The shifting loyalties and rivalries for affection within these groups, the 'triangles of tension', and preoccupation with who-likes-who and who-betrayed-who that dominated the group of friends in Margaret Atwood's *Cat's Eye*, these are less commonly found among the boys' than the girls' cliques.

But it would be a great mistake to emphasize these differences so much that we neglect the fact that the overlap between boys and girls in their interactions with friends – at least in the early years – is great. Billy and Jonathan in John Gottman's study (quoted on page 109) are, after all, disclosing their fears and sharing their excitement, they are building an elaborate shared fantasy together . . . the qualities that are often stressed as *female* are very clear in their extended games.

In our own research, there were also gender differences in the occurrence of pretend games with a violent theme; this play was associated with children's attentional problems and conduct disorder – and these problems were more frequent in boys. Among the boys without such problems, violent pretend play was extremely rare, and it was almost never observed among the girls.[27]

Conversations about inner states   What about the conversations between friends about feelings, and inner states, that have been found to be consistently related to more mature understanding of others? Here we have found in studies both in the US and in London, that girls talked with their friends more frequently about feelings and inner states; in both the Pennsylvania study, and the London study interestingly, such talk between girls was more likely to be about *shared* referents, and indeed often happened in the context of shared pretence: 'We're pretending we're sisters!' 'We're frightened 'cos we've lost our Mummies!'[28] Talking about feelings, and about what people are thinking is more common among girls, according to some, but not all, studies, just as some studies report that girls perform more successfully on theory-of-mind tasks and emotion-understanding assessments.[29] And other research suggests that self-disclosure (relatively rare, of course, with this young age group) is more common among the girls than the boys. Sharing secrets, which by six years or so is common among girls, is less frequent among boy–boy friends. However, the individual differences here again are marked, among both girls and boys. I've just talked to six-year-old Ben about his best friends, and the conversation went like this:

JUDY: Have you got a best friend, Ben?
BEN: Zack and Carlo are my best friends.
JUDY: Do you ever tell them secret things – talk about secrets?
BEN: [firmly] *Yes*. Because I trust them.

Perhaps most striking was that among our longitudinal findings, there were not significant gender differences in the insight, liking or conflict which girls and boys reported about their school friendships at seven years old; moreover, the links between their preschool experiences, social cognitive abilities and early friendships and these later relationships (described in Chapter 4) were largely similar for both boys and girls.[30] The developmental patterns, that is, were not different for boys and girls.[31] Other evidence on children's perceptions of friendship processes also indicates that there were not gender differences in five-year-old children's perceptions of the importance of validation and conflict or in the stability of their friendships.[32]

In studies of slightly older children, gender differences have been reported for pro-social behaviour, for intimacy and for the forms that conflict and aggression take between friends.[33] Girls are reported to show more frequent pro-social behaviour in their friendships (helping, sharing, caring), but also more 'relational' aggression (behaviour that threatens to hurt another child's friendships, relationships, status or reputation) than boys. When conflicts arise, girls may intensify them by divulging confidential intimate information to outsiders; boys show more overt aggression. Greater intimacy in girls' friendships has been documented from age six onwards, and increases over time; female friends are reported to share personal information and engage in intimate conversations with one another at an earlier age than boys,[34] and by adolescence they have had more experience of taking part in supportive conversations. The greater intimacy of girls' friendships, it has been suggested, intensifies reactions to conflicts, making them more difficult to resolve: when confidential information has been exchanged in an intimate friendship, each member of the friendship pair is vulnerable to more emotional harm if this information is divulged to an outsider. This makes very close friendships between girls potentially more fragile than the friendship between boys.[35] So paradoxically, although girls' skills at conciliation may be greater, in this respect their friendships can have this particular dimension of vulnerability.

If you talk directly to young children about their friendships, among the five- and six-year-olds at least, many of the 'expected' differences between boys' and girls' same-gender friendships are simply not evident. For instance, that notion of boys having 'extensive' networks of friends, and girls having smaller but 'intensive' cliques has failed to be supported in two recent studies.[36] The girls actually had larger numbers of dyadic friendships at school. One difference that has shown up in some research, however, is that many boys may well have difficulty in dealing with conflict within their friendships in ways that do not jeopardize the relationship. The skill with which Eleanor and Sara (in the example on pages 109–10) dealt with their disagreements in their pretend play over which party to go to, how to deal with the luggage, and so on was quite impressive. When the acrimony increased over whether it was to be a sun-tan or a hoola party, Eleanor comes up with a neat compromise, that they should split up at the crossroads en route, 'then we'll be with each other for a little bit, and we won't for a little while. So that's cooperating . . .' When conflict again increases both girls suggest compromises: Sara suggests 'Let's just not go to a party', and then Eleanor deflects another dispute over who will phone to cancel the plans by suggesting they each call their own party. Their friendship weathered many such problems, and they remained close friends for the four years we studied them.

It is interesting, in relation to how friends resolve disagreements, that Gary Ladd and his colleagues noted that among the five-year-olds whose perceptions of friendship they studied, the relations between conflict in the friendship and the child's adjustment difficulties was stronger for boys than girls.[37] Ladd and his colleagues interpret this pattern thus: that when adapting to school, boys are more adversely affected by conflict in their friendships; the boys had fewer close dyadic ties than the girls, and may thus have fewer resources to turn to when they have difficulty in their close friendships. Findings reported by Jeffrey Parker and Steve Asher[38] fit with such a hypothesis. They found boys reported more difficulty in resolving conflicts with their friends.

Girl–boy friendships

If everything associated with girls is a source of public disgust and denigration to young boys in their playground games, isn't it very unlikely that close friendships between boys and girls can develop, or be maintained? If the separation of boys and girls in group settings grows during the first few years at school, what happens to friendships that began when the children were even younger? Do toddlers and young preschoolers form cross-gender friendships, and if so, do these founder later on, in the face of the shifting interests and public disapproval of the other gender that are so rife among the five-, six- and seven-year olds?

Toddlers in day care have the opportunity to form friendships with either boys or girls. And those that do form close relationships *form them equally often with children of the same or the opposite gender.* Carollee Howes' studies in Los Angeles, described in Chapter 2, show that these early friendships are not linked to the gender of the other child. But when Carollee Howes followed these children with early friendships over the next few years, she found an interesting pattern of stability and change.[39] While on average the percentage of cross-gender friendships in the sample as a whole dropped from 53 per cent to 15 per cent over the next three years, this was not because the early cross-gender friendships dissolved. Rather, it was the *new* friendships that the children formed in preschool with children that they had not known earlier in day care, that were likely to be with children of the same gender.

Howes's initial hypothesis had been that friendships between children of the same gender would prove more stable than those cross-gender friendships which had formed in the second or third year of life, given the disapproval and mockery of the peer group that met relationships that crossed gender boundaries. But this idea was not supported. Rather, girl–girl and girl–boy friendships from this early period were very likely indeed to be maintained over the transition to preschool, but boy–boy friendships were not. Here is how Howes summed up her results:

> . . . cross-gender friendships formed in the toddler period were likely to be maintained into preschool. The same children who tended to form same-gender friendships with newcomers to the peer group as preschoolers were also able to maintain their cross-gender friendships in the context of a peer group becoming increasingly gender-associated.

She concluded that girls may well be doing 'more of the "work" of friendship maintenance', and suspected that the resiliency of the cross-gender friendships could well be attributable to the children in these relationships having highly compatible play styles. In cross-gender, but not same-gender friendships, she found that the children were particularly well matched in terms of their social skills. If your companion is particularly interesting as a partner, and the two of you can share your favourite games with ease and comfort, it seems to matter little that he or she is of the other gender. At least this appears to be so in kindergarten: John Gottman found, in a door-to-door survey of parents, that there was a dramatic decline in cross-gender friendships with increasing age between kindergarten (when 67 per cent of friendship choices were same-sex) to fourth grade (when 84 per cent were same same-sex) – results that are echoed in other studies.[40]

In our own research on close friends in south London, we have followed 160 children from the preschool period over the transition to 'big school', filming and recording the children talking with their friends at school and with their families at home. We chose to focus on children who already had a particular friend, according to their mothers and teachers, and we confirmed these adult reports by observations of the children's choice of companions at school.[41] Nearly a quarter of the four- to five-year-old friends are cross-gender pairs, and we are watching with interest to see how these friendships last, in the context of the increasing gender segregation the children will face in their next years at school.

Cross-gender friendships that survive into the school years all too often are driven 'underground' during the school day. Katy and Jake, two seven-year-olds taking part in our Pennsylvanian research who had lived in the same neighbourhood all their lives, and who played together very frequently during the weekends and breaks in school hardly talked at school, even when they were in the playground together. When I asked Katy why, she said simply 'We'd both get teased. He doesn't want to be called "Sissy" – and we both hate the jokes about kissing and stuff . . .'

Early romance

There can be something very special about some cross-gender friendships. Indeed, John Gottman sees some of these friendships as 'very similar to many marriages' in the intensity of the children's expressed emotions. One pair of four-year-olds that he studied, Eric and Naomi (who we saw was frightened of the dark, in Chapter 4), lived across the street from one another and had been best friends for several years:

They considered themselves engaged to be married. Apparently Eric had discussed the wedding plans with his mother, who expressed her eagerness for him to be on his own, in the classic way mothers do, by telling him she would be happy to dance at his wedding. He took her literally and told Naomi:

E: Hey, do you know . . . You see where my, where my, when me . . . and when you and me are married . . . um my mother is going to dance in the wedding.
N: Yeah.

Their affection for one another was common in their play, and it was often directly expressed:

E: Do you know, I love you and I'm going to marry you, Naomi.
N: I love you too and I'm going to marry you [*voice breaking with emotion*]. I hope you'll give me a ring.

Eric and Naomi had elaborate plans for their life together, which John Gottman notes certainly involved living together and sharing the same bed.[42]

Cross-gender friendships in children can be particularly emotional and intimate, and high in self-disclosure, when compared with either boy–boy or girl–girl friendships. And if you ask around, you may well hear similar stories of the intensity of girl–boy friendships. My colleague's five-year-old boy, whose close friendship with a girl was disrupted when his mother had to move to a different city in the course of her career, missed his friend acutely. He continued to phone her several times a week *for a year*, even though he made new friends and was very happy in his new school. Such intense cross-gender friendships are probably quite unusual, especially as children grow beyond five or six years; John Gottman's comment on cross-gender friendships in older children is that 'we have no idea what functions such rare and special relationships serve.' However we shouldn't forget that romantic attachments can start very early, and with very little to go on! Annie Dillard, in *An American Childhood*, recalls an early passion:[43]

I was seven. I had fallen in love with a red-haired fourth-grade boy named Walter Milligan. He was tough, Catholic, from an iffy neighborhood. Two blocks beyond our school was a field . . . where boys played football. I parked my bike on the sidelines and watched Walter Milligan play. As he ran up and down the length of the field, following the football, I ran up and down the sidelines, following him. After the game, I rode my bike home, delirious. It was the closest we had been, and the farthest I had travelled from home.

(My love lasted two years and occasioned a bit of talk. I knew it angered him. We spoke only once. I caught him between classes in the school's crowded hall and said, 'I'm sorry'. He looked away, apparently enraged; his pale freckled skin flushed. He jammed his fists in his pockets, looked down, looked at me for a second, looked away, and brought out gently, 'That's okay.' That was the whole of it: beginning, middle, end.)

And Mark Twain's *Autobiography* is full of examples of his romantic devotion to girls as a child, several of which reappear in *Tom Sawyer*.[44] Becky Sharp, for instance, has a model in the girl Laura Wright who the young Sam Clemens (Mark Twain) met on a boat on the Mississippi; he remembered her 48 years later with such clarity as:

> that slip of a girl – that instantly elected sweetheart out of the remotenesses of interior Missouri. I was not four inches from that girl's elbow during our waking hours for the next three days . . . I could see her with perfect distinctness in the unfaded bloom of her youth, with her plaited tails hanging from her young head and her white summer frock puffing about her in the wind of that ancient Mississippi time . . .

Clearly they are not to be dismissed, these early friendships of girl and boy.

Conclusions on gender and friendship

- Evidence on gender differences in children's *group* play and conflict at school must be considered separately from evidence on gender differences in friendship.
- In group situations, children begin after 30–36 months to choose to play with same-sex partners, and these preferences increase with age; they are reported from very different cultures, worldwide.
- The idea that there are 'two cultures', one of boys and one of girls, has been developed from studying children in group situations, and shouldn't be extrapolated to children's intimate dyadic relationships, with friends or siblings. Even where average group-differences are found, we should recognize the wide range of individual differences *within* gender groups, and the great overlap between boys and girls in interaction measures.

- We don't have hard evidence (such as clear biological evidence) for the explanation for the early stages of gender segregation. Observations of children outside the school situation (e.g., within their families, with their siblings in their neighbourhoods) give a picture of much less separation between young boys and girls.
- As regards friends: few consistent gender differences in observational measures of young close friends are reported. In conflict, girls submit and resolve more than boys; in pretend, after the age of six some studies report girls engage in more elaborate play, and the themes of their play differ. Some, but not all, studies report that talk about feelings and mental states is more frequent in girl–girl friendship pairs than in boy–boy pairs.
- In young children, gender differences in children's perceptions of their friendships are not found. Studies of older children report gender differences in aspects of pro-social behaviour, and in intimacy (girls more). By adolescence girls engage more often in supportive inter-actions with their friends.
- Girl–boy friendships from toddlerhood are likely to be maintained into preschool years, if circumstances allow. Nearly a quarter of our London friendships were cross-gender among the five-year-olds, and these cross-gender friendships can be particularly intense.

8

Parents and friends

From parents to peers?

The idea that how children relate to other children is crucially influenced by their own relationships with their mothers and fathers is one with a long history. It stems in part from Freud's ideas on the core significance of the mother–child relationship as the foundation for the way in which our personalities and our emotional security develop, and it is central to the views of attachment theorists, following John Bowlby's ideas and writing. It is a notion that also fits with the idea that we learn styles of relating to others from our early experiences of how others relate to us – the 'social learning' view.

According to attachment theorists, children's first attachments are in an important sense the prototypes for their later relationships, as children and as adults. Our expectations for the way people will relate to us, our responsiveness and sensitivity to others, our confidence in ourselves as people who are *lovable* and *likeable*, our trust in the affection and support of others: all these are seen as growing from the kind of relationships we have with our mothers and fathers.[1] It is such a central idea in our culture that we often just take it for granted. Yet by now, we do have plenty of studies of children that should enable us to make well-informed judgements on how reasonable an idea it is, as far as children's relationships with other children are concerned. We'll look first at two extreme examples which provide evidence for connections between children's early attachment experiences and their later relationships with other children.

Children from institutions

The first example concerns children who have not had the opportunity to form attachments with parent figures in infancy, but have spent their early years in institutions. Do the friendships of these children differ from those of children who grew up in families? The findings of two research programmes illustrate the links between early experiences of social deprivation and later peer relationships.

First, Barbara Tizard and Jill Hodges studied adopted children who had spent their early years in institutions in which attachments between caregivers and children were actively discouraged, and in which the turnover of caregivers was in any case so high that the children were very unlikely to form close child–caregiver relationships. When they were adopted away from these institutions, many of these children formed good relationships with their adoptive parents. Yet their early institution experiences cast a long shadow, in the sense that the peer relationships of the children as eight-year-olds, and even as 16-year-olds, were much more likely to be unsatisfactory than those of children who had grown up in ordinary families.[2] The picture of these children, able to form close relationships with their adoptive families, yet frequently disliked by their peers and teachers at school, is a striking one. It seems that the experience of those early months in the institution, and the lack of opportunity to form a close relationship with a parent figure were linked to real difficulties later on in the children's relations with other children.

The second example concerns Romanian children who were 'rescued' from the extremely deprived circumstances of Romanian institutions, after the fall of the regime of the dictator Ceaucescu, and adopted into UK families.[3] The children were adopted after varying lengths of time in these profoundly adverse institutional conditions, and the study by Michael Rutter and his colleagues examined the significance of these differing experiences of deprivation for the children's later development. The great majority of the children had been placed in the institutions in very early infancy; the sample was large (111 children) and a comparison group of 50 children adopted within the UK were also studied. The conditions in the Romanian institutions had ranged 'from poor to appalling': the children had experienced no personalized caregiving, very little talking from the caregivers, harsh physical environments (for instance, washing consisted of being hosed down with cold water). Most of the children were in a poor physical state on arrival in the UK, severe malnutrition was the rule, chronic respiratory and intestinal infections and skin disorders were common. They were severely developmentally impaired on all measures, with about half being below the third percentile on a broad developmental assessment.

The striking and welcome news when the children were followed up at age four was that the catch-up in both physical growth and cognitive level appeared nearly complete for the children who had come to the UK before six months old. The developmental catch-up was also impressive – though not complete – for the children who were adopted between 6 and 24 months. The strongest predictor of cognitive catch-up was the length of time the children had remained in the institution before adoption into the UK: the shorter the time in institution, the greater the 'catch-up' after adoption. The recovery – in terms of cognitive and physical development – of the children adopted into supportive and loving families was remarkable.

However the picture was not so encouraging in terms of the children's social development. First, at six years, attachment problems (specifically a lack of differentiation between adults, and over-friendliness to strangers), inattention/hyperactivity and autistic-like symptoms were significantly more likely among the ex-institution children. But a crucial factor was how long they had remained in the institution. As at the four-year assessment, those who had been removed from the institutions before six months were likely to be well functioning (70 per cent), but those who had suffered prolonged time in the institutions were most likely to be showing problems. And problems with peers, from parental reports, were significantly higher in the children who had been late adopted.

In terms of the children's ability to form friendships, the most notable information came from the visits to the children when they were 11 years old. At this stage, an extended interview with the children about their best friends was carried out, which focused on the quality of their friendships – in particular the intimacy of the relationship, the children's emotional openness, and the coherency and terms with which the children talked about their relationship with their best friend. First, whether or not the children *had* a best friend was related to their time in the institution, with the late adoptees (adopted after 24 months) significantly less likely than the rest of the sample or the control-group children to have a best friend. Second, the quality of the children's friendships differed: the adopted children described less intimacy in the relationship, they were less emotionally open, and less 'psychological' and more 'concrete' in their accounts of their friends. Less insight, less coherency, fewer references to feelings or thoughts characterized their accounts.

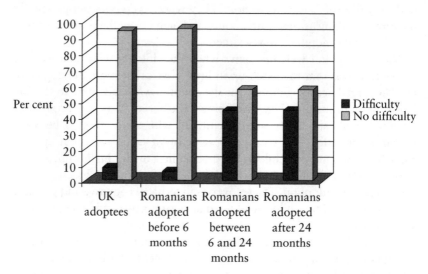

Figure 3 Romanian Adoptees Study: percentage of children by adoptee group with or without difficulty making friends
(From Kreppner and the English and Romanian Adoptees Study Team, 2003)

They also showed less social understanding in standard assessments. The individual differences in these friendships were quite marked, and the researchers found that among the predictors of these differences three factors stood out: the length of time the children had been in the institution, the quality of their attachment to their adoptive parents as six-year-olds, and whether they had had peer problems at six years. Prolonged deprivation had an adverse effect on the children's friendship intimacy and trust, on the children's references to mental and emotional states, and the way they were able to talk in a coherent and organized way about the relationships (which psychologists see as the way they are able to 'represent' their relationship). The pattern over time in these links is shown in Figures 3 and 4. Even after the effects of poor past peer relations and the children's verbal abilities were taken into account, the early severe deprivation continued to exert significant effects on the children's friendship – ten years later. And this effect was not explained by the level of malnutrition the children had suffered, nor their developmental delay when adopted.

It is a dramatic story, which highlights the importance of children's early social experience, for these children who had missed out on early loving relationships with a parent, and who had not had the foundation in early

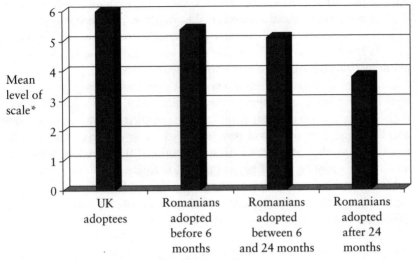

* Scale combined frequency and quality of reference

Figure 4 Romanian Adoptees Study: references to mental states and feelings during interviews about friends
(From Kreppner and the English and Romanian Adoptees Study Team, 2003)

life of sensitive reciprocal exchanges. Of course we cannot rule out the possibility that they had also suffered underlying neurological problems.

And there is one more thread in the developmental story of these children who were adopted from institutions in Romania which echoes the themes we've considered in this book – concerning the important connections between early social understanding and pretend play, in children's developing intimacy with other children. When the Romanian adoptees were four years old, one of the assessments concerned their pretence and social role-play, and their shared enjoyment of engagement in joint pretence with the adult interviewer. A notable difference was found between the Romanian and UK adoptees. The Romanian children engaged in less pretend play, less interactive role-play, showed less shared enjoyment of the play, and made fewer references to mental states. The differences were not explained by general cognitive or verbal ability. The differences in engagement in pretence and social role-play were observed *even among the children adopted before they were six months old.* As we have seen, shared pretend play is a key feature of young children's friendships, and being an effective play companion is central to the development of relationships with other children. Whether we consider joining in shared pretence to reflect a social or a cognitive ability, the differences among these four-year-olds in their play behaviour were important precursors of their later problems in friendship. Experiences even in the first few months of life apparently cast a long shadow over children's subsequent intimate relationships.

And other studies of children who spent their early months in orphanages or residential care support this finding: Even when after adoption the children had made great gains in terms of their mental development and language, they often had problems with other children. The picture from these studies of children from institutions, then, suggests that the attachment story may well be on target, for children who have suffered extreme deprivation, and that the problems the children showed in engaging in joint pretend play was part of the developmental pattern linking early attachment to problems in friendship.

Children with very troubled relationships with their parents

The second example of a link between parent–child and peer relationships concerns children who have very troubled, disturbed relationships with their parents. These children are much more likely to have some difficulties in their relations with the children around them than children who have enjoyed warm and supportive parent–child relationships.[4] High levels of conflict, and aggressive, punitive relations between parents and children are particularly clearly associated with children's difficulties in their relations with other children. Those who are very aggressive and violent with the other children at school, for instance, are more likely to have frequent violent fights at home with their parents, and to have been punished very harshly.

But most children, thank goodness, have not suffered the extremes of early deprivation of institutions, and most do not have major difficulties in their relationships with their parents. They may be very shy, they may be rather aggressive and demanding, or very active and restless, but most are not *disturbed*. And most parents are not unloving or harsh; they are usually trying to do the best they can in the face of complicated, stressful lives. To what extent are differences within the 'normal' range of family relationships linked to differences in the quality of children's relations with other children? And even when, as in the case of seriously troubled children, there are unquestionable links between relations within and outside the family, can we be clear about what underlies these connections?

Ordinary families, attachment to parents, and social life at nursery school

At the Elmwood Preschool, one of the centres in which we are working in London, four-year-old Bella is always sought after by the other children. She has a special friend, Shelly, and the two of them are often joined by a group of others. Bella is a key figure in the dramas that evolve in the playhouse in the corner of the centre – she is full of confidence and ideas about how the story should develop and who should be who. When her mother Jan leaves her at the centre each morning, Bella runs in very cheerfully to meet all her friends. She has a serene relationship with her mother, who enjoys her company hugely. And it has always been, Jan tells me, an easy relationship. Even as a one-year-old, Jan says, Bella was happy to meet and play with new people, and loved social events like the mother-and-toddler group, as long as her mother was around in the background. In the language of psychologists, Bella's attachment to her mother was secure, and she managed the balance between exploring the new worlds of unfamiliar children and adults, and keeping contact with her mother easily and without distress. How should we see the link between Bella's secure attachment to her mother as a baby and toddler, and her social success with her friends at preschool? Does this kind of secure relationship with a parent in babyhood guarantee that a child will happily develop good relations with other children?

What we know most about from research is the pattern linking children's attachments to their mothers, and the way they get along in the *group scene* of nursery school or kindergarten, that is, how attachment is related to how well-accepted or popular children are. We know much less about links to *friendship* – as opposed to popularity in the group, or how children behave with unfamiliar children. There is now an impressive body of research that documents links between the security of the attachments children form with their parents in their first two years, and their 'social success' at preschool. The picture from this research on parent–child attachment and both group social-relations and friendship has recently been reviewed and a 'meta-analysis' carried out by Barry Schneider and his colleagues which puts together all the research studies that had been conducted between 1970 and 1998.[5] This approach enables the researchers to assess how strong the link between attachment and peer relations may be (the 'effect size' of the association), and to come to a conclusion about how general the findings are. Very usefully, they examined the associations for both peer-group acceptance, and separately for friendship.

First, the findings on attachment and peer relations   The idea here
is that children who are secure in their attachment to their mothers are
likely to be more socially competent at nursery school, getting along well
with the other children, joining in with others to play in cooperative ways,
and not getting into constant battles with other children. It is a story that
makes good sense, whether we like to think in terms of social skills (what
you have learned in your interactions with your mother) or in terms
of expectations for intimate relationships with others along the lines
the attachment researchers have outlined (what your expectations are
about relationships, that are built on some kind of 'internal model' of
relationships). As expected, the meta-analysis found evidence for a relation
between secure attachment to mother, and later successful peer relations.
However, the effect size was small, and Schneider and his colleagues conclude that this link cannot be interpreted as causal. The small effect size,
they point out, is consistent with the idea that attachment is only one of
many influences on peer relations. Around 25 per cent of the studies in
their meta-analysis included other aspects of parent–child relationships
and child or mother characteristics, and many of these accounted for
additional variation in the children's peer relations – beyond what was
explained by attachment quality.

So, for instance, children's temperament, childcare experience and
attachment to caregivers in childcare, mothers' depression, attitude to
parenting, parenting practices, psychosocial adjustment and observed
warmth and emotional expressiveness with their children have all been
linked to some aspects of children's interactions with peers.[6] In those
studies in which both attachment and other parent-and-child variables
were included, these predicted different aspects of children's interactions
with peers.[7] Attachment predicted sharing, pro-social behaviour, while
previous experience with peers predicted the verbal interactions between
children and peers.

Second, the findings on attachment and friendship   Here, Schneider
and his colleagues predicted that the evidence for ties between parent–
child attachment quality and friendship would be stronger than that
for group relations. The bonds of family life, they point out, are more
similar to the trust and intimacy of close friendships than to the skills
involved in negotiating relations with a group of peers (a point made in
an earlier review by Jay Belsky and Jude Cassidy).[8] Many fewer studies
of friendship than group relations were available for the meta-analysis
by Schneider and his colleagues, and there were some problems with the
differences in the measures used in different studies. However, the general

finding was clear: *the association between secure mother–child attachment and quality of friendship was strong.*

Importantly, the links between attachment quality and friendship increased with the children's age – that is, the friendships of middle childhood and adolescence were particularly strongly related to the individuals' attachments to their mothers. The processes of intimacy, loyalty and commitment which become increasingly significant in friendships as children grow up are just those that we would expect to be associated with the quality of child–parent attachment relationships.

What is not yet clear

This is striking evidence, especially when taken in conjunction with the findings from children deprived of early attachment relationships, in institutions. However, there are still problems with drawing causal conclusions about the nature of the connections between early family relations and friendships. And there are some interesting complexities to the results of research that this straightforward story does not explain.

Complications to the story   Not only do we still have relatively little research on friendship, as opposed to group popularity, to go on, but there are some inconsistencies in the findings.[9] It appears that *some* aspects of parent–child relationships may prove to have connections over time with *some* features of children's friendships. If we look at how specific features of the child–parent relationship are linked to specific aspects of friendship, some of the patterns make good sense.

A good candidate is how children deal with conflict with their friends. Among the children we studied in Pennsylvania, those who had as three-year-olds enjoyed a high degree of involvement with their mothers were more likely to use compromise and negotiation in their arguments with their friends than the children who had been less close to their mothers. And those who grew up in families in which their parents were frequently angry or distressed handled conflict with their friends quite differently. They tended not to reason with their friends, but simply to protest or lash out. Mothers' strategies in disputes with their children as 33-month-olds were also correlated with children's constructive conflict management with their friends. Specifically, the mother's use of 'other-oriented reasoning' (reasoning about the conflict that took account of the other person's needs, feelings, desires, etc.) with her two-year-old predicted the child's use of compromise or submission with a friend at six years, independently of the

child's verbal fluency and emotional understanding. The evidence for links
between parent–child conversations about emotions, children's developing
social understanding, and their engagement in joint pretend play with
their friends is a second candidate for specific aspects of parent–child
relationships being associated with specific aspects of friendship.[10]

An interesting example of these complexities in connections between
parents' characteristics and children's friendships is the recent information
on links between parents' own friendships and their children's friendships.[11] Sandra Simpkins and Ross Parke investigated how the quality of
mothers' and fathers' friendships were related to those of their children,
and found that there were systematic associations between these friendships and both the children's perceptions of their own friendships, and
also observed behaviour of child and friend. However, it was clear that
gender of both parent and child had to be taken into account. Girls'
friendships were more clearly related to their parents' friendships than
those of boys. But the positive features of girls' friendships (resolution
of conflict, help, validation of the friend) were related to the positive
qualities of their fathers' friendships, while the conflict in the girls' friendships were related to the quality of their mothers' friendships. Parke
and Simpkins suggest that these differences may be related to the greater
intimacy and smaller network of girls' friendships.

This matter of father/mother differences brings up the general issue
of how father–child and mother–child relationships may carry different
implications for children's friendships. Those few studies that have
included fathers as well as mothers find striking differences in the links
between how children relate to the other kids at school, and their attachments to their fathers and mothers (note that Schneider and his colleagues
found only seven studies that included a focus on fathers). Children's relationships with their fathers in some cases show a closer link to these peer
relationships than do their relationships with their mothers. In fact some
studies find no connections between children's relationships with their
mothers and their peers, but do find links to father–child relationships.[12]

Why should this be? Several lines of evidence indicate that fathers have
a particularly strong impact on children's emotional expressiveness, and
in their capacity to regulate their anger and distress – which is important
in maintaining close friendships, and indeed peer relations in general.
There's also evidence that fathers contribute significantly to children's
emotional understanding, and capacity to maintain playful interactions.[13]
John Gottman and his colleagues found that fathers' acceptance of their
children's emotional displays was more predictive of their children's
friendships than mothers' management of children's emotional displays.

To add to the complexity, these patterns appear to differ for boys and for girls. Already this evidence for mother/father differences suggests that it is not simply the case that 'all good things go together'. The connections between children's close relationships within the family and their social relations outside the family are not reducible to a simple motif like 'a good attachment to your mother means all other relationships are likely to be good'. Moreover, the research is full of examples that don't fit the simple story. One study will find the predicted links for girls but not boys, another will fail to find the pattern for girls but does so for boys. One study will find links at one age, but not six months later – or vice versa. It is often argued that there are grounds for expecting that same-gender relationships (father–son, and mother–daughter) will be stronger than different-gender relationships (father–daughter, mother–son): here the 'classical' theories of identification between individuals suggest that those who have gender in common will identify more strongly with each other than different-gender pairs.[14] And there is evidence from studies of middle childhood and of adolescence that fathers are more involved with their sons and mothers more involved with their daughters.[15] Research on peer relations also indicates that fathers' behaviour is especially likely to be linked to sons' peer relationships, while mothers' behaviour is more closely linked to daughters' peer relationships.[16]

The complexities of the links between parent–child and child–friend relationships certainly do not decrease as children grow up. Clare Stocker studied seven-year-old friends and their relationships with both their parents in Colorado, and found very different patterns of links for mothers and for fathers – and like some of the research on younger children, she reports more links between father–child and friendship than for mother–child relations.[17] And in Michael Lewis's research on nine-year-olds whose attachment to their mothers had been documented eight years earlier, no connection at all was found with the number of close friends the nine-year-olds had.[18]

So there is still much we have to learn about the nature and extent of links between parent–child relationships and children's close friendships later on. Perhaps we should not be surprised. After all, a *relationship* involves two people, and what happens between a child and his friend will be profoundly affected by *who that friend is*, as well as (probably) influenced by the kind of early family relationships he has experienced. And the qualities of a child's personality that are important in his relationship with his mother may not be the same qualities that come to the fore in his relationships with his friend. We all enjoy different relationships, *in which we do, of course, behave differently*. Inevitably there is a special intimacy and warmth to some relationships that is absent from others. Why should we expect a simple carry-over from one to another relationship for our children? Finally, as Susan Lollis and her Canadian colleagues put it:[19] 'The "lessons" that children learn from their parents may not be completely transferable to peers because children must also learn to expect differences between peers and parents and to interact differently with peers than they do with parents.'

Explaining the links

Where connections are found – as in Bella's relations with her mother and her social success at school (p. 125), how are these associations to be explained? People have attributed the connections between parent–child and peer relations to all sorts of aspects of what parents do.[20]

Emotional expressiveness and understanding   Some argue that it is the openness and freedom with which parents express their own emotions that foster children's confidence and understanding in their relations with other children. The suggestion is that children in these families are themselves more expressive and open in their emotions, and are better able to understand other people's feelings. The notion that the way children learn to understand feelings (their own and those of other people) and to manage their own anger and frustration may be centrally important in their interactions with other children is certainly plausible. This notion gets plenty of support from our own studies. As we've seen, differences in children's understanding of feelings and their grasp of why other people behave the way they do are clearly linked to differences in the way they relate to their friends – how they manage disputes, and the skill with which they share elaborate make-believe.

   And here the evidence of links between mother–child attachment, emotional understanding and children's conversational experiences becomes important. Ross Thompson and his colleagues have shown that mother–child pairs with secure attachment relationships engage in discourse that includes more frequent references to emotion and more moral evaluatives, suggesting that a secure attachment fosters the understanding of emotions.[21] In one study, mothers were asked to discuss with their children incidents in the past: the emotion-laden discourse about the child's past in which the securely attached mother–child pairs engaged, Thompson argues, may make emotions more accessible and less threatening for a child. Other research that links the security of mother–child attachment, discourse between mother and child about inner states, and the children's social understanding is that of Elizabeth Meins and her colleagues. Mothers of the securely attached children in their study had shown particular sensitivity to their children's current level of understanding and used more 'mental-state' terms in talking to them, a propensity the researchers called 'mind-mindedness', which was correlated with the children's understanding of inner states. In these programmes of research the complex links between the quality of children's attachments, the conversational world in which they grow up, and their developing understanding of feelings are beginning to be mapped out.

It is important to recognize that relationships other than that of parent and child may also be significant here. In the next chapter, we look at the evidence suggesting that what happens between siblings and between other family members (not directly involving the child) may be of key importance, for instance.

Parents' disciplinary strategies   Others propose that how parents discipline their children is linked to the way children relate to their peers – here the suggestion is that more 'democratic' styles of discipline by parents foster children's understanding of the point of view of others.[22] The evidence on links between early mother–child conflict management and children's later conflict strategies with their friends (see above) fits this argument.

Parents' own adjustment   Yet another view is that what governs the connections between parent–child and peer relations is the parents' own adjustment and well-being. Parents who are stressed or disturbed cannot relate to their children – it is suggested – in a way that fosters the children's confidence and sensitivity to *others*. And we should remember that any association between what parents do with their children and the children's relations with their friends could result from something else that's common to both of them.

Genetics   So, for instance, genetics could underlie the sociability of both a parent and her child, for instance.[23] Comparisons of parent–child pairs in which children are adopted and those in which they are biologically related are a powerful way of testing this idea, and they have shown genetic influence on a wide range of parent behaviour. We don't know yet how substantial is the part that genetics plays in the kinds of connections between parent–child and peer relationships that have been found. But we certainly cannot rule out the possibility.

The 'management' view   Another idea is that parents can directly influence their children's experiences with other children and their friendships, by influencing their opportunities to meet and play with other children, by mediating in their quarrels with their companions, and by supervising, instructing or counselling them over problems with their peers.[24] There are strong echoes here of the 'parents as pals' themes that were prominent in advice to parents in the 1920s and 1930s.

But it is not clear how much parents actually do these things, or whether such direct involvement by parents actually influences the quality of children's close relationships with others. It is characteristic of our ignorance of children's real lives that our answers to these questions are pretty limited. We know that if you bring mothers and children into a situation in which there are other children, the extent to which mothers become involved in the children's play, and the ways in which they do or do not attempt to help their own children to become part of the others' play or sort out quarrels differ greatly. Mothers of children who are popular (in their own schools) tend to encourage their children to join in the others' play without disrupting it, while mothers whose children are not seen as popular by their classmates tend to use more intrusive tactics to get their child involved. We also know that mothers' own reports on what they do at home when their children have a playmate over are linked to the children's popularity in the classroom. Parents who say that they use strategies involving direct (controlling) supervision, as opposed to less intrusive, more indirect strategies of supervision, tend to have children who are less well liked at school. Of course, these accounts don't give us definitive evidence on whether parents influence children, or vice versa – it is that thorny issue of what the direction of influence may be, between children's behaviour and personality, and parents' actions and responses to them.

Helping the play   Once children are beyond the toddler stage, it is not at all clear that parental involvement in play is a help to the development of children's close relationships with other children. Much is currently made of parental 'scaffolding' of children's play. But while this may help in organizing the anarchic interactions between a group of several toddlers or two-year-olds, it is questionable whether parental involvement in their play fosters the relationship between slightly older children who are on the way to becoming friends. Recall that the core of young friends' play is often joint pretend. Adults are, quite simply, pretty hopeless at participating in the shared fantasies of children. Even devoted, eager mothers tend to join in with the kind of didactic suggestions that act as real dampers on the play between friends. John Gottman and his colleagues left tape-recorders on in the rooms in which pairs of young friends were playing alone, as part of a study of friendship.[25] Among a host of interesting findings, he reports that when either child's mother happened to enter the room *the children's shared pretend play took a nose-dive.* The quality of intimacy and shared excitement that makes joint fantasy such a core part of young children's friendship simply does not survive the presence of an adult – even a loved mother!

So the picture of the usefulness of parental 'management' of the positive side of children's peer relations is as yet far from clear, and we cannot leap confidently from what research there is to give firm advice to parents about how to foster their children's peer relationships. This research rather gives us some modest hints about what might be helpful for parents, which are summarized in the Appendix.

Directions of influence

In any weighing of the evidence for or against the idea that parents directly contribute to problems or success in children's relationships outside the family, there are two key issues to be considered. The first is that children themselves contribute to the difficulties in any parent–child relationship. Children are born with very different personalities and temperaments. Some are clearly much more difficult than others, as any parent with more than one child will know. Even in the early months, some children are more irritable, restless, hard to comfort or to amuse than others. Their parents need huge resources of patience, humour and other sources of emotional, financial, practical support to weather the storms and steer everyone through to calmer waters. Difficult parent–child relationships can of course develop as a *consequence* of harsh, unloving, insensitive parenting. But in a relationship between two people, both are implicated in the nature of that relationship. So the personalities and ways of interacting of hard-to-manage children can contribute to difficult relationships both with their parents and with their peers. They may be contrary, obstinate, uncooperative, irritable and unpleasant with both parents and peers – not fun to be with for either peers or parents! And this difficult behaviour can be responded to by anger, by parents or peers increasing their distance, by sharper punishments. The link between the quality of the relationships with parents and peers is unlikely to be in a simple way due solely to how the parents have handled their child.

The second issue is that if children have problems in their relations with other children, they may well show their unhappiness and insecurity about these relations by becoming difficult at home. That is, the direction of the influence may not be family-to-peer relations, but peer-to-family relations. If we watch what happens over time, we can often get clues about the direction of effects. When Ben a five-year-old in our London studies started school, he was teased and mocked at school, and ignored in recess. As the weeks went by, he became sulky, moody and tearful at home, and it was increasingly hard for his parents to relate to him. The timing of changes here should alert us to the possibility that those school experiences contributed to the troubles at home. In the case of Kelly, usually a cheerful and sociable child, it was the break-up of her close relationship with another six-year-old that led to her becoming moody or withdrawn at home. Friendship problems can certainly lead to unhappiness that shows up at home.

In contrast, if a child whose parents are in major conflict begins to be aggressive or withdrawn with the other children at school, again the direction of influence seems clear.[26] In real life, of course, difficulties at home and with peers outside the family are likely to exacerbate each other. And for those children with very disturbed relationships either at home or with other children, there are likely to be connections both ways between family and peer relations – family to peer and peer to family.

To interfere or not?

Trouble between children is often the catalyst for parents to become involved in their children's exchanges with other children. As children grow up, there are big changes in parents' views on becoming involved in their children's disputes with their friends. In the Newsons' Nottingham study of 700 families, in which mothers were interviewed repeatedly during the children's childhood from one year old to 16 years, these changes with children's age became clear.[27] When the children were four, there was more 'interference' in quarrels by the more highly educated, upper-middle-class mothers than by the other mothers (who came from a very wide range of backgrounds). More mothers who took the line 'let them settle their own differences' were found among the less well-educated mothers. The more middle-class mothers were in fact more than twice as likely to intervene when their children quarrelled with their friends as not to intervene. But by seven years, these highly educated mothers were much less likely to intervene directly, though they were quite likely to engage in discussion with the children of incidents they had witnessed – talking with the children about what had happened, later. The comments of the mother of seven-year-old Larry illustrate this attitude: 'If he's outside my door . . . and I hear a quarrel, and I know Larry's definitely in the wrong, I wouldn't go out and tell him and make him look small; but I would have it in my mind, to bear in mind to mention it to him after.'

The realities of family life

The message that parents in a key sense influence the quality of their children's peer relationships is implicit in much of the discussion of differences in children's relations with their peers. Yet as we have seen the evidence in favour of such a message is not simple when it is differences within the 'normal' range that are at issue. What is more, the research all too often distances us from the realities of the lives of many parents and children, especially the experiences of those who are likely to be 'failing' to provide the recommended support for their children's peer relations.

Consider Lisa, living in a housing project in a deprived part of London, whose five-year-old Jonah is taking part in one of our studies. Lisa has, as well as Jonah, his three-year-old sister Sissy – and little support from their father who left them about six months ago. He comes around quite often and fetches Jonah from day care every now and then, but Lisa cannot rely on him for regular or predictable help. The family lives on the fourth storey of a large block of apartments standing in a bleak inner-city area. There are plenty of older kids who live in the block, to be found playing soccer in the passageways and on the scrubby grass between the block and the busy main road, but Lisa is, very reasonably, anxious about letting Jonah out to play alone. She babysits two children of her neighbours, a two-year-old and an 8-month-old; this gives her, as she says, 'just enough cash to keep going'. But having the four of them puts real constraints on what she can do for Jonah's social life. She makes heroic efforts to 'do' things with the four children, struggling down with a double stroller for the younger two, and cajoling Jonah and Sissy to walk as far as the nearest park. But through the gloomy days of autumn and winter they are all frequently marooned upstairs in the apartment. And there the continual noise of the kids, the endless squabbles between Sissy and the visiting two-year-old, the cramped space, would devastate most of us.

Not surprisingly, Jonah doesn't have visiting friends over to play, and in fact he doesn't have close friends in the neighbourhood. He goes to a day-care centre most days, except on those days when Lisa cannot face the hassle of getting everyone downstairs and across the road. But it is a pretty chaotic day-care centre, and he hasn't made any real friends there. In a couple of months he will start primary school, but he will have to face that new and demanding world without the experience of cooperative play with other children that can be so supportive, or the reassuring presence of friends he already knows.

The contrast with Jason, also participating in our study, who lives only a few blocks away, is striking. Jason and his three-year-old sister live with their parents in a quiet street of small nineteenth-century terrace houses, each with a small garden. He goes to a private preschool where he has two good friends; both of these he sees regularly outside school. They come to play in his playroom or garden, or he visits them. These visits are often a family affair, as his mother is friendly with the parents of both boys, and says her own relationships with them developed in part because of the children's friendships. Jason is all set for a smooth transition to primary school, as all three boys are making the change together. The difference between the prospects for Jonah and for Jason is all too clear. Already at four years, the impact of poverty and neighbourhood on Jonah's opportunities to make relationships outside the family is poignantly evident.

Poverty, neighbourhood and networks

In poor neighbourhoods, like that in which Jonah is growing up, the possibility of making stable friendships is likely to be affected not only by the lack of opportunity to meet other children and start a friendship.[28] In addition, the frequent moves that families are forced to make, the difficulties that parents such as Lisa, without transport, face in arranging for the children to come to each other's homes, the cramped and difficult circumstances of the homes and probably also the restricted network of friends to which the children's mothers belong all add up to increase problems in making and keeping friends. These limitations have been described by Joyce Epstein, working with children in Maryland who are growing up in widely varying circumstances.[29] She has looked at how community, school and neighbourhood affect *who* children make friends with, and concludes that we have to move beyond ideas on mothers' attachment and their parenting strategies, to include the wider world in which children are growing up, if we are to understand, and eventually help, children's difficulties in their friendship networks.

We don't yet have good research on how these social circumstances affect the quality of those close relationships that children are able to form. But we do know something of the impact of social circumstances on children's popularity and rejection at school, and on their patterns of companionship outside school. The story is a sad one. Charlotte Patterson and her colleagues, studying eight- to ten-year-olds in Virginia, asked how chronic family adversity and acute life events affected children's popularity and their companionship.[30] What they found was startling. The probability of rejection by peers was only 8 per cent among children whose families suffered no adversities (such as financial hardship, chronic illness or unemployment) or recent life events. But it rose from this low level to about 35 per cent among children who had several adverse family background experiences, and to an astonishing 75 per cent for the children who had both extreme chronic family adversities *and* severe recent life events. While nothing is known of how the children's friendships (as opposed to their popularity within the group, and companionship outside school) were affected by these circumstances, it seems extremely unlikely that their close relationships were buffered from the negative impact of these family events and background.

The question of how far the relationships between parents and children are implicated in these associations is an extremely sensitive one. As far as young children are concerned, to assume that parents are the primary mediators of young children's opportunities for social contact – because they decide on where the family will live, and control their children's access to other kids – may be reasonable for families in the middle and upper classes. But it is hardly reasonable for those at the lower end of the social and economic spectrum. For Lisa to manage to foster Jonah's relationships with other children would take extraordinary resources (personal, social and economic), which are simply not available to her right now. The deck is stacked too high against Lisa. Two scientists who have studied the links between parents' networks and support for their children's peer contacts in various communities in upstate New York, Cochran and Davila, summed it up succinctly:[31] 'The networks of the poor and undereducated parents and children (who make up 20–25% of all families in the United States) are largely constructed for them by their life circumstances.'

And this impact does not diminish as children grow up. Clearly they are less dependent on their parents for access to peers, and to some extent the opportunities for escape from the constraints and limitations on friendship of the immediate neighbourhood will increase. But some studies in the US find parents' socio-economic status continues to predict the size and nature of children's friendship network up to adolescence. And the sequelae of the greater freedom that age brings presents new problems for parents concerned for the kind of friends with whom their children become involved.

Trouble-making friendships

Almost everyone here keeps their kids to themselves; they don't let their children play with other children, or at least they try to prevent it.

The comments of a mother in a low-income area in Cochran and Davila's upstate New York study, are echoed again and again in conversations with mothers who live in poor city neighbourhoods. Parents' worries about the safety of their children in high-risk neighbourhoods include a clear concern about the negative influence of the children and adults around. They worry about their own kids picking up bad language, early exposure to drugs and violence from these others, and they are especially concerned about the subversive influence of friendship with other children who are allowed to run wild. In notable contrast to mothers in more comfortable middle-income neighborhoods, who see other children around as a source of companionship and friendship, these parents are really concerned to limit their children's exposure to the other children.

As children reach seven or eight years, this concern often becomes more acute; the children are still (relatively) responsive to their parents' views on who they should spend time with, and (relatively) restricted in their movements outside the home. The concern is often focused on a developing friendship with a particular child. Here is the account given by the mother of Barney, a seven-year-old in the Nottingham study of the Newsons, who was apparently in danger of being terrorized into a life of crime by his delinquent friend.[32]

Well, this boy, he's been taking Barney to the shops, and saying to Barney 'I'm going to smash your face in if you don't go in that shop and pinch money out the till'; and he come home one day, Saturday it was, and he come in, and he was crying, he was, and I said 'What's the matter wi' you?' And he says 'Bill Barton's going to smash me face in'. I says 'What for? What's he going to do that for?' He says 'Cause I won't go into Fine Fare and pinch money out the till'. And anyway, I went down and told his mother, and she just laughed and sort of well – I couldn't care-less attitude.

Barney's mother laid down the law about stopping the two boys meeting: 'If he comes to the door now and knocks on the door for him, I says "He's not coming, you're to keep away from him!" '

Usually, the reasons underlying mothers' discomfort about their children's friendships are more mundane (superficially, at least). The friend is dirty, uses bad language, is rude, rowdy or quarrelsome. Parents of young school-aged children are only too aware of how vulnerable their children are to outside influences, and that they may, as the Newsons comment:[33] 'all too easily be swayed by children who do not share the same standards, particularly when the behavior of the other child has the spice of novelty and adventure just because it is less controlled and less constrained by adult pressures'.

What is often at issue here is not just a concern about dirt and bad language, but an anxiety about deeper matters. Mothers are trying their hardest to establish standards in social and moral issues with their children, and a friendship with a child who plainly disregards such standards is a real threat. 'It wasn't so much her language, it was just her *way of life*', one mother says. The root of the matter, the Newsons comment, is that such friendships undermine the parent's own hard-won authority over her child. Here is how the mother of seven-year-old Scott, in their study, described her dilemma:

> One little lad I did [discourage]. I put me foot down about it, I told Scott to come in on one occasion, and this lad said 'Tell her to shut her mouth!' – and I mean he was only a matter of 6 years of age, and I said 'We'll have no more, go and play in your own street and your own house.' He sort of looked at Scott, and he said 'Take no notice of her, come on' – and Scott was between the devil and the deep, he didn't know whether to come in or whether to show he was clever and go with him. So afterwards I said 'That's finished, he comes here no more.' I've managed to ease him off.

Of course, parents also discourage friendships on many other grounds – perhaps less dramatic than the seduction into deviance. Often these are more 'psychological' grounds: they can be friendships in which the parents feel their child is being too dominated or pressured by the other child, or friendships in which they feel the other child is disturbed, or unkind. One mother in our Pennsylvanian study commented to me that she really wanted to edge her son away from his relationship with a new friend, because she'd found them pulling flies to bits, and teasing a pet mouse (not in the interests of scientific enquiry, she felt, but with sadistic glee).

These kinds of anxiety about friendship are evident in every kind of neighbourhood or community, and are not solely a matter important for those living in poverty or social stress. Indeed they are rather common. In the Nottingham study, 35 per cent of the parents of the seven-year-olds had already discouraged some specific friendships. This figure rose considerably among families who lived in or near neighbourhoods that were 'rougher' than the mothers found acceptable. More generally, a notable 72 per cent of mothers said that they *would* take action to restrict their child's friendship if they were not happy with it.

Conclusions

- Children's social experiences in infancy and early childhood show notable links with the kinds of friendships they form later. Evidence from children who spent their early months and years in institutions supports the ideas of attachment theorists concerning the importance of early attachment relationships.
- The study of Romanian adoptees highlights the connections between emotion understanding, shared pretend play abilities and experiences, and later friendship quality that have been documented for family-reared children.
- The meta-analysis of research studies with information on parent–child attachment quality and later friendship further supports the idea that mother–child attachment relationships are linked to friendship quality; these links increase with the age at which friendship is assessed.
- It is likely however that particular aspects of parent–child relationships – not solely attachment security – are associated with particular aspects of friendship. A number of inconsistencies and uncertainties about family-to-friend associations remain: for example it is not clear how father–child relationships are implicated, and some differences in parent-to-child associations are reported for boys and girls.
- Explaining the links between parent–child and friendship relationships: a wide range of very different processes have been suggested, including parental influence on emotional expressiveness and understanding, disciplinary strategies, 'management' of children's friendships by parents, and genetics. All may well contribute to the complex processes of influence.
- Direction of effects: we should not assume that the direction of influence in these associations is exclusively parent-to-child. Children's

personalities and adjustment may well contribute to both the parent–child relationship and the friendship. Children's problems with their friends may contribute to difficulties at home.

- While the evidence for links between parents' relationships with their children and the quality of the children's friendships is considerable, we should recognize the impact of adverse social circumstances and stress on both family and friend relationships.

Parents are not the only family members involved in children's social lives. Around 80 per cent of children grow up with brothers and sisters, and these turn out to be potentially quite significant in relation to early friendships. It is to these siblings we turn next.

9

Siblings and friends

Sara, who has just whacked her younger brother on the head and refused to let him play with her, discusses moral transgressions with me, while her brother retreats miserably to complain to his mother. When I ask Sara 'What if you didn't let Jane [her friend] play with you . . . ?', a stricken look crosses her face. 'Oh I'd *never* stop her playing – her feelings'd be hurt . . .'

The moral sensibility of children is often more finely tuned where their friends are concerned than it is in relation to their siblings. Recall Kevin, like Sara a participant in our Pennsylvanian study, whom we quoted in Chapter 2, saying it was fine for him to take a toy from his older sister Alice, but that he would NEVER take a toy from his friend Jeff. That conversation continued like this:

JUDY: How about if Alice took a toy from you – would that be OK or not OK?

KEVIN: Not OK! I would be pissed off, and I would kick her!

JUDY: Why?

KEVIN: [outraged] Because she'd be taking something from me. Because she'd be stealing it. A CRIME!

JUDY: What about if Jeff took something from you?

KEVIN: [cheerfully] That would be OK . . . because I wouldn't mind. Because he's my friend.

The differences in Kevin's relations with his sister and with Jeff are very clear. He is endlessly squabbling with Alice; her superior skills of argument and her disparaging comments frequently reduce him to fury and tears. When he was three years old they played quite a lot together, and there are still favourite shared fantasy games they play (he is a champion leader of the football band while she twirls and tosses her baton). She still is a concerned comforter when he falls off his bike or is ill. But the shared games are becoming less frequent, though the fights continue, noisily.

With Jeff, Kevin's friend for over two years, there are long, quiet, gossipy conversations (we eavesdropped on their gossip in Chapter 3, page 34), and a continuing game which involves, mysteriously, both Robin Hood and Captain Hook. Alice has no part in this, and is bored with the computer game which the boys also play together for long chunks of time. Kevin handles disagreements and conflict with Alice and with Jeff very differently. He makes some attempt to reason and justify his position when he is arguing with Jeff; it is almost always to get his own way, rather than to achieve a compromise, but there is some negotiation, some give-and-take. In his disputes with Alice, in contrast, he usually furiously refuses to comply, screams prohibition and insults, and rarely reasons – it is enough to try the patience of his loving mother.

And the balance of power within the two relationships is quite different: Alice manages to dominate their conversations and play, and rarely submits to his suggestions, while Jeff is a compliant companion. The emotions involved in the two relationships are very different too. Kevin rarely gets angry or distressed when he is playing with Jeff; there is a happy, even tenor to their communication, which builds every now and then to a crescendo of laughter.

Is it unusual for the same child to relate so differently to friend and sibling? And if such differences are quite common, does this mean that in general, sibling relationships do not influence the kind of friendship children form – or vice versa?

The case for links between sibling and friend relationships

We might well expect to find links between children's relationships with their siblings and their friends. A case for finding connections can be made on several different grounds. First, if we assume that a warm, secure attachment between child and parent is the crucial template for later relationships, we would predict that a child with a happy secure relationship with his mother would form a positive, warm relationship both with his sibling, and with a friend. We saw in the last chapter that there is evidence that children with secure attachments to their mothers are likely to have warm positive friendships. There is some evidence too for positive sibling relationships to be associated with secure parent–child attachments, though it is not a simple or consistent story.[1]

Second, there is the argument that children learn, within their families, certain styles of relating to other people and certain expectations about how others will relate to them. Again, we might expect these 'lessons' to apply to styles of relating both to siblings and to other children outside the family – the social learning account. More specifically, people often suggest that children will learn ways of relating to other children from their experiences with their siblings that will either help or hinder them in building relationships with other children. It is argued, for instance, that only children, who have not had experience playing, sharing and conversing with siblings from an early age will have more difficulty in the world of peers than children who have grown up with brothers and sisters. 'They'll learn to share', 'They'll learn to sort out quarrels'; such optimistic comments are often made by prospective parents who see these benefits of having more than one child.

Then there is also the argument that a child's particular personality is likely to *elicit* similar reactions from other people – both siblings and friends. An easygoing, happy-go-lucky, extroverted child is likely to be a good companion for both siblings and peers, and to have, as a result, friendly relations with both. One study of five- to ten-year-olds showed that the temperamental characteristic of sociability was systematically linked to both the quality of children's close friendships and their sibling relationships.[2]

Most recently, we've learned that young children who have had experiences of cooperative play with a friendly older sibling are particularly likely to be skilled at understanding feelings and other minds. Longitudinal research shows that the experience of cooperative play – especially shared pretend play – with an older sibling contributed to children's mind-reading and emotion understanding, independently of their verbal ability.[3] Research with siblings also shows that individual differences in discourse about inner states (mental states and feelings) with siblings were related to assessments of mind-reading, in very different samples of children.[4] A parallel point is made from the evidence on links between conflict between siblings and social understanding: Children whose older siblings had engaged in frequent 'other-oriented' reasoning when they were in disputes with their younger siblings (that is, reasoning that took account of the other person's wishes, feelings or intentions) were more successful on mind-reading tasks than those whose siblings had not reasoned in this way.[5]

These findings suggest that it is not simply *having a sibling around* that is important in the development of social understanding, but the quality of that sibling relationship and particular interactions between the children that matter, in terms of developmental influence on children's social understanding. The relevance for children's friendships is that these skills of understanding other people's emotions and thoughts are, as we've seen, importantly linked to the quality of friendship and peer relations in later years. Playing (especially joint make-believe) with an older sibling provides a wonderful forum for children to begin to understand other children, and discourse about inner states is especially likely during this play. So in an indirect way, certain experiences with siblings are likely to foster the understanding that is important in coordinating pretend with another child, so significant in friendships between young children, and in the growth of valuable skills for sorting out disagreements.

The case against links between the relationships

Against these arguments, a quite different case can be made. Friendship is, after all, so *different* from the bond with a brother or sister. Although both are intimate relationships, in that children know both their siblings and their friends quite well, and are familiar with what amuses, excites or upsets them, there are key differences between the two relationships. There is a mutual commitment of interest, affection and support between good friends. In contrast, not all siblings feel that way about each other as years of research on siblings have shown![6] With friends, there is no rivalry for parents' love and attention, and no long history of competition or jealousy, as there can be with siblings.

Children choose their friends, and are usually strongly committed to making the friendship continue. When problems or disagreements arise, as we've seen, children often attempt to solve these disagreements in a way that ensures the friendship is not jeopardized. As in the case of Kevin's relations with Alice, the same is very often not true of conflict between siblings. The relationship between siblings is no-holds-barred: If children feel irritated or provocative towards a brother or sister, they usually simply show that hostility. They aren't going to lose their sibling by expressing their mean feelings (even if they'd quite like to, occasionally). A sibling is there for life.

Choice doesn't enter into sibling relations – a child is simply stuck with his or her brothers or sisters. And while, as we've seen, children often choose as friends those children who are similar to them, it is the *differences* between siblings that are often so striking.[7] And research on brothers and siblings has shown that the more different they are in temperament from one another, the more conflicted their relationship is likely to be in early childhood.[8]

The feelings that siblings have for each other are likely, then, to be very different from those of friends. There is often an emotional ambivalence between sisters and brothers – affection but also jealousy, irritation and yet admiration, competitive feelings and concern, the closeness of intimate knowledge and shared experience, yet also an eagerness to distance self. There are also very great individual differences between siblings in their feelings for each other and in how they get along. Observational studies have documented a striking range in the proportion of friendly, positive interactions and of hostile interactions in siblings' interactions.[9] Some are close, supportive, interested, affectionate, some outright hostile ('I wish Jack wasn't IN this family', one five-year-old complained to me about her brother). Other brothers and sisters are simply uninterested and cool about each other.

This great range of differences helps to explain why there is little evidence that simply having a sibling, versus being an only child, is associated with the kind of friendship a child forms. Having a sibling can mean very different things. It can mean growing up with someone who is a great companion, full of ideas for playing, supportive when you are upset, always there when you need someone. Or it can mean growing up with someone who endlessly disparages you, takes your things, needles and teases you, takes your parents' attention away. Given these huge differences, the key question becomes not whether having a sibling or being an only child affects a child's friendships or vice versa, but *how* the *kind* of sibling relationship a child experiences connects with the sort of friendships he or she develops.

The case for expecting simple global connections between sibling and friend relationships becomes weaker still when we recognize that a child with more than one sibling can have very different kinds of relationship with his various brothers and sisters, as any parent with more than two children knows.[10] Here's how a mother in our Pennsylvanian study sees her six-year-old son's relations with his two brothers:

> Tom and he get along ever so well – they can play for hours without a fight- he loves to do things with Tom. He said to me the other day 'Tom has the *best* ideas Mom!' But with Charley he just doesn't do well . . . they seem to always rub each other the wrong way, you know . . . Charley's a bit, well, bossy, and he can't stand it . . .

And, of course, the same child can have a range of friendships which differ from one another in important ways, as we saw in Chapter 3. Given these differences in children's relations with their various friends and different siblings, it appears rather unlikely *in principle* that we will find simple connections between how children get along with their brothers, sisters and friends. What does the research focused on the details of siblings' and friends' relationships show?

Patterns across relationships

First, we have to take into account of the developmental stage of the children, which plays a major role in the kind of links across children's relationships with siblings and friends. Recall Laurie Kramer's study, described in Chapter 4. The three-year-old children in that study who had close friendships were particularly friendly to their newborn siblings, and continued to be so over the months that followed.[11] Kramer argued that the friendship buffered the children against the trauma of events surrounding the arrival of the sibling.

However, it would be hazardous to extrapolate from what happens between three-year-olds and their baby siblings to the relations between school-aged or adolescent siblings and their friendships. With the three-year-olds and their baby siblings, the two individuals have strikingly different powers of understanding and communication, and clearly the roles of the older and baby siblings in their interaction is very different. Harmony in the exchange between a three-month-old baby and a preschooler is a very different matter from harmony in the exchange between a 12-year-old and an older adolescent sibling. The degree of harmony in the first case is very much in the hands of the firstborn child: indeed we know that how firstborns behave towards their new baby siblings can tell us a lot about how their relationships will develop over the next year or so.[12] But between the older children in the second case, harmony is likely to be influenced by *both* children to a much greater extent, by the history of what has happened between them, and the wider social world in which they live. The connections between sibling relationship and friendship are likely to be very different at different periods of children's lives.

Most studies that have included a close examination of both sibling and friend relationships have focused on slightly older children than those in Kramer's study. In these studies the picture of differences in Kevin's relations with his sister Alice and with his friend Jeff turns out to be not unusual. In our Pennsylvanian research we were able to study the children with their brothers and sisters over the years from two till seven, and with their friends as four-year-olds, as kindergartners, and as first graders. There were some links across the two relationships, but not many. Children who engaged in long connected conversations with their siblings were likely to do so with their friends. And children who were very likely to deal with conflict by simply shouting or hitting, rather than reasoning or negotiating often did this with both siblings and friends. (They tended to come from families in which there was a lot of anger and conflict between the other family members, too).

But the differences between the relationships were striking. There was little consistency in the emotional qualities of children's relations with friend and sibling. A child who was continually at loggerheads with a brother or sister often enjoyed a warm relationship with a friend. And some children in our studies who had very close relationships with their siblings had relatively distant or 'cool' relations with their friends. In Kevin's case we might assume it is the gender differences in the two relationships that are key to explaining the differences. But the picture of differences that we found with Kevin is often evident when children have same-sex siblings and same-sex friends. Other studies of young children report that same lack of simple associations across the relationships.[13]

A close look at differences in sibling and friend relationships

Further evidence on the differences between the two relationships in children of this age-range came from our research in London of children from widely differing backgrounds, which included detailed assessments of the children's social understanding and language, and those of their friends, as well as naturalistic observations of children with their friends and with their older siblings, recorded when they were playing and talking with no observer present.[14]

Three points stand out from these observations and assessments. First, the observations revealed differences in three key features of the two relationships: there was more conflict between the siblings than between the same children with their friends, but also more cooperative pretend play, and there was more 'failed' communication between the children with their friends than there was between them and their older siblings. It is very likely that the older siblings, with their greater language and socio-cognitive skills, played a particularly important part in maintaining the extensive shared pretend play narratives, and also the smoother communication between the siblings. (Note, however, that the relative age gap between the siblings did not affect the findings.)

Second, and most importantly, there were *no* significant correlations between children's sibling and friend relationships in terms of their shared pretend play, their connected communication and their conflict. This was the case when we looked at how each individual child behaved in the two relationships – the same child who engaged in frequent and elaborate make-believe with his friend did very little with his sibling, for instance. It was also the case when we looked at the dyadic measure of what the two children were doing as a *pair* – there was no relation between how a pair of child-and-friend behaved together, and how the pair of same-child-and-sibling interacted.

The third point concerns the ways in which children's language skills and powers of social understanding were linked to their behaviour in these two different relationships. Here we examined the correlations between the various measures of social understanding, language ability and social background, and the interactions they had with their close friend and with their older sibling. The question at issue was the following: are language skills particularly important for the relationship with your friend, and less important for your sibling relationship? How are your powers of mind-reading and understanding feelings linked to what happens in your relations with your friend, and with your sibling?

The pattern of results was this. Children's powers of social understanding (an aggregate of measures of mind-reading and emotion understanding) were correlated with their cooperative pretend play with both sibling and friend. Those children with greater understanding of mind and emotion were engaging in more cooperative pretend in both relationships. (As we've seen, this association could reflect the important role of social understanding in maintaining a shared fantasy with another child, and it could also reflect the 'fostering' of social understanding that takes place in such shared make-believe with another child.) However while their language ability was also importantly related to their cooperative pretend with their friends, it was *not* associated with differences in the shared pretend with a sibling.

Similarly, the social background of the child (socio-economic status) was correlated with their shared pretend with their friends: children from more middle-class, educated families, were engaging in more frequent and extended cooperative pretend with their friends.[15] But shared pretend with a sibling was not related to the children's language ability or their social background. Again, it seems likely that such shared cooperative pretend with an older sibling can be maintained and developed by the older child, and is independent of the younger sibling's language ability or the siblings' social background.

These findings bring us back to the point that what happens in a relationship depends crucially on both members of the dyad, and also reminds us that the way in which children *use* their powers of understanding in particular relationships differs. Children's sophistication of pretend play, their discourse about mental states and their management of conflict all differ in different relationships – they are not correlated.[16] The emotional context of particular relationships is key to the use that children make of their understanding, in interaction, and may be key to the further fostering of this understanding.

Siblings and friends in middle childhood

With slightly older children, there are again links between some aspects of the relationships but not others. Clare Stocker and I studied five- to ten-year-olds' relationships with siblings, with friends, and their acceptance in their peer groups,[17] and as noted above, we found that the children's temperamental characteristics did contribute to the quality of both friendships and sibling relationships. However, only four of 24 correlations between measures of the two relationships were significant, and only one of these significant correlations was positive – mothers who described their children's relationship with the sibling as positive were also more likely to describe their friendship as positive (so, this could be an effect of having both relationships rated by the same person). The other three correlations were negative. Children who were described as competitive and controlling in their sibling relationship were likely to be described as having very positive friendships.

In a later study in Colorado, Clare Stocker and her colleagues studied seven- and eight-year-olds, and children growing towards adolescence.[18] She found that children who were particularly *controlling* with their siblings were also controlling and less positive about their friends, when interviewed, than other children. Those who were particularly cooperative with their siblings were likely to be especially cooperative and affectionate with their friends. But the story was not a simple one. These children tended to spend less time with friends and to be involved in fewer activities with them. The 'companionship' side of the relationship was quite low. It could be that children who have close relationships with their siblings choose to spend less time with their friends; it could also be that the parents of these children were less motivated to arrange for their children to play with their friends than those in families in which siblings quarrelled endlessly and did not like playing together.

This fits with the idea that there may be some 'compensatory' patterns across the two relationships. That is, children who have rather unsatisfactory (to them) relations with their siblings may be particularly likely to develop important friendships instead. There is indeed evidence in this direction among school-aged children. For instance, in the Stocker and Dunn study just described, the firstborn children who were especially competitive and dominant with their younger siblings were more friendly and positive with their friends than other children.

At first sight, this picture differs from the one that Clare Stocker's later research revealed; but it could be that birth order explains the differences. The significance of dominating, controlling behaviour to a sibling may be different for a firstborn and a later-born child. Controlling behaviour towards a younger sibling is just what we would expect from a firstborn, and it is clearly not incompatible with developing a warm relationship with a friend. For a second-born child to be controlling towards an older sibling, in contrast, is quite unusual, and it may well suggest a combative, bossy personality. Such a bossy child could well be less likely to be a cooperative, good companion for a friend. In Clare Stocker's later study the children were mostly later-born, whereas in our earlier study the children were firstborn.

So birth order may be important in the kinds of connections between the two relationships. So too may gender. Morton Mendelson in Canada found that among kindergartners, hostile and difficult sibling relationships were associated with *particularly positive* friendships for same-sex siblings (whether boy–boy or girl–girl pairs), but this was not so for siblings who were boy-girl pairs.[19] It is possible that a child who has a very difficult relationship with a sibling of the same gender is particularly motivated to seek out friends, though a child who has a warm relationship with an opposite-gender sibling may still want to form a close friendship with a child who shares his or her gender (the norm, of course, for children of this age).

The impact of friendship on siblings

The lesson that the connections between sibling and friend relationships are likely to be different at different periods of children's lives was brought home to us with particular vividness in the comments that children between eight and fourteen years and their mothers made to us in the research in Cambridge, England, in which we had followed the children from their toddlerhood to their adolescence.[20] Here is eight-year-old Shelley, talking to me about her relationships with her older sister Carey:

> We used to do tons of things together . . . everything, really. [When did that change, do you think?] It changed really when she started spending time with Phoebe – that's her best friend . . . She and Phoebe just didn't let me do *anything* with them – still don't . . . and they tease me and laugh at me . . . Carey and me just don't talk together anymore like we used to . . .

The story of how Carey's friendship with Phoebe has changed the relationship between the sisters was the first example of many that we heard as we interviewed the families we'd studied since before the second-born children's second birthdays. These accounts, quite simply, surprised us. We did not expect to hear so often that friendship had had this impact on family relations – diminishing the closeness of the siblings. But overwhelmingly this was the picture that emerged when we asked the children, their siblings and their mothers whether they felt there had been changes in how siblings got along. If they said there had been changes, we asked them to what they attributed the changes they described. What we heard, again and again, was that there had been a marked decrease in closeness between the siblings when one of the siblings was between seven and nine years old – the age at which many children make a transition to junior school in England. It was to the new friendships that so many children formed around this time, that all three family members attributed the decrease in sibling warmth and closeness.

Among the ten-year-olds that we talked to, for instance, the majority of the children spontaneously referred to friends (their own or those of their siblings) as having affected their relations with their siblings, and in a striking 85 per cent of these comments the children said that the friendship had had a negative impact on their sibling relationship.

In some cases it was a story of one sibling becoming increasingly involved with a friend, and losing interest in the sibling as she did so. In other cases, the tension between the siblings arose because the friend of one sibling showed a lot of interest and attention to the other sibling, and this caused resentment and hostility between the siblings. Thus Wendy described what happened to her relationship with her younger sister Kelly:

> Well, when I started secondary school, I made friends with this girl Joy, and whenever Joy came back here with me after school, Kelly used to hang

about with us, and she and Joy used to do all this silly stuff together . . . I tried to make Kelly stay out of the room, but she would keep coming in, and then I got fed up with Joy paying her so much attention, wanting to take Kelly with us when we went out, and stuff like that . . . I think that's when things started to go badly between Kelly and me . . .

This pattern began to be evident among children when they were eight years old. It was increasingly powerful by the time they reached 10 and 12 years old, regardless of the children's birth order. The pattern was related to gender too – it was especially clear in families with firstborn boys and younger sisters. Gender differences had not been important in the relationships between the siblings when the children were preschoolers, but by 12 to 13 years, the firstborn boys were reporting less warmth and intimacy with their younger sisters than the firstborn girls. And both children and mothers saw this pattern as linked to the ties the boys were forming with other boys and a male peer group outside the family. It was linked, too, to the neighbourhood and social class of the families. The decrease in closeness between the siblings, and the close ties to the peer group, were clearest in the families growing up in poor, low-income neighbourhoods. The increasing impact of the wider social world on the children's family life, as well as on the nature of their relationships with other children is again highlighted.[21] Understanding children's close relationships is not simply a matter of family dynamics; the outside world becomes increasingly significant as children reach middle childhood and the teenage years.

Siblings, friends and adjustment

What about children who have real problems in their relations with the other kids at school? Do their relations with their siblings provide any support for them? One study of children who were regarded by the other kids as social misfits, and isolated from their peers, provides some encouraging news here. Patricia East and Karen Rook, working in southern California, found that support from a favourite sibling for such children meant that they were less anxious and worried than children who were socially isolated at school and did not have such supportive siblings. But the effect was not a big one.[22] The lesson is that protection from difficulties in the peer group can sometimes, but not always, be found through close relations with a sibling, just as popularity with the group doesn't always buffer children from a difficult relationship.

Only children and their friends

The stereotyped view of only children – held by both parents and children in our culture – is that children who grow up without siblings are spoilt, selfish, difficult with other children, and are likely to have fewer friends than children with siblings. Trouble in making and keeping friends is seen as one theme in the problems they develop, growing up alone with their parents. But this is a stereotype that has not stood the test of the few careful studies that have compared the social lives of only children and those with brothers and sisters. There is not good evidence that children from one-child families have social handicaps – indeed they may well be better at developing close relationships with other adults who are not part of their immediate families.[23] The autobiographies and biographies of writers who grew up as only children give us vivid accounts of their intense friendships with other children, and these should surely add to our scepticism about the portrayal of only children as having more problems in making or sustaining friendships.

So, the evidence from studies of children with their friends and family and from the experience of writers highlights the complexity and difference in children's relationships with their siblings and their friends. It suggests that we shouldn't expect simple, global links between these relations. But this does not mean that the experiences of children growing up with brothers and sisters may not be important, in relation to friendship. Certain kinds of experiences with an older sibling (pretend play is a prime candidate) are particularly likely to foster understanding other people, and this kind of understanding contributes to the communication, coordination, and self-disclosure between young friends. But it is only one factor in the complex chemistry of what makes two children good friends.

10

Implications

Three themes have run through this book. The first concerns the nature of very young children's close relationships with other children, the second the question of how our understanding of children's cognitive and emotional development can be illuminated by studying their friendships, and the third, the issue of individual differences in the quality of children's friendships – what lies behind such differences, and what evidence there is that friendships can influence children's development. What have we learned, and what questions and challenges are raised by considering young friends?

The nature of young children's friendships

The first question with which this book began was 'Do very young children have friendships?' The answer to that first question, from the exemplary work of Carollee Howes, Hildy Ross and their colleagues is yes, and it is an answer that challenges the conventional developmental story that children don't form important friendships until they are seven, eight or nine years old. In the affection and mutual interest, the increasingly complex shared play of toddlers and very young preschoolers the groundwork is laid for the first signs of intimacy in preschool children – the shared imaginative worlds, the talk about feelings and mental states, the shared sense of what is funny and what is unfair, the understanding of the other child that is apparent in the ways in which conflict and disagreements are addressed and comfort offered to the distressed. Among the lessons on the *nature* of these very early friendships from the observational research the following deserve attention:

- The pleasure, enjoyment and excitement that children express with their friends – the evident importance of the relationship to them.

- The significance of the shared pretend play of three-, four- and five-year-old friends, and its links to the affective quality of the relationship.
- The changes, with development, in the friendships of young children, with increase in intimacy, new powers of resolving conflict, new concerns with the social group in which the friendship exists, and its pressures on the relationship.
- The support and comfort that young friends can provide, and the distress children express following separation from their friends.
- Friendship is a relationship between two individuals, and this is one reason (among several) why we shouldn't expect simple 'spillover' from a child's relationship with parent or with sibling to friendship. The contribution of both individuals to the friendship is illustrated clearly in the research into longitudinal patterns of friendship – the 'old friends/new friends' research described in Chapter 4.
- The growing intimacy between friends, paradoxically, is a contributor to the vulnerabilities and fragilities of friendships – part of the story of girls' friendships in particular (Chapter 7).
- The effects of early adversities (such as institutional rearing) are especially evident in children's problems in close relationships with other children, and the emotional understanding that is so closely tied to these.
- These lessons are encapsulated by Vivian Paley, in her book *Bad Guys Don't Have Birthdays* in which she talks of the interlocking of the three Fs: Fantasy, Friendship and Fairness. Then she adds a fourth F – the fear of losing one's special place with someone.

Friendship and the growth of understanding others

The second theme was the issue of how the study of friends could illuminate some general developmental principles, in particular the growth of children's understanding of others and their moral sensitivity. If the first message of the book is that friendship, with all its emotional power, can develop remarkably early, the second is that this emotional power is tied closely to the growth of new understanding of other people. Perhaps the most general lesson from studying children with their friends concerns the connections between children's emotional engagement and their cognitive development. Take three examples. First, the example of conflict: in the context of a friendship in which they care about the other child, are concerned for the feelings of the other, and want to maintain the relationship, children attempt to conciliate, negotiate, make compromise more frequently and with more success than in their other relationships, such as those with their siblings or parents. They reveal, and possibly develop, such relatively mature cognitive abilities because of the emotional quality of their relationship.

The second example, which has run through the book, concerns sharing an imaginative world. The cognitive challenges that are implicated in this shared pretend include the discussion of what the imaginary characters in the shared narrative would be *thinking, knowing, feeling*, and how these inner states are related to the characters' actions. A host of studies have demonstrated the associations between engaging in discourse about inner states and success on later formal assessments of social understanding. What the friendship research has shown is that such talk is especially likely to take place in the context of the intimate play and conversation of friends, and that the experience of shared pretence between friends contributes independent variance to a wide range of later socio-cognitive outcomes. The research highlights the social processes involved in the 'work of the imagination', in Paul Harris's phrase,[1] and importantly the significance of the *shared* nature of this imaginative work. Again, it is the role of emotion in the relationship between friends that must not be ignored, if we are to appreciate fully these developmentally significant processes.

And the third example concerns the development of moral understanding and sensitivity. Friendship, the findings of the research show, is a context in which moral understanding is demonstrated very early, and individual differences in friendship are associated with differences in moral development. *Because they care about the friend*, children see clearly how a friend may be suffering, and they care more about their friends in distress because they understand the links between their friends' experiences and their feelings. Piaget's original argument about the important role of peers in moral development focused primarily on the power relations between children of more-or-less equal status, and their understanding of reciprocity between peers.[2] Here we have emphasized, instead, the key importance of children's emotional ties to their friends in the growth of their moral understanding.

Developmental influence, and individual differences in friendship?

Such associations between friendship and developmental outcome are easy to interpret as causal. But we have to be very cautious about drawing inferences about causal influence. We have seen that friendships differ strikingly in quality – the third theme of the book – and it is reasonable to argue that these differences have to be taken into account in any attempt to document developmental influence. So too the identity of friends has to be included in any such attempt. But throughout the book we have noted that it is not appropriate to draw firm conclusions about causal influence from correlations between quality of friendship, and children's developmental outcome. Correlations have been found for various aspects of positive friendship interactions and children's later friendships, their moral understanding and sensibility, and between negative features of friendship and children's later troublesome behaviour at school.[3] These associations are certainly consistent with the idea that friendship quality affects the children's development, they show us which causal hypotheses are plausible, and they can stimulate ideas on what social processes may be implicated (as in the evidence on discourse about inner states being more frequent in certain friendships – those high in shared imaginative play). But to make progress in testing causal hypotheses we need experimental studies, intervention studies and longitudinal research that examines how changes in friendship may be linked to changes in children's behaviour, and vice versa. Berndt, for instance has emphasized the value of an experimental approach in which a researcher could train children who had low-quality friendships in skills that could improve the quality of their friendships, and then investigate how such interventions affected other aspects of the children's social adjustment.[4]

Challenges and questions

Beyond the intractable causal questions, there are many straightforward questions to which we don't yet have answers. Developmentally, the picture of children's friendships is very much in broad brush-strokes. We don't know, for instance, whether the significance of similarity between friends changes with development. The recent work on preschoolers suggests that similarity in language ability, and in the families' educational background is important in the early years,[5] while gender becomes important later, as does race.[6] Perceptions of similarity are important at all ages that have been studied, though with age children become more aware of the ways in which they differ from their friends. On the question of whether the significance of children's personality characteristics for their friendships changes with age, little is known, though some research suggests that assertiveness and dominance are attractive features for

preschool friends, while in middle childhood close friendship is linked
to sociability, pro-social behaviour, as well as emotional supportiveness
and emotional understanding. We still know little about the relation of
conceptions of friendship to the quality of actual friendship. We also know
relatively little about the phases of friendship (from initial acquaintance,
through deepening friendship, to weakening of ties or breakdown of the
friendship), and whether these change developmentally.

Cultural differences in children's friendships?

A particularly striking gap in our knowledge of children's friendship concerns possible cultural differences. It is a gap that reflects the focus in
most research on North American and European communities. In 1996
Lothar Krappmann commented that there was hardly any information
on cultural differences in childhood friendships, even though cultural
diversity in adult friendships has been discussed extensively by anthropologists.[7] The picture has hardly changed today. While several authors
discuss how friendship is a context for the acquisition for cultural roles
from the wider culture,[8] others emphasize the independence of peer cultures from the adult world (see for instance the ethnographic studies of
peer cultures).[9] What we lack is systematic investigation of whether friendships do differ in culturally diverse settings. To what extent and in what
ways are children's friendships 'culturally embedded' (the themes of their
shared pretend are very likely indeed to reflect the wider culture).[10] And
does the extent of 'cultural embeddedness' change with age? We know that
the mores of the wide world impact increasingly on sibling relationships
in middle childhood[11] – perhaps this is so for friendships too. Conceptions
of friendship have been studied in Germany, Iceland, China, and generally
the results parallel those found in English speakers, but some of the differences raise further questions. Thus Monika Keller and her colleagues
found that young Chinese children appeared to use pro-social reasons
in decisions about action with friends earlier than Western children.[12] It
may be that the collectivist orientation of the Chinese educational system
supports an early development of pro-social reasoning.[13]

   That important features of friendship are found in strikingly different
cultures is indicated by the programme of research by Doran French
and colleagues on Indonesian and American friendships.[14] Many of the
characteristics of friendship were found to be similar in the two cultures
– provision of intimacy and companionship for instance. Similarity of
friends to one another was also found in Indonesia for aggression, social

withdrawal, social preference and achievement. The findings on aggression parallel those from the US, however the *differences* between the Indonesian and US friends on withdrawal illustrate the difficulties in comparing friendship between two complex cultures. As the researchers point out, in Indonesia even friendless and rejected children are rarely alone, and we need to know more about how social withdrawal exists in Indonesian culture before we can fully unravel the meaning of this construct for friendship.

Influences on individual differences

While some of the sources of individual differences in children's close friendships are becoming clear, there is still much we don't know. Brothers and sisters, for instance, can have very different relationships with their friends, and we have only just begun to investigate these 'within-family' differences.[15] On this third theme of the book, individual differences, however one message is clear. Friendships differ in important ways, and these differences make any simple answers to the question of what impact friendships have on children's development likely to be misleading. These differences, and the independence of friendship from family relationships surely should lessen feelings of responsibility or guilt that parents may feel as they catch glimpses of the dramas (and sometimes traumas) of their children's intense relationships outside the family. We can indeed do something about the extremes of loneliness and bullying. But so much of our children's social world is in a real sense outside the family, and therein lies much of its importance and interest. Friendship is the crucible in which so much learning about the social world – and indeed about ourselves – is likely to take place. It deserves our attention.

Appendix

How can parents help children over friendship difficulties?

For many of the troubles that children experience in their friendships – jealousy, exclusion from a clique, dominance, competitiveness – parents can do little directly to help, though of course their general support, sympathy and love can be enormously important as a buffer for the child. But the case of bullying deserves special mention.

Bullying

As we saw in Chapter 6, bullying which causes extreme suffering and loss of self-confidence often goes on without parents or teachers being aware. The signs that a child might be being bullied have now been identified from a number of studies, and it is certainly helpful for parents to be given this information. The signs include the following:

A child not wanting to travel on the school bus, but begging to be driven.
Complaining of feeling ill every morning, and not wanting to go to school.
Beginning to play truant.
Beginning to do poorly at school work.
Coming home with books, papers or clothes destroyed.
Becoming withdrawn, stammering, losing confidence.
Asking for money, beginning to steal.
Unexplained bruises or scratches.
Crying at night, wetting the bed or having nightmares.
Refusing to discuss what is wrong.

What can parents do, if they think a child might be being bullied? The advice from the researchers is that parents should first ask directly 'I think you are being bullied or threatened. I'm worried about you; let's talk about it.' Say that you are there to listen at any time of day or night, when she or he feels ready to talk. It is important to keep a careful eye on the signs – some children become so desperate that they get to the point of running away from home or taking an overdose.

Most important is the reassurance you can give, that the child will be protected if he tells an adult about it. Tell the school authorities, and make sure they actually do something about the problem. Make alternative arrangements about the travel to school if that is a problem. What not to say: fight back; sort it out for yourself; learn to stand up for yourself. Encouraging children to fight back is now seen as inappropriate, because the end result is likely to be two aggressive children – both the bully and the victim, and the victim may well get seriously physically hurt.

Problems other than bullying

For other issues in children's friendships, such as how to deal with quarrels among very young friends, how to foster a network of companions for young children, how to help a child with a particular problem, some helpful pointers have emerged from the studies we have been discussing.

Talking things over

First, in general, discussions that help children to understand relationships between people, and to reflect on their own responses and the feelings of others, are likely to be helpful. If a child is having difficulties with a particular child, it could well help to discuss and give advice *outside the actual situation*, to discuss possible options for handling teasing or provocative actions before the child arrives. Incidents in which trouble had occurred earlier could be discussed, with a focus on why the other child acts this way. Counselling diplomacy may well help, as in the examples given by several of the mothers in the Nottingham study:

> If I sense that she wants to get out of a situation but she wants to be polite as well, I try to suggest a way out that she could use.

> Well, we try to show her, you know how to *make* friends rather than fall out with them all the time. [What sort of thing do you say?] Well, ask them if you can play with them, rather than forcing yourself, and, er, do what they do. Don't try to be the boss all the time, you know, do what *they* want to do – fall in, you know.

For children who easily lose control and become angry with their playmates, again *discussion* can help, as the next two examples (from Pennsylvania and Nottingham respectively) illustrate:

> He does lose it – gets furious if he's frustrated, and flings himself around, and the other kids just don't like it, and leave him to it. We've talked about it, and I think he's *maybe* managing to stop himself more . . .

> I've told him that if he feels himself getting really cross he should walk out of the situation before he comes to blows, because I've *told* him he has this strong temper and is a strong child, and that he certainly mustn't hit or frighten children smaller or not so strong as himself *because* of this . . . er . . . and it's sort of one of the things he's learning to live with . . .

Nice things that other children do can be highlighted, with an emphasis on how much the child must be liked: 'That was a nice thing for Kerry to do, to give you that. She must like you a lot.' Children's attributions about their own success or failure with peers can also usefully be discussed, to build up children's confidence in their own likeability.

Don't blame yourself

Second, parents should remember not to blame themselves for the ups and downs in their children's lives with their peers. As I've tried to show, the tendency to blame parents for their children's difficulties with peers seems way out of balance with the evidence. There is a real distinction between serious problems with peers, and minor hiccups in the course of friendship. If a parent is facing what is really a minor hiccup, she shouldn't feel guilty or anxious. If as a parent you think there is a serious issue to be faced, don't feel that you have to face it alone. Get help.

Things change, often for the better

Third, it is easier to foster friendships among the preschoolers and kindergartners than the older children. If you've tried and things are still rather bleak in your child's world, remember that children's relations with other children can change quite dramatically with time. Psychologists often emphasize the continuities in patterns over time; while these can be striking – as in the instance of the children who were brought up in institutions that we described earlier – within the range of experiences of children growing up in families, the changes over time in their peer relations can be notable. A change of school, a new set of children met in another context – these can mean new sources of confidence and support. Children can be 'labelled' unkindly by their peers, and this 'reputation' can damage their chances of making new friendships as they move through the school. A change of school can mean the opportunity to escape this reputation, a chance to start anew, and can really help the possibility of making friends. It has been shown, for instance, that children who have the reputation within school as being *loners* or *aggressive* are just as able to form good friendships outside school as children who are popular in the classroom (see East and Rook, 1992).

These hints are offered more as common-sense generalities than as the fruits of careful research into how parents can foster children's peer relations. With the exception of studies on extremely troubled or difficult children, we lack such research.

Notes

1 Friends matter

1. This incident is drawn from an observation in our research on friends in Pennsylvania: Dunn (1995); Dunn et al. (1991).
2. Relationships involve successions of interactions between two individuals known to each other, and the nature of these interactions is influenced by the history of past interactions and the participants' expectations for the future. For discussion of definition of friendship in childhood see Rubin, Bukowski and Parker (1998). In adolescence and adulthood, commitment is also seen as an important feature of relationships (Hinde, 1979; 1995).
3. Acceptance as a one-way construct, see Berndt (1984); Bukowski and Hoza (1989).
4. Criteria of companionship, intimacy and affection originated in the study of adult friendships (Weiss, 1974).
5. Children talk about friendship, referring to companionship, intimacy and affection (Bigelow, 1977; Buhrmester, 1990; Furman and Buhrmester, 1985).
6. For recent reviews of research on popularity, acceptance and rejection by the peer group, see Rubin et al. (1998).
7. For Blum's discussion see Blum (1987).
8. See Bretherton et al. (1986).
9. Child participating in our London research on friendships, see Cutting and Dunn (1999), Dunn and Cutting (1999).
10. For Piaget's arguments concerning the significance of peers in moral development, see Piaget (1932/1965).
11. For Isaacs's observations and interpretations of the behaviour and conversations of the children in the Malting House School, see Isaacs (1937).
12. For brief description of historical changes in parental concerns and advice to parents in urban America, see Renshaw and Parke (1992).
13. Throughout the book, the quotations from children and mothers come from our research studies, otherwise noted. Children's names are changed, to preserve anonymity. These studies are described in the following sources:

a. Studies in Cambridge, England: Dunn and Kendrick (1982); Dunn (1988).
b. Studies in Pennsylvania: Dunn et al. (1991); Dunn (1993); Maguire and Dunn (1997).
c. Studies in London: Dunn and Cutting (1999); Cutting and Dunn (1999); Dunn, Cutting and Demetriou (2000); Hughes and Dunn (1997); Hughes, White, Sharpen and Dunn (2000).
d. Studies in Bristol: Dunn, Davies, O'Connor and Sturgess (2000).

2 Beginnings

1. For the study by Burlingham and Freud of children brought up in the Hampstead Nursery in London during the Second World War, which includes detailed records of the children's behaviour, see Burlingham and Freud (1944).
2. Ibid., p. 23.
3. Ibid., p. 41.
4. Dunn and Kendrick (1982).
5. For the studies in Cambridge involving siblings, see Dunn (1988).
6. For attachment to siblings: see Stewart (1983); Stewart and Marvin (1984); Teti and Ablard (1989); Dunn (1988).
7. Ibid.
8. Ibid.
9. For Howes's studies of friendship in toddlers and preschoolers, see Howes (1988); Howes et al. (1992); Howes (1996).
10. The Pennsylvania Study of Social Understanding, see Dunn et al. (1991).
11. Corsaro (1985).
12. Ross and Lollis (1989).
13. Ross et al. (1992).
14. Hartup et al. (1988); Hinde et al. (1985).
15. Dunn and Wooding (1977).
16. For research on the increase in imitation, see Eckerman (1993), Howes (1992); on the development of cooperation and the differentiation of self and other during the second year, see Brownell and Carriger (1990); also Harter (1998); on the increase in reciprocal games, see Howes (1988), Ross, Lollis and Elliot (1982).
17. Ibid.
18. For developmental changes in self-control and emotion regulation in toddler-hood, Calkins et al. (1999). For a review, see Thompson (1991); Brenner and Salovey (1997); Denham et al. (2002).
19. Dunn (1988).
20. See Howes et al. (1989).
21. Dunn (1988).

22. Dunn and Dale (1984).
23. Intersubjectivity: see Trevarthen and Hubley (1978) for discussion of 'primary intersubjectivity', and Trevarthen (1989) for discussion of the development of 'secondary intersubjectivity', towards the end of the second year.
24. See Goncu (1993).
25. See Garvey (1990).
26. Ibid., p. 82.
27. Dunn and Dale (1984).
28. For Gottman's studies of young friendship, see Gottman and Parker (1986).
29. Harris (2000).
30. Taylor (1999).
31. Gopnik (2001).
32. For this evidence, see Custer (1996); Hickling et al. (1998); Joseph (1998). For an alternative view of whether young children understand the mental state of characters in pretense, see Lillard (1998). The apparent contradictions between the findings of Joseph (1998) and Lillard (1998) are attributable in part to the significance of whether, in the story on which children are asked to make judgments of mental states, it is established initially that the characters are *pretending* (in which case the children are more likely to be successful in reasoning about the characters' mental representations). As Gopnik (1998) points out, it appears that children's concept of pretence involves an association with intentional action (as Joseph shows); however for very young children pretence can also involve cases that are simply acting 'as if'.
33. Quotation is from Bruner (1986, p. 66). See also Bruner (1990) for the exposition of this argument; see also Feldman (1992).
34. See Lewis et al. (1994).
35. Gopnik (2001).
36. Griffiths (1935).
37. See note 11.
38. See, e.g., data from the NICHD childcare study, Zerwas and Brownell (2003). For further evidence that children play in more complex ways with friends than non-friends, see Hinde et al. (1985), Doyle (1982); for evidence that children cooperate more with friends, see Charlesworth and La Freniere (1983); that they negotiate more in resolving conflicts with friends than non-friends, see Hartup and Laursen (1991), Hartup (1992).
39. For the study of children rescued from concentration camps, discussed in Chapter 5, see Freud and Dann (1951).
40. For evidence on increase in length of sequences of pretend, see Goncu (1993); on developmental 'tuning' of conversation to understanding of companion, see Shatz and Gelman (1973).
41. See Howes (1996).
42. Eisenberg and Fabes (1998).
43. Dunn (1988).

44. For Murphy's classic study of children's social and emotional development, see Murphy (1937).
45. For Blum's discussion of the development of concern for others, and his observations of Sarah, see Blum (1987).
46. Sebanc (2003).

3 Friends within a social world: the early school years

1. For the Pennsylvania Study of Social Understanding see Dunn et al. (1991).
2. Also children from observations in the Pennsylvania study.
3. For the increasingly key role of gossip in friendship: see Gottman (1986a); Gottman (1986b); quotations from pp. 166–7. Also see Gottman and Mettetal (1986).
4. Ibid.
5. See Isaacs (1937).
6. For research on children's conflict management, see Dunn (1996); Tesla and Dunn (1992); Dunn and Herrera (1997).
7. Ibid.
8. Increase in conciliation, see Ross and Conant (1992). Also, references to conflict management in note 6 above.
9. See Tesla and Dunn (1992).
10. Ibid.
11. Increase in talk about feelings, memories etc, see Bartsch and Wellman (1995); Brown and Dunn (1992); Brown et al. (1996); Wellman et al. (1995). For studies on children's interest in and conversations about emotions (their own and those of others) see Bartsch and Wellman (1995); Brown and Dunn (1991); Dunn and Brown (1994); Dunn, Brown and Beardsall (1991); Dunn (1988); for overviews of research see Harris (1994); Saarni et al. (1998).
12. For the evidence that conversations about mental states were twice as common with friends as with mothers, by 47 months of age, see Brown et al. (1996).
13. Updike (1965), p. 76.
14. For Gilligan's consideration of relationships and the development of morality, see Gilligan and Wiggins (1987). For the Pennsylvania study of moral sensibility, see Dunn, Brown, and Maguire (1995). For evidence on links between moral development and friendship from the London research, see Dunn, Cutting and Demetriou (2000).
15. For Kochanska's moral stories see Kochanska (1993).
16. Garvey (1990), p. 88.
17. Goncu et al. (2000).
18. Garvey (1990).
19. See note 3.
20. Dillard (1988), pp. 124–5.

4 Differences in children's friendships: links with social understanding

1. Sebanc (2003).
2. Pennsylvania study friendship dimensions, see Maguire and Dunn (1997).
3. Dimensions of friendship: For a meta-analysis of 'features of children's friendships', see Newcomb and Bagwell (1996); for discussion of measuring friendship perceptions and the dimensions of friendships, see Furman (1996). See also Berndt (1996).
4. For the Nottingham study, see Newson and Newson (1980). See also Newson and Newson (1970), for the research on the same children at four years old.
5. Similarities in friends; for summaries, see Rubin et al. (1997); also Hartup and Abecassis (2002). See also Haselarger et al. (1998).
6. Dunn and Cutting (1999).
7. Hartup and Abecassis (2002).
8. Newson and Newson (1980), p. 180.
9. Dunn, Brown, Slomkowski, Tesla and Youngblade (1991).
10. For a clear and succinct account of the research on children's understanding of other minds, and the controversies about the developmental story, see Astington (1994). See also Wellman (1990), Perner (1991). For a meta-analysis of recent studies, see Wellman et al. (2001).
11. For deception studies, see Sodian and Frith (1992); Chandler et al. (1989).
12. See note 10.
13. For emotion understanding in two- to four-year-olds, see Denham (1986). For findings on emotion understanding in the Pennsylvania Study see Dunn, Brown, Slomkowski, Tesla and Youngblade (1991); Dunn and Brown (1994); Brown and Dunn (1996). For general discussion of interest and growing understanding that children show in relation to other people's emotions during infancy and toddlerhood, see Bretherton et al. (1986). For an overview, see Harris (1994).
14. Dunn, Brown, Slomkowski, Tesla and Youngblade (1991).
15. Findings from the Pennsylvanian study on early social understanding and friendship interactions: Slomkowski and Dunn (1996); Herrera and Dunn (1997); Maguire and Dunn (1997); Dunn (1995).
16. The London Friendship Study: For early social understanding related to later friendship, see Dunn and Cutting (1999); Dunn, Cutting and Fisher (2002); see also Hughes and Dunn (1997).
17. For Ladd's findings on friendship and the transition to school, Ladd (1990). Also Ladd and Kochenderfer (1996).
18. Howes (1996) proposes that early representations of friendships may influence subsequent friendships.
19. Pretend play as a context for talk about inner states; Astington and Jenkins (1995); Howe (1991); Youngblade and Dunn (1995a); Hughes and Dunn (1997).

20. References to mental states more frequent with friends: Brown et al. (1996).
21. See note 19.
22. For family talk about feelings shown to be related to later social understanding, see Dunn, Brown and Beardsall (1991); Dunn, Brown, Slomkowski, Tesla and Youngblade (1991); Brown et al. (1996). For similar findings, see Moore et al. (1994). See also Meins and Fernyhough (1999), Peterson and Siegal (2000).
23. Importance of identity of friends in older children, see Hartup (1996).
24. Howes (1996).
25. Arsenio and Lover (1995). For Piaget's views on peers in moral development, see Piaget (1932/1965).
26. Mannarino (1976). See also McGuire and Weisz (1982).
27. Interview based on Slomkowski and Killen's (1992) interview. For findings see, Dunn, Cutting and Demetriou (2000).
28. Dunn (1995); Dunn, Cutting, and Demetriou (2000); Hughes and Dunn (2000); Hughes et al. (2001).
29. For current friendship problems related to difficulties in social understanding; Rubin, Bukowski and Parker (1998).
30. Costs of social understanding: for evidence on associations with later sensitivity to criticism, see Cutting and Dunn (2002); for evidence that response to failure and criticism has long-term consequences, see Dweck (1986); Buhrans and Dweck (1995).
31. Genetics, shyness and sociability: see Loehlin (1992).
32. Pike and Atzaba-Poria (2003). For the Manke study, see Manke et al. (1995).
33. Stocker and Dunn (1990).
34. For the twin study reporting genetic influence on theory-of-mind scores, see Hughes and Cutting (1999); for the study reporting little genetic influence on theory of mind, see Hughes et al. (2004). For the study reporting genetic influence on behavioural items reflecting theory of mind skills, see Ronald et al. (2004).
35. Howes (1996).
36. See note 17.
37. Hartup (1996). See also Azmitia and Montgomery (1993).
38. Howes (1996).
39. Talk about deviance with friends: Hughes et al. (2000); Dunn and Hughes (2001).

5   With a little help from my friends

1. Brontë (1994), *Jane Eyre*. For biographical accounts, see Gerin (1967); Gaskell (1978).
2. For Freud and Dann's study of the holocaust children, see Freud and Dann (1951).

3. Stepfamily research: Dunn et al. (1998); Dunn and Deater-Deckard (2001).
4. For the Californian study of divorce, see Wallerstein and Kelly (1980).
5. For the English study, see Jenkins and Smith (1990).
6. Hetherington (1999).
7. Newcomb and Bagwell (1996).
8. Dunn and Deater-Deckard (2001).
9. Barbee et al. (1990).
10. Increases in seeing friends as supportive with age, see Buhrmester (1990); Buhrmester and Furman (1987); Newcomb (1990); Parker and Gottman (1989).
11. Schadler and Ayers-Nachamkin (1983).
12. For summary and discussion of Harris's research on coping strategies, see Harris (1989).
13. Denton and Zarbatany (1996).
14. Dunn and Deater-Deckard (2001).
15. For Kramer's study of the birth of a sibling, see Kramer and Gottman (1992).
16. Sibling birth and children's adjustment, see Dunn and Kendrick (1982); also Gottlieb and Mendelson (1990); Stewart et al. (1987); Vandell (1987).
17. Paley (1988).
18. For Gottman's account of Eric and Naomi's friendship, see Gottman (1986b), quotation p. 159.
19. For the studies of the significance of friendship for children starting school, see the research of Gary Ladd, e.g., Ladd (1990; 1999). Also Ladd and Kochenderfer (1996).
20. For summary of shyness research, see Rubin et al. (2002).
21. Howes (1988; 1996).
22. For the study of physiological changes in children experiencing separation from their friends, see Field (1984).
23. Newsons' study of Nottingham families: see Newson and Newson (1980).
24. Berndt (1996).
25. For the study of school children's depression and friendships, see Goodyer et al. (1989).

6   Intrigues, bullying, rejection and loneliness

1. For the study of six-year-olds' friendships in the playground, see Tamplin (1989).
2. Atwood (1990).
3. Trollope (1999); Greene (1992, pp. 60–1).
4. For research on victimization within friendships, see Crick and David (2002). For research on bullying, see Olweus (1993). Also Smith et al. (1999); Rigby (2002).

5. Wolke et al. (2000).
6. Hodges et al. (1995).
7. Olweus, 1978; Perry et al. (1992).
8. Sutton et al. (1999).
9. A number of large-scale intervention studies have been carried out on bully-victim problems in schools: see for instance Olweus's studies in Norway (Olweus, 1993); an intervention programme aimed at students, teachers and parents was carried out and assessed in 42 primary and junior high schools in Norway. The results were encouraging, with substantial reductions in the levels of bullying and being bullied. See also a large-scale intervention in Sheffield in 16 primary and seven secondary schools (Smith and Sharp, 1994).
10. Victimization and friendship, see Canadian study: Hodges et al. (1999). See also Hodges et al. (1997).
11. Hartup and Stevens (1997).
12. For research on non-aggressive victims versus aggressive victims, see Malone and Perry (1995).
13. Peer rejection: for recent comprehensive review of research see Rubin et al. (1997). For the correlates of peer rejection, see also Asher and Coie (1990). For Trollope's account of his schooldays, see Trollope (1999).
14. See note 13. For a review of the research on the relations between popularity, rejection and friendship, see Rubin et al. (1998).
15. Rubin et al. (1998).
16. McGuire and Weisz (1982).
17. Kaye (1991).
18. Hoza (1989).
19. Newcomb and Bagwell (1996).
20. See note 13.
21. For genetics of hyperactivity, see Brown (2003).
22. For the research on children's interpretation of ambiguous behaviour, and links between a tendency to misattribute the causes of behaviour, and aggression, see Dodge et al. (1986). For Dodge's research on the groups of children, see Dodge et al. (1990).
23. See for example Hymel et al. (1990); Hymel et al. (1993).
24. East and Rook (1992).
25. See note 13.
26. Tamplin (1989).
27. Sullivan (1953).
28. For recent research on loneliness, see Asher and Paquette (2003); Rotenberg and Hymel (1999).
29. Renshaw and Brown (1993); Ladd (1999).
30. See note 28.
31. Ibid.
32. Ibid.

33. Those without friends report more loneliness: Parker and Asher (1993); Renshaw and Brown (1993).
34. Boivin and Hymel (1997); Ladd et al. (1996).
35. See note 28.
36. Asher et al. (1984).
37. Goodyer et al. (1989).

7   Girls, boys and friendship

1. Studies that involve recording and analysing the conversations between women friends and those between men friends report marked differences between the two sexes. Linguist Jennifer Coates reports, for instance, that the talk between women friends frequently involved sharing of personal experiences, and discussion of highly personal issues (Coates, 1986; see also Coates, 1996). Women friends' talk combines and overlaps – they often speak at the same time, not in a competitive way, but on the same theme. They also use questions frequently, not as information-seeking, but for checking a shared perspective. Their conversations are full of 'tag' questions like 'don't you think?', 'isn't it?', 'right?' – questions that offer the other person an opportunity to give their view. Controversy and disagreement is damped down in many of these conversations, for instance by the use of 'hedging' comments like 'sort of' or 'maybe'. In contrast studies of men friends' conversations emphasize the differences in topic (more impersonal), in the roles as 'experts', and the lack of overlapping turns. These conversational differences between men and women reflect, Deborah Tannen argues, deep differences in social relations (Tannen, 1990).
2. Flannery and Watson (1993).
3. Paley (1984).
4. Serbin et al. (1994).
5. Maccoby and Jacklin (1987).
6. Martin and Fabes (2001).
7. Serbin et al. (1982).
8. Paley (1984)
9. Thorne (1993).
10. Whiting and Edwards (1988).
11. Harkness and Super (1985).
12. Benenson et al. (1997). Also Benenson et al. (2001). But see recent evidence suggesting that although there is evidence that boys tend to play in larger peer groups than do girls (Ladd, 1983; Ladd et al. 1990), the evidence on friendships does not fit this pattern (Ladd et al. 1996).
13. Maccoby (1988). Also Maccoby (1990).
14. Golombok and Hines (2002).
15. Baron-Cohen (2003).

16. Ellis et al. (1981).
17. Wulff (1988).
18. Thorne (1993).
19. Opie and Opie (1969).
20. Goodenough (1987).
21. DiPietro (1981), commented on by Jacklin (1981).
22. Thorne (1993).
23. Schofield (1982).
24. Gender differences in friends' handling of conflict: Dunn and Herrera (1997).
25. For the Pennsylvania study, see Maguire and Dunn (1997); see also Astington and Jenkins (1995). For John Gottman's examples, and discussion of the significance of the gender differences, see Gottman (1986b: quotation p. 161). For the evidence on violent themes in pretend play: See Dunn and Hughes (2001).
26. Gottman and Parker (1986), p. 161.
27. See note 25.
28. Girls engage in more conversations about inner states, and shared referents: In Pennsylvania see Brown et al. (1996); in London see Hughes and Dunn (1998).
29. Girls did better on emotion understanding tasks at three years and at six years, in study by Brown and Dunn (1996). See also Zahn-Waxler et al. (1984); also evidence on girls' causal attributions about emotions see Eisenberg and Fabes (1998). Girls did better on theory of mind tasks in Dunn and Cutting (1999).
30. See note 29.
31. No gender differences in patterns of longitudinal findings from preschool to school: see Dunn et al. (2002).
32. Ladd et al. (1996).
33. Research on average differences in friendship of older boys and girls. Gender differences in intimacy: Bigelow (1977). Also Buhrmester and Praeger (1995). For summaries of gender differences in friendship, see Buhrmester (1996), also Ruble and Martin (1998), Maccoby (1998). For relational aggression, see Crick (1995), Crick (1996), Sebanc (2003).
34. Buhrmester and Furman (1987). Newcomb (1990).
35. Benenson and Christakos (2003).
36. See Parker and Seal (1966).
37. Ladd et al. (1996).
38. Parker and Asher (1993).
39. Howes and Phillipsen (1992).
40. Gottman (1986a; 1986b).
41. London friendship study: Dunn and Cutting (1999).
42. Gottman (1986b).
43. Dillard (1988). Quotation concerning pretend, p. 125. Quotation concerning gender, p. 42.
44. Twain (1966).

8 Parents and friends

1. Attachment theory: Bowlby (1971); Bowlby (1973). For discussion of recent research and theory, see Thompson (1998). See also Dunn (1993).
2. Hodges and Tizard (1989).
3. Follow up of Romanian adoptees, see Rutter and the English and Romanian Adoptees Study Team (1998). For the friendship differences between the Romanian and UK adoptees, see Kreppner and the English and Romanian Adoptee Study Team (2003). For the differences in pretend play at four years, see Kreppner et al. (1999).
4. Studies of the correlates of peer rejection are reviewed in Asher and Coie (1990). See also Parke and Ladd (1992).
5. Schneider et al. (2001).
6. Links with peer relations: significance of child temperament, see Bates, Maslin and Frankel (1985). For links with day care experience, see Howes (1991). For links with attachment to caregiver, see Howes and Wu (1990). For evidence on links between peer relations and maternal depression, see Rubin et al. (1991). For links between peer relations and parents' emotional expression, see Denham and Auerbach (1995), Parke and Ladd (1992). For links with parenting attitudes, see Adams (1994). For links with parenting practice, see Youngblade and Belsky (1992). For links with parents psycho-social adjustment, see Lyons-Ruth et al. (1993).
7. Lieberman (1977).
8. Belsky and Cassidy (1995).
9. Inconsistent findings on family-friendship links: in four-year-olds and five-year-olds, compare Park and Waters (1989); Youngblade et al. (1993); Youngblade and Belsky (1992).
10. For evidence on links between parental conflict strategies and children's conflict management with friends from Pennsylvania study, see Herrera and Dunn (1997); Slomkowski and Dunn (1992). For references on family discourse about emotions, social understanding and later friendship, see Chapter 4, note 19; also Dunn (1995).
11. For the relations between mothers' and fathers' friendships and those of their children, see Simpkins and Parke (2001).
12. For references on the different patterns of links between children's peer relations and mother–child and father–child relationships, see for instance MacDonald and Parke (1984); Youngblade et al. (1993).
13. Fathers' acceptance of children's emotional displays a better predictor of children's friendship than mothers' management of children's emotions, see Gottman et al. (1997). Fathers contribute to children's emotion under-standing, regulation and capacity to maintain friendships, see Parke (1997).
14. Theories about identification, see Bronfenbrenner (1960).
15. Evidence that fathers in middle childhood were more involved with sons, and mothers more involved with their daughters, see Crouter and Crowley (1990); for similar findings for adolescence, see Harris and Margolin (1991).

16. Evidence that fathers' behaviour is likely to be related to boys' peer relations, while mothers' more closely linked to girls' peer relations: see Isley et al. (1999); MacDonald and Parke (1984); Youngblade and Belsky (1992).
17. Stocker's research is reported in Stocker and Mantz-Simmons (unpublished).
18. Lewis and Feiring (1989).
19. Lollis et al. (1992), quotation on p. 256.
20. For review and discussion of the mechanisms linking parent and peer relationships, see Parke and Ladd (1992).
21. For the research by Thompson and his colleagues, see Laible and Thompson (1998), and also Laible and Thompson (2000). For research by Meins's group, see Meins et al. (1998).
22. Parke and Ladd (1992).
23. For consideration of the part that genetics plays in links between family measures and child outcome, see for example, Braungart et al. (1992); Plomin and Neiderhiser (1992); Rowe (1989).
24. For views and research on parental management of peer relations, see Parke and Ladd (1992) especially chapters 8 and 9.
25. Gottman's studies are reported in Gottman and Parker (1986).
26. Evidence for links between friendships and marital conflict: Parke et al. (2001); Wasserstein and LaGreca (1996); Hetherington and Stanley-Hagan (1999).
27. Parents' involvement in their children's quarrels, see Newson and Newson (1980). Quotations on p. 205.
28. Neighbourhoods, poverty and contact with other children: Parke and Ladd (1992).
29. Epstein (1986).
30. Poverty and rejection by peers: Charlotte Patterson's study in Charlottesville, Virginia: Patterson et al. (1992).
31. For the up-state New York study: Cochran and Davila (1992).
32. Quotation from the Nottingham study, Newson and Newson (1980, p. 211). Discouraging certain friendships: quotations from the Nottingham study: Newson and Newson (1980, p. 207).
33. Newson and Newson (1980).

9 Siblings and friends

1. Evidence that secure attachment to mother is associated with positive sibling relationships: some results fit this pattern, e.g., Teti and Ablard (1989); see also Bosso (1985). However other findings in the Teti and Ablard study do not fit the predicted pattern. Also, note that siblings differ in their attachment to their mothers: 36 per cent of siblings in the Teti and Ablard study, and a similar proportion in the study by Ward et al. (1988) differed. See also Abramovitch et al. (1986).
2. Stocker and Dunn (1990).

3. Sibling cooperative play and especially joint pretend is correlated with high levels of social understanding: Dunn et al. (1991); Youngblade and Dunn (1995a).
4. Discourse about mental states is related to performance on theory of mind assessments: Brown et al. (1996). For similar findings in a very different, socially deprived sample, see Hughes and Dunn (1997).
5. For the relation of social understanding to conflict management, see Dunn, Slomkowski, Donelan-McCall and Herrera (1995).
6. Sibling relationships: for evidence for hostility see for instance Brody (1998); Brody et al. (1992); Dunn and Kendrick (1982); Dunn (1988).
7. Differences between siblings: nature and extent, see Dunn and Plomin (1990).
8. Temperament mismatch and sibling conflict, see Munn and Dunn (1989).
9. For the striking range of individual differences in sibling relationships, see for instance Dunn and Kendrick, 1982; Dunn, Slomkowski and Beardsall (1994).
10. For evidence that sibling relationships differ within the same family, see Jenkins et al. (2003).
11. Kramer and Gottman (1992).
12. Dunn and Kendrick (1982).
13. Abramovitch et al. (1986).
14. London Friendship Study, see Dunn and Cutting (1999).
15. Socio-economic status, maternal education, and social understanding, see Cutting and Dunn (1999).
16. Evidence of lack of correlation across children's various relationships, see Brown et al. (1996); Slomkowski and Dunn (1992); Youngblade and Dunn (1995a).
17. Stocker and Dunn (1990).
18. Stocker and Mantz-Simmons (unpublished).
19. Mendelson and Aboud (1991, April).
20. Longitudinal findings from Cambridge Sibling Study: see Dunn, Slomkowski and Beardsall (1994); Dunn, Slomkowski, Beardsall and Rende (1994).
21. Impact of socio-economic status on siblings in middle childhood, see Dunn, Slomkowski and Beardsall (1994).
22. East and Rook (1992).
23. Falbo (1979).

10 Implications

1. Harris (2000).
2. Piaget (1965).
3. Evidence that negative features of friendship were associated with increased later self-reported disruptive behaviour at school, see Berndt (1996).
4. Berndt (1996).

5. For correlations between friends in language ability and family background, see Dunn and Cutting (1999).
6. See Aboud and Mendelson (1996).
7. For consideration of cultural diversity in adult friendships, see Cohen (1966) for a study of adult friendship in 65 societies for which ethnographic material is available; Eisenstadt (1956); Wolf (1966). These studies distinguish between different types of friendship, and parallels are drawn with the community structures of the societies studied. Paine (1969; 1970) points out that all the types of friendship categorized in these accounts can be found within Western societies. For a general discussion of these issues see Krappmann (1998).
8. See for instance, Corsaro (1985) and Fine (1981; 1987).
9. For 'ethnographic' approaches to children's peer cultures, see Corsaro (1985); Corsaro and Rizzo (1988); Davies (1982); Fine (1987).
10. Dunn and Hughes (2001).
11. Siblings and socio-economic status, see Dunn, Slomkowski, Beardsall and Rende (1994).
12. For evidence on Chinese children, see Keller et al. (1993).
13. Krappmann (1998).
14. For French's programme of research on friendship in Indonesia, see French et al. (2003).
15. For approaches to 'within-family' differences in siblings' adjustment and response to family conflict, see O'Connor et al. (2001).

References

Aboud, F. E., and Mendelson, M. J. (1996). Determinants of friendship selection and quality: Developmental perspectives. In W. M. Bukowski, A. F. Newcomb, and W. W. Hartup (eds.), *The company they keep: Friendship in childhood and adolescence* (pp. 87–112). New York: Cambridge University Press.

Abramovitch, R., Corter, C., Pepler, D. J., and Stanhope, L. (1986). Sibling and peer interaction: A final follow-up and a comparison. *Child Development*, 57, 217–29.

Adams, D. L. (1994, unpublished). An investigation of the interrelationships among security of attachment, parenting attitudes, and the development of competence. Virginia Beach, VA.

Arsenio, W., and Lover, A. (1995). Children's conceptions of sociomoral affect: Happy victimizers, mixed emotions, and other expectancies. In M. Killen and D. Hart (eds.), *Morality in everyday life* (pp. 87–128). Cambridge: Cambridge University Press.

Asher, S. R., and Coie, J. D. (1990). *Peer rejection in childhood*. New York: Cambridge University Press.

Asher, S. R., Hymel, S., and Renshaw, R. D. (1984). Loneliness in childhood. *Child Development*, 55, 1456–64.

Asher, S. R., and Paquette, J. A. (2003). Loneliness and peer relations in childhood. *Current Directions in Psychological Science*, 12, 75–8.

Astington, J. W. (1994). *The child's discovery of the mind*. New York/London: Harper Collins/Fontana.

Astington, J. W., and Jenkins, J. M. (1995). Theory of mind development and social understanding. *Cognition and Emotion*, 9, 151–65.

Atwood, M. (1990). *Cat's eye*. London: Virago Press.

Azmitia, M. M., and Hesser, J. (1993). Why siblings are important agents of cognitive development: A comparison of siblings and peers. *Child Development*, 64, 430–44.

Azmitia, M. M., and Montgomery, R. (1993). Friendship, transactive dialogues, and the development of scientific reasoning. *Social Development*, 2, 202–21.

Bacon, F. (1625). Of friendship. In G. S. Haight (ed.), *Essays* (pp. 109–18). New York: Walter J. Black.

Barbee, A. P., Gulley, M. R., and Cunningham, M. H. (1990). Support seeking in personal relationships. *Journal of Social and Personal Relationships*, 7, 531–43.

Baron-Cohen, S. (2003). *The essential difference: Men, women, and the extreme male brain*. London: Allen Lane.

Bartsch, K., and Wellman, H. M. (1995). *Children talk about the mind*. Oxford: Oxford University Press.

Bates, J. E., Maslin, C. A., and Frankel, K. A. (1985). Attachment insecurity, child–mother interaction, and temperament as predictors of behavior-problem ratings at age three years. In I. Bretherton and E. Waters (eds.), *Monographs of the Society for Research in Child Development* (vol. 50, pp. 167–93).

Belsky, J., and Cassidy, J. (1995). Attachment theory and evidence. In M. Rutter and D. Hay (eds.), *Development through life* (pp. 373–402). Oxford: Blackwell.

Benenson, J., Apostoleris, N., and Parnass, J. (1997). Age and sex differences in dyadic and group interaction. *Developmental Psychology*, 33, 538–43.

Benenson, J., and Christakos, A. (2003). The greater fragility of females' versus males' closest same-sex friendships. *Child Development*, 74, 1123–9.

Benenson, J., Nicholson, C., Waite, A., Roy, R., and Simpson, A. (2001). The influence of group size on children's competitive behavior. *Child Development*, 72, 921–8.

Berndt, T. J. (1984). Sociomeric, social-cognitive, and behavioural measures for the study of friendship and popularity, *Friendship in normal and handicapped children* (pp. 31–52). Norwood, NJ: Ablex.

Berndt, T. J. (1996). Exploring the effects of friendship quality on social development. In W. M. Bukowski, A. F. Newcomb, and W. W. Hartup (eds.), *The company they keep*. Cambridge: Cambridge University Press.

Bigelow, B. J. (1977). Children's friendship expectations: A cognitive-developmental study. *Child Development*, 48, 246–53.

Blum, L. (1987). Particularity and responsiveness. In J. Kagan and S. Lamb (eds.), *The emergence of morality in young children* (pp. 306–37). Chicago: University of Chicago Press.

Boivin, M., and Hymel, S. (1997). Peer experiences and social self-perceptions: A sequential model. *Developmental Psychology*, 33, 135–45.

Bosso, R. (1985). Attachment quality and sibling relations. *Dissertation Abstracts International*, 47, 1293-B.

Bowlby, J. (1971). *Attachment and loss, volume 1: Attachment*. London: Hogarth Press (reprinted. by Penguin, 1978).

Bowlby, J. (1973). *Attachment and loss, volume 2: Separation*. New York: Basic Books.

Braungart, J. M., Plomin, R., and Fulker, D. W. (1992). Genetic mediation of the home environment during infancy: A sibling adoption study of the HOME. *Developmental Psychology*, 28, 1048–55.

Brenner, E., and Salovey, P. (1997). Emotion regulation during childhood. In P. Salovey and D. Sluyter (eds.), *Emotional literacy and emotional development* (pp. 168–92). New York: Basic Books.

Bretherton, I., Fritz, J., Zahn-Waxler, C., and Ridgeway, D. (1986). Learning to talk about emotions: A functionalist perspective. *Child Development*, 57, 529–48.

Brody, G. H. (1998). Sibling relationship quality: Its causes and consequences. *Annual Review of Psychology*, 49, 1–24.

Brody, G. H., Stoneman, Z., McCoy, J. K., and Forehand, R. (1992). Contemporaneous and longitudinal associations of sibling conflict with family relationship assessments and family discussions about sibling problems. *Child Development*, 63, 391–400.

Bronfenbrenner, U. (1960). Freudian theories of identification and their deviations. *Child Development*, 31, 15–40.

Brontë, C. (1994) *Jane Eyre*. London: Penguin.

Brown, G. W. (2002). Social roles, context and evolution in the origins of depression. *Journal of Health and Social Behavior*, 43, 255–76.

Brown, G. W., and Harris, T. (1978). *Social origins of depression: A study of psychiatric disorder in women*. London: Tavistock Press.

Brown, J. R., and Dunn, J. (1991). 'You can cry, mum': The social and developmental implications of talk about internal states. Special issue: Perspectives on the child's theory of mind: II. *British Journal of Developmental Psychology*, 9, 237–56.

Brown, J. R., and Dunn, J. (1992). Talk with your mother or your sibling? Developmental changes in early family conversations about feelings. *Child Development*, 63, 336–49.

Brown, J. R., and Dunn, J. (1996). Continuities in emotion understanding from three to six years. *Child Development*, 67, 789–802.

Brown, J. R., Donelan-McCall, N., and Dunn, J. (1996). Why talk about mental states? The significance of children's conversations with friends, siblings, and mothers. *Child Development*, 67, 836–49.

Brown, K. (2003). New attention to ADHD genes. *Science*, 301, 160–1.

Brownell, C. A., and Carriger, M. S. (1990). Changes in cooperation and self–other differentiation during the second year. *Child Development*, 61, 1164–74.

Bruner, J. S. (1986). *Actual minds, possible worlds*. Cambridge, MA: Harvard University Press.

Bruner, J. S. (1990). *Acts of meaning*. Cambridge, MA: Harvard University Press.

Buhrmester, D. (1990). Intimacy of friendship, interpersonal competence, and adjustment during preadolescence. *Child Development*, 61, 1101–11.

Buhrmester, D. (1996). Need fulfillment, interpersonal competence, and the developmental contexts of early adolescent friendship. In W. M. Bukowski, A. F. Newcomb, and W. W. Hartup (eds.), *The company they keep* (pp. 158–88). Cambridge: Cambridge University Press.

Buhrmester, D., and Furman, W. (1987). The development of companionship and intimacy. *Child Development*, 58, 1101–13.

Buhrmester, D., and Praeger, K. (1995). Patterns and functions of self-disclosure during childhood and adolescence. In K. J. Rotenberg (ed.), *Disclosure processes in children and adolescents* (pp. 10–56). Cambridge: Cambridge University Press.

Bukowski, W. M., and Hoza, B. (1989). Popularity and friendship: Issues in theory, measurement, and outcome. In T. J. Berndt and G. W. Ladd (eds.), *Peer relationships in child development* (pp. 15–45). New York: Wiley.

Burhans, K. K., and Dweck, C. S. (1995). Helplessness in early childhood: The role of contingent worth. *Child Development*, 66, 1719–38.

Burlingham, D., and Freud, A. (1944). *Infants without families*. London: Allen and Unwin.

Calkins, S. D., Gill, K. L., Johnson, M. C., and Smith, C. L. (1999). Emotional reactivity and emotional regulation strategies as predictors of social behavior with peers during toddlerhood. *Social Development*, 8, 310–34.

Chandler, M., Fritz, A. S., and Hala, S. (1989). Small-scale deceit: Deception as a marker of two-, three- and four-year-olds' theories of mind. *Child Development*, 60, 1263–77.

Charlesworth, W. R., and La Freniere, P. (1983). Dominance, friendships and resource utilisation in preschool children's groups. *Ethology and Sociobiology*, 4, 175–86.

Coates, J. (1986). *Women, men and language*. London: Longman.

Coates, J. (1996). *Women talk: Conversations between women friends*. Oxford: Blackwell.

Cochran, M. M., and Davila, V. (1992). Societal influences on children's peer relationships. In R. D. Parke and G. W. Ladd (eds.), *Family–peer relationships: Modes of linkage* (pp. 191–212). Hillsdale, NJ: Erlbaum.

Cohen, Y. A. (1966). Patterns of friendship. In Y. A. Cohen (ed.), *Social structure and personality* (pp. 351–86). New York: Holt, Rinehart and Winston.

Corsaro, W. A. (1985). *Friendship and peer culture in the early years*. Norwood, NJ: Ablex.

Corsaro, W. A., and Rizzo, T. A. (1988). 'Discussione' and friendship: Socialization processes in the peer culture of Italian nursery school children. *American Sociological Review*, 53, 879–94.

Crick, N. R. (1995). Relational aggression. The role of intent attributions, feelings of distress, and provocation type. *Development and Psychopathology*, 7, 313–22.

Crick, N. R. (1996). The role of overt aggression, relational aggression, and prosocial behavior in the prediction of children's future social adjustment. *Child Development*, 67, 2317–27.

Crick, N. R., and Nelson, D. A. (2002). Relational and physical victimization within friendships: Nobody told me there'd be friends like these. *Journal of Abnormal Child Psychology*, 30, 599–607.

Crouter, A. C., and Crowley, M. S. (1990). School age children's time alone with fathers and single and dual-earner families: Implications for the father–child relationship. *Journal of Early Adolescence*, 10, 296–312.

Custer, W. L. (1996). A comparison of young children's understanding of contradictory mental representations in pretense, memory and belief. *Child Development*, 67, 678–88.

Cutting, A. L., and Dunn, J. (1999). Theory of mind, emotion understanding, language and family background: Individual differences and inter-relations. *Child Development*, 70, 853–65.

Cutting, A. L., and Dunn, J. (2002). The cost of understanding other people: Social cognition predicts young children's sensitivity to criticism. *Journal of Child Psychology and Psychiatry*, 43, 849–60.

Davies, B. (1982). *Life in the classroom and playground*. London: Routledge and Kegan Paul.

Denham, S. (1986). Social cognition, prosocial behavior, and emotion in preschoolers: Contextual validation. *Child Development*, 57, 194–201.

Denham, S., and Auerbach, S. (1995). Mother–child dialogue about emotions and preschoolers' emotional competence. *Genetic, Social and General Psychology Monographs*, 121, 313–37.

Denham, S., von Salisch, M., Olthof, T., Kochanoff, A., and Caverley, S. (2002). Emotional and social development in childhood. In P. K. Smith and C. H. Hart (eds.), *Blackwell handbook of childhood social development* (pp. 307–28). Oxford: Blackwell.

Denton, K., and Zarbatany, L. (1996). Age differences in support processes in conversations between friends. *Child Development*, 67, 1360–73.

Dillard, A. (1988). *An American childhood*. New York: Harper and Row.

DiPietro, J. A. (1981). Rough and tumble play: A function of gender. *Developmental Psychology*, 17, 50–8.

Dodge, K. A., Pettit, G. S., McClaskey, C. L., and Brown, M. A. (1986). Social competence in children, *Monographs of the Society for Research in Child Development* (vol. 2, serial no. 213). Chicago: University of Chicago Press.

Dodge, K. A., Price, J. M., Coie, J. D., and Christopoulos, C. (1990). On the development of aggressive dyadic relationships in boys' peer groups. *Human Development*, 33, 200–70.

Doyle, A. (1982). Friends, acquaintances and strangers: The influence of familiarity and ethnolinguistic background on interactions. In K. H. Rubin and H. S. Ross (eds.), *Peer relations and social skills in childhood* (pp. 229–52). New York: Springer-Verlag.

Dunn, J. (1988). *The beginnings of social understanding* (first edn.). Cambridge, MA: Harvard University Press.

Dunn, J. (1993). *Young children's close relationships: Beyond attachment* (first edn., vol. 4). Newbury Park, CA: Sage.

Dunn, J. (1995). Studying relationships and social understanding. In P. Barnes (ed.), *Personal, social and emotional development of children* (pp. 336–47). Oxford: Blackwell/Open University.

Dunn, J. (1996). Arguing with siblings, friends, and mothers: Developments in relationships and understanding. In D. I. Slobin, J. Gerhardt, A. Kyratzis, and J. Guo (eds.), *Social interaction, social context, and language: Essays in honor of Susan Ervin-Tripp* (pp. 191–204). Mahwah, NJ: Erlbaum.

Dunn, J., and Brown, J. R. (1994). Affect expression in the family, children's understanding of emotions, and their interactions with others. Special issue: Children's emotions and social competence. *Merrill-Palmer Quarterly*, 40, 120–37.

Dunn, J., Brown, J. R., and Beardsall, L. (1991). Family talk about feeling states and children's later understanding of others' emotions. *Developmental Psychology*, 27, 448–55.

Dunn, J., Brown, J. R., Slomkowski, C., Tesla, C., andYoungblade, L. (1991). Young children's understanding of other people's feelings and beliefs: Individual differences and their antecedents. *Child Development*, 62, 1352–66.

Dunn, J., Brown, J. R., and Maguire, M. (1995). The development of children's moral sensibility: Individual differences and emotion understanding. *Developmental Psychology*, 31, 649–59.

Dunn, J., and Cutting, A. (1999). Understanding others, and individual differences in friendship interactions in young children. *Social Development*, 8, 201–19.

Dunn, J., Cutting, A., and Demetriou, H. (2000). Moral sensibility, understanding others, and children's friendship interactions in the preschool period. *British Journal of Developmental Psychology*, 18, 159–77.

Dunn, J., Cutting, A., and Fisher, N. (2002). Old friends, new friends: Predictors of children's perspectives on their friends at school. *Child Development*, 73, 621–35.

Dunn, J., and Dale, N. (1984). I a Daddy: 2-year-olds' collaboration in joint pretend with sibling and with mother. In I. Bretherton (ed.), *Symbolic play: The development of social understanding* (pp. 131–58). San Diego, CA: Academic Press.

Dunn, J., Davies, L., O'Connor, T., and Sturgess, W. (2000). Parents' and partners' life course and family experiences: Links with parent–child relationships in different family settings. *Journal of Child Psychology and Psychiatry*, 41, 955–68.

Dunn, J., and Deater-Deckard, K. (2001). *Children's views of their changing families*. York: York Publishing Services/Joseph Rowntree Foundation.

Dunn, J., Deater-Deckard, K., Pickering, K., O'Connor, T., Golding, J., and the ALSPAC Study Team (1998). Children's adjustment and pro-social behaviour in step-, single and non-step family settings: Findings from a community study. *Journal of Child Psychology and Psychiatry*, 39, 1083–95.

Dunn, J., and Herrera, C. (1997). Conflict resolution with friends, siblings, and mothers: A developmental perspective. *Aggressive Behavior*, 23, 343–57.

Dunn, J., and Hughes, C. (2001). 'I got some swords and you're dead!': Fantasy and friendship in young 'hard to manage' children. *Child Development*, 72, 491–505.

Dunn, J., and Kendrick, C. (1982). *Siblings: love, envy and understanding.* London: Grant McIntyre Ltd.

Dunn, J., and Plomin, R. (1990). *Separate lives: Why siblings are so different* (first edn.). New York: Basic Books.

Dunn, J., Slomkowski, C., and Beardsall, L. (1994). Sibling relationships from the preschool period through middle childhood and early adolescence. *Developmental Psychology,* 30, 315–24.

Dunn, J., Slomkowski, C., Beardsall, L., and Rende, R. (1994). Adjustment in middle childhood and early adolescence: Links with earlier and contemporary sibling relationships. *Journal of Child Psychology and Psychiatry and Allied Disciplines,* 35, 491–504.

Dunn, J., Slomkowski, C., Donelan, N., and Herrera, C. (1995). Conflict, understanding, and relationships: Developments and differences in the preschool years. Special issue: Conflict resolution in early social development. *Early Education and Development,* 6, 303–16.

Dunn, J., and Wooding, C. (1977). Play in the home and its implication for learning. In B. Tizard and D. Harvey (eds.), *The biology of play.* London: Heinemann Medical Books.

Dweck, C. S. (1986). Motivational processes affecting learning. *American Psychologist,* 41, 1040–8.

East, P. L., and Rook, K. S. (1992). Compensatory patterns of support among children's peer relationships: A test using school friends, nonschool friends, and siblings. *Developmental Psychology,* 28, 163–72.

Eckerman, C. O. (1993). Imitation and toddlers' achievement of coordinated action with others. In J. Nadel and L. Camaioni (eds.), *New perspectives in early communicative development* (pp. 116–56). New York: Routledge and Kegan Paul.

Eisenberg, N., and Fabes, R. (1998). Prosocial development. In W. Damon (ed.), *Handbook of child psychology* (vol. 3, pp. 701–78). New York: Wiley.

Eisenstadt, S. N. (1956). *From generation to generation: Age groups and social structure.* Glencoe, IL: Free Press.

Ellis, S., Rogoff, B., and Cromer, C. C. (1981). Age segregation in children's social interaction. *Developmental Psychology,* 17, 399–407.

Epstein, J. L. (1986). Friendship selection: Developmental and environmental influences. In E. Mueller and C. Cooper (eds.), *Process and outcome in peer relationships* (pp. 129–60). New York: Academic Press.

Epstein, J. L. (1992). Neighbourhoods, poverty and contact with other children. In R. D. Parke and G. W. Ladd (eds.), *Family–peer relationships: Modes of linkage.* Hillsdale, NJ: Erlbaum.

Falbo, T. (1979). Only children, stereotypes, and research. In M. Lewis and L. Rosenblum (eds.), *The child and its family* (pp. 127–42). New York: Plenum Press.

Field, T. (1984). Separation stress of young children transferring to new schools. *Developmental Psychology,* 20, 786–92.

Fine, G. A. (1981). Friends, impression management and preadolescent behaviour. In S. R. Asher and J. M. Gottman (eds.), *The development of children's friendships* (pp. 29–52). Cambridge: Cambridge University Press.

Fine, G. A. (1987). *With the boys: Little League baseball and preadolescent culture*. Chicago: University of Chicago Press.

Flannery, K. A., and Watson, M. W. (1993). Are individual differences in fantasy play related to peer acceptance levels? *Journal of Genetic Psychology*, 154, 407–16.

French, D. C., Jansen, E. A., Riansari, M., and Setiono, K. (2003). Friendships of Indonesian children: Adjustment of children who differ in friendship presence and similarity between mutual friends. *Social Development*, 12, 605–21.

Freud, A., and Dann, S. (1951). An experiment in group upbringing. *Psychoanalytic Study of the Child* (vol. 6). New York: International Universities Press.

Furman, W. (1996). The measurement of friendship perceptions: Conceptual and methodological issues. In W. M. Bukowski, A. F. Newcomb, and W. W. Hartup (eds.), *The company they keep: Friendship during childhood and adolescence* (pp. 41–65). New York: Cambridge University Press.

Furman, W., and Buhrmester, D. (1985). Children's perceptions of the personal relationships in their social network. *Developmental Psychology*, 21, 1016–24.

Garvey, C. (1990). *Play*. Cambridge, MA: Harvard University Press.

Gaskell, E. C. (1978). *The life of Charlotte Brontë*. Oxford: Oxford University Press.

Gerin, W. (1967). *Charlotte Bronte*. Oxford: Oxford University Press.

Gilligan, C., and Wiggins, G. (1987). The origins of morality in early childhood relationships. In J. Kagan and S. Lamb (eds.), *The emergence of morality in young children* (pp. 277–305). Chicago: University of Chicago Press.

Golombok, S., and Hines, M. (2002). Sex differences in social behavior. In P. K. Smith and C. H. Hart (eds.), *Blackwell handbook of childhood social development* (pp. 117–36). Oxford: Blackwell.

Goncu, A. (1993). Development of intersubjectivity in the dyadic play of preschoolers. *Early Childhood Research Quarterly*, 8, 99–116.

Goncu, A., Mistry, J., and Mosier, C. (2000). Cultural variation in the play of toddlers. *International Journal of Behavioral Development*, 24, 321–9.

Goodenough, R. G. (1987). Small group culture and the emergence of sexist behavior. In G. Spindler and L. Spindler (eds.), *Interpretive ethnography of communication* (pp. 409–45). Hillsdale NJ: Erlbaum.

Goodyer, I. M., Wright, C., and Altham, P. M. (1989). Recent friendships in anxious and depressed school age children. *Psychological Medicine*, 19, 165–74.

Gopnik, A. (1998). Wanting to get it right: Commentary on Lillard and Joseph. *Child Development*, 69, 994–5.

Gopnik, A. (2001). The meaning of make-believe. *Science*, 292, 57.

Gottlieb, L. N., and Mendelson, M. J. (1990). Parental support and firstborn girls' adaptation to the birth of a sibling. *Journal of Applied Developmental Psychology*, 11, 29–48.

Gottman, J. M. (1986a). The observation of social process. In J. M. Gottman and J. G. Parker (eds.), *Conversations of friends: Speculations on affective development* (pp. 51–100). Cambridge: Cambridge University Press.

Gottman, J. M. (1986b). The world of coordinated play: Same- and cross-sex friendship in young children. In J. M. Gottman and J. G. Parker (eds.), *Conversations of friends* (pp. 139–91). Cambridge: Cambridge University Press.

Gottman, J. M., Katz, L. F., and Hooven, C. (1997). *Meta-emotion: How families communicate emotionally*. Mahwah, NJ: Erlbaum.

Gottman, J. M., and Mettetal, G. (1986). Speculations about social and affective development: Friendship and acquaintance through adolescence. In J. Gottman and J. Parker (eds.), *Conversations of friends: Speculations on affective development* (pp. 192–237). Cambridge: Cambridge University Press.

Gottman, J. M., and Parker, J. G. (1986). *Conversations of friends: Speculations on affective development*. Cambridge: Cambridge University Press.

Greene, G. (1992). *A sort of life*. Harmondsworth: Penguin Books.

Griffiths, R. (1935). *A study of imagination in early childhood*. London: Kegan Paul.

Harkness, S., and Super, C. M. (1985). The cultural context of gender segregation in children's peer groups. *Child Development*, 56, 219–24.

Harris, K. M., and Margolin, S. P. (1991). Fathers, sons and daughters: Differential paternal involvement in parenting. *Journal of Marriage and the Family*, 53, 531–44.

Harris, P. L. (1989). *Children and emotion*. Oxford: Blackwell.

Harris, P. L. (1994). The child's understanding of emotion: Developmental change and the family environment. *Journal of Child Psychology and Psychiatry*, 35, 3–28.

Harris, P. L. (2000). *The work of the imagination*. Oxford: Blackwell.

Harter, S. (1998). The development of self-representations. In W. Damon and N. Eisenberg (eds.), *Handbook of child psychology* (vol. 3, Social, emotional and personality development, pp. 553–617). New York: Wiley.

Hartup, W. W. (1992). Conflict and friendship relations. In C. U. Shantz and W. W. Hartup (eds.), *Conflict in child and adolescent development* (pp. 186–215). Cambridge: Cambridge University Press.

Hartup, W. W. (1996). The company they keep: Friendships and their developmental significance. *Child Development*, 67, 1–13.

Hartup, W. W., and Abecassis, M. (2002). Friends and enemies. In P. K. Smith and D. Hart (eds.), *Blackwell handbook of childhood social development* (pp. 285–306). Oxford: Blackwell.

Hartup, W. W., and Laursen, B. (1991). Relationships as developmental contexts. In R. Cohen and A. W. Siegel (eds.), *Context and development* (pp. 253–79). Hillsdale, NJ: Erlbaum.

Hartup, W. W., Laursen, B., Stewart, M. I., and Eastensen, A. (1988). Conflict and the friendship relations of young children. *Child Development*, 59, 1590–1600.

Hartup, W. W., and Stevens, N. (1997). Friendships and adaptation in the life course. *Psychological Bulletin*, 121, 355–70.

Haselarger, G. J. T., Hartup, W. W., van Lieshout, C. F. M., and Riksen-Walraven, J. M. A. (1998). Similarities between friends and nonfriends in middle childhood. *Child Development*, 69, 1198–1208.

Herrera, C., and Dunn, J. (1997). Early experiences with family conflict: Implications for arguments with a close friend. *Developmental Psychology*, 33, 869–81.

Hetherington, E. M. (1999). Should we stay together for the sake of the children? In E. M. Hetherington (ed.), *Coping with divorce, single-parenting, and remarriage: A risk and resiliency perspective* (pp. 93–116). Hillsdale, NJ: Erlbaum.

Hetherington, E. M., and Stanley-Hagan, M. (1999). The adjustment of children with divorced parents: A risk and resiliency perspective. *Journal of Child Psychology and Psychiatry*, 40, 129–40.

Hickling, A., Wellman, H. M., and Gottfried, G. M. (1998). Preschoolers' understanding of others' mental attitudes toward pretend happenings. *British Journal of Developmental Psychology*, 15, 339–54.

Hinde, R. A. (1979). *Towards understanding relationships*. London: Academic Press.

Hinde, R. A. (1995). A suggested structure for a science of relationships. *Personal Relationships*, 2, 1–15.

Hinde, R. A., Titmus, G., Easton, D., and Tamplin, A. (1985). Incidence of 'friendship' and behavior with strong associates versus non-associates in preschoolers. *Child Development*, 41, 234–45.

Hodges, E. V. E., Boivin, M., Vitaro, F., and Bukowski, W. M. (1999). The power of friendship: Protection against an escalating cycle of peer victimization. *Developmental Psychology*, 35, 94–101.

Hodges, E. V. E., Malone, M. J., and Perry, D. G. (1995). *Behavioral and social antecedents and consequences of victimization by peers*. Paper presented at the presentation at biennial meetings of the Society for Research in Child Development, Indianapolis, IN.

Hodges, E. V. E., Malone, M. J., and Perry, D. G. (1997). Individual risk and social risk as interacting determinants of victimization in the peer group. *Developmental Psychology*, 33, 1032–9.

Hodges, J., and Tizard, B. (1989). Social and family relationships of ex-institutional adolescents. *Journal of Child Psychology and Psychiatry*, 30, 77–98.

Howe, N. (1991). Sibling-directed internal state language, perspective-taking, and the sibling relationship. *Child Development*, 62, 1503–12.

Howes, C. (1988). Peer interaction of young children. *Monographs of the Society for Research in Child Development*, 53, serial no. 217.

Howes, C. (1991). A comparison of preschool behaviors with peers when children enroll in child-care as infants or older children. *Journal of Reproductive and Infant Psychology*, 9, 105–15.

Howes, C. (1992). *The collaborative construction of pretend*. Albany: State University of New York Press.

Howes, C. (1996). The earliest friendships. In W. M. Bukowski, A. F. Newcomb, and W. W. Hartup (eds.), *The company they keep: Friendship in childhood and adolescence* (pp. 66–86). New York: Cambridge University Press.

Howes, C., and Phillipsen, L. (1992). Gender and friendship: Relationships within peer groups of young children. *Social Development*, 1, 230–42.

Howes, C., Unger, O., and Matheson, C. (1992). *The collaborative construction of pretend: Social pretend play functions*. Albany: State University of New York Press.

Howes, C., Unger, O., and Seidner, L. B. (1989). Social pretend play in toddlers: Parallels with social play and with solitary pretend. *Child Development*, 60, 77–84.

Howes, C., and Wu, F. (1990). Peer interactions and friendships in an ethnically diverse school setting. *Child Development*, 61, 537–41.

Hoza, B. (1989). Development and validation of a method for classifying children's social status based on two types of measures: Popularity and chumship. Unpublished manuscript. (Cited by A. F. Newcomb and C. L. Bagwell (1996), The developmental significance of children's friendship relations. In W. M. Bukowski, A. F. Newcomb, and W. W. Hartup (eds.), *The company they keep* (pp. 289–321). Cambridge: Cambridge University Press.)

Hughes, C., Cutting, A. L., and Dunn, J. (2001). Acting nasty in the face of failure? Longitudinal observations of 'hard to manage' children playing a rigged competitive game with a friend. *Journal of Abnormal Child Psychology*, 29, 403–16.

Hughes, C., and Dunn, J. (1997). 'Pretend you didn't know': Preschoolers' talk about mental states in pretend play. *Cognitive Development*, 12, 477–99.

Hughes, C., and Dunn, J. (1998). Understanding mind and emotion understanding: Longitudinal associations with mental state talk between friends. *Developmental Psychology*, 34(5), 1026–37.

Hughes, C., and Dunn, J. (2000). Hedonism or empathy?: Hard-to-manage children's moral awareness, and links with cognitive and maternal characteristics. *British Journal of Developmental Psychology*, 18, 227–45.

Hughes, C., Jaffee, S., Happe, F., Taylor, A., Caspi, A. and Moffitt, T. E. (2004). Origins of individual differences in theory of mind: From nature to nurture? *Child Development* (in press).

Hughes, C., White, A., Sharpen, J., and Dunn, J. (2000). Antisocial, angry and unsympathetic: 'Hard to manage' preschoolers' peer problems, and possible social and cognitive influences. *Journal of Child Psychology and Psychiatry*, 41, 169–79.

Hymel, S., Bowker, A., and Woody, E. (1993). Aggressive versus withdrawn unpopular children: Variations in peer and self-perceptions in multiple domains. *Child Development*, 64, 879–96.

Hymel, S., Wagner, E., and Butler, L. J. (1990). Reputational bias: View from the peer group. In S. R. Asher and J. D. Coie (eds.), *Peer rejection in childhood* (pp. 156–86). New York: Cambridge University Press.

Isaacs, S. (1937). *Social development in children: A study of beginnings.* New York: Harcourt Brace.

Isley, S., O'Neil, R., Clatfelter, D., and Parke, R. D. (1999). Parent and child expressed affect and children's social competence: Modelling direct and indirect pathways. *Developmental Psychology*, 35, 547–60.

Jacklin, C. N. (1981). Methodological issues in the study of sex-related differences. *Developmental Review*, 1, 226–73.

Jenkins, J., and Smith, M. (1990). Factors protecting children living in disharmonious homes: Maternal reports. *Journal of the American Academy of Child and Adolescent Psychiatry*, 29, 60–9.

Jenkins, J., Turrell, S. L., Kogushi, Y., Lollis, S., and Ross, H. S. (2003). A longitudinal investigation of the dynamics of mental state talk in families. *Child Development*, 74, 905–20.

Joseph, R. M. (1998). Intention and knowledge in preschoolers' conception of pretend. *Child Development*, 69, 966–80.

Kaye, C. D. (1991, unpublished). Do low-accepted children benefit from having friends? Doctoral dissertation, University of Texas, Dallas.

Keller, M., Schuster, P., and Edelstein, W. (1993). Universelle und differentielle Aspeckte in der Entwicklung sozio-moralischen Denkens. Ergebnisse einer Untersuchung mit isladnischen und chinesischen Kindern [Universal and differential aspects of the development of socio-moral reasoning. Results from a study of Icelandic and Chinese children]. *Zeitschrift fuer Sozialisationnsforschung un Erziehungssoziologie*, 13, 149–60.

Kochanska, G. (1993). Towards a synthesis of parental socialization and child temperament in early development of conscience. *Child Development*, 64, 326–47.

Kramer, L., and Gottman, J. M. (1992). Becoming a sibling: 'With a little help from my friends'. *Developmental Psychology*, 28, 685–99.

Krappmann, L. (1998). Amicitia, drujba, shin-yu, philia, Freundschaft, friendship: On the cultural diversity of a human relationship. In W. M. Bukowski and A. F. Newcomb (eds.), *The company they keep: Friendship in childhood and adolescence* (pp. 19–40). New York: Cambridge University Press.

Kreppner, J. M. (2003). Friendship quality, friendship representations, and understanding of mental and emotional states in children following severe emotional deprivation. Doctoral dissertation, University of London.

Kreppner, J. M., and the English and Romanian Adoptees Study Team (2003, April). *Children's understanding of Friendship following early institutional rearing: An 11-year follow up*. Presented at the Biennial meetings of the Society for Research in Child Development, Tampa, FL.

Kreppner, J. M., O'Connor, T. G., Dunn, J., Andersen-Wood, L., English and Romanian Adoptees (ERA) Study Team (1999). The pretend and social role play of children exposed to early severe deprivation. *British Journal of Developmental Psychology*, 17, 319–32.

Ladd, G. W. (1983). Social networks of popular, average and rejected children in school settings. *Merrill-Palmer Quarterly*, 29, 283–307.

Ladd, G. W. (1990). Having friends, keeping friends, making friends, and being liked by peers in the classroom: Predictors of children's early school adjustment? *Child Development*, 61, 1081–1100.

Ladd, G. W. (1999). Peer relationships and social competence during early and middle childhood. *Annual Review of Psychology*, 50, 333–59.

Ladd, G. W., and Kochenderfer, B. (1996). Linkages between friendship and adjustment during early school transitions. In W. M. Bukowski, A. F. Newcomb, and W. W. Hartup (eds.), *The company they keep* (pp. 322–45). Cambridge: Cambridge University Press.

Ladd, G. W., Kochenderfer, B., and Coleman, C. (1996). Friendship quality as a predictor of young children's early school adjustment. *Child Development*, 67, 1103–18.

Ladd, G. W., Price, J. M., and Hart, C. H. (1990). Preschoolers' behavioral orientations and patterns of peer contact: Predictors of social status? In S. R. Asher and J. D. Coie (eds.), *Peer rejection in childhood* (pp. 90–115). New York: Cambridge University Press.

Laible, D. J., and Thompson, R. A. (1998). Attachment and emotional understanding in preschool children. *Developmental Psychology*, 34, 1038–45.

Laible, D. J., and Thompson, R. A. (2000). Mother–child discourse, attachment security, shared positive affect, and early conscience development. *Child Development*, 71, 1424–40.

Lewis, C., Freeman, N. H., Hagestad, C., and Douglas, H. (1994). Narrative access and production in preschoolers' false belief reasoning. *Cognitive Development*, 9, 397–424.

Lewis, M., and Feiring, C. (1989). Early predictors of childhood friendship. In T. J. Berndt and G. W. Ladd (eds.), *Peer relationships in child development*. New York: Wiley.

Lieberman, A. F. (1977). Preschoolers' competence with a peer: Relations with attachment and peer experience. *Child Development*, 48, 1277–87.

Lillard, A. S. (1998). Wanting to be it: Children's understanding of intentions underlying pretense. *Child Development*, 69, 981–93.

Loehlin, J. C. (1992). *Genes and environment in personality development*. Newbury Park, CA: Sage.

Lollis, S. P., Ross, H. S., and Tate, H. (1992). Parents' regulation of children's peer interactions: Direct influences. In R. D. Parke and G. W. Ladd (eds.), *Family–peer relationships: Modes of linkage* (pp. 255–81). Hillsdale, NJ: Erlbaum.

Lyons-Ruth, K., Alpern, L., and Repacholi, B. (1993). Disorganised infant attachment classification and maternal psychosocial problems as predictors of hostile-aggressive behavior in the preschool classroom. *Child Development*, 64, 572–85.

Maccoby, E. E. (1988). Gender as a social category. *Developmental Psychology*, 24, 755–65.

Maccoby, E. E. (1990). Gender as a social category. In S. Chess and E. Hertzig (eds.), *Annual progress in child psychiatry and child development*. New York: Brunner/Mazil.

Maccoby, E. E. (1998). *The two sexes: Growing up apart, coming together*. Cambridge, MA: Bellknap.

Maccoby, E. E., and Jacklin, C. N. (1987). Gender segregation in childhood. In H. W. Reese (ed.), *Advances in child development and behaviour* (vol. 4). Orlando, FL: Academic Press.

MacDonald, K., and Parke, R. (1984). Bridging the gap: Parent–child play interaction and peer interactive competence. *Child Development*, 55, 1265–77.

Maguire, M., and Dunn, J. (1997). Friendships in early childhood, and social understanding. *International Journal of Behavioral Development*, 21, 669–86.

Malone, M. J., and Perry, D. G. (1995, March). Features of aggressive and victimized children's friendships and affiliative preferences. Paper presented at the Society for Research in Child Development, Indianapolis, IN.

Manke, B., McGuire, S., Reiss, D., Hetherington, E. M., and Plomin, R. (1995). Genetic contributions to adolescents' extrafamilial social interactions: teachers, best friends, and peers. *Social Development*, 4(3), 238–56.

Mannarino, A. P. (1976). Friendship patterns and altruistic behaviour in preadolescent males. *Developmental Psychology*, 12, 555–6.

Martin, C. L., and Fabes, R. A. (2001). The stability and consequences of young children's same-sex peer interactions. *Developmental Psychology*, 37, 431–46.

McGuire, K. D., and Weisz, J. R. (1982). Social cognition and behaviour correlates of preadolescent chumship. *Child Development*, 53, 1478–84.

Meins, E., and Fernyhough, C. (1999). Linguistic acquisitional style and mentalising development: The role of maternal mind-mindedness. *Cognitive Development*, 14, 363–80.

Meins, E., Fernyhough, C., Russell, J. T., and Clarke-Carter, D. (1998). Security of attachment as a predictor of symbolic and mentalising abilities: A longitudinal study. *Social Development*, 7, 1–24.

Mendelson, M. J., and Aboud, F. E. (1991, April). *Kindergartners' personality, popularity and friendships*. Paper presented at the Poster presentation at the biennial meetings of the Society for Research in Child Development, Seattle, Washington.

Moore, C., Furrow, D., Chiasson, L., and Patriquin, M. (1994). Developmental relationships between production and comprehension of mental terms. *First Language*, 14, 1–17.

Munn, P., and Dunn, J. (1989). Temperament and the developing relationship between siblings. *International Journal of Behavioral Development*, 12, 433–51.

Murphy, L. B. (1937). *Social behavior and child personality: An exploratory study of some roots of sympathy*. New York: Columbia University Press.

Newcomb, A. F., and Bagwell, C. L. (1996). The developmental significance of children's friendship relations. In W. M. Bukowski, A. F. Newcomb, and W. W. Hartup (eds.), *The company they keep* (pp. 289–321). Cambridge: Cambridge University Press.

Newcomb, M. D. (1990). Social support and personal characteristics: A developmental and international perspective. *Journal of Social and Clinical Psychology*, 9, 54–68.

Newson, J., and Newson, E. (1970). *Four years old in an urban community*. Harmondsworth: Penguin Books.

Newson, J., and Newson, E. (1980). *Seven years old in an urban community*. Harmondsworth: Penguin Books.

O'Connor, T., Dunn, J., Jenkins, J., Pickering, K., and Rasbash, J. (2001). Family settings and children's adjustment: Differential adjustment within and across families. *British Journal of Psychiatry*, 179, 110–15.

Olweus, D. (1978). *Aggression in the schools: Bullies and whipping boys*. Washington, DC: Hemisphere Press (Wiley).

Olweus, D. (1993). *Bullying: What we know and what we can do*. Oxford: Blackwell.

Opie, I., and Opie, P. (1969). *Children's games in street and playground*. Oxford: Clarendon Press.

Paine, R. (1969). In search of friendship: An exploratory analysis in 'middle-class' culture. *Man*, 4, 505–24.

Paine, R. (1970). Anthropological approaches to friendship. *Humanitas*, 6, 139–59.

Painter, G. D. (1971). *Marcel Proust: A biography*. London: Chatto and Windus.

Paley, V. G. (1984). *Boys and Girls: Superheroes in the doll corner*. Chicago: University of Chicago Press.

Paley, V. G. (1988). *Bad guys don't have birthdays: Fantasy play at four*. Chicago: University of Chicago Press.

Park, K., and Waters, E. (1989). Security of attachment and preschool friendships. *Child Development*, 60, 1076–81.

Parke, R. D. (1997). *Fatherhood*. Cambridge, MA: Harvard University Press.

Parke, R. D., Kim, M., Flyr, M., et al. (2001). Managing marital conflict: Links with children's peer relationships. In J. Grych and F. Fincham (eds.), *Interparental conflict and child development: Theory, research and application* (pp. 291–314). New York: Cambridge University Press.

Parke, R. D., and Ladd, G. W. (1992). *Family–peer relationships: Modes of linkage*. Hillsdale, NJ: Erlbaum.

Parker, J. G., and Asher, S. R. (1993). Friendship and friendship quality in middle childhood: Links with peer group acceptance and feelings of loneliness and social dissatisfaction. *Developmental Psychology*, 29, 611–21.

Parker, J. G., and Gottman, J. M. (1989). Social and emotional development in a relational context: Friendship from early childhood to adolescence. In T. J. Berndt and G. W. Ladd (eds.), *Peer relationships in child development* (pp. 95–131). New York: Wiley.

Parker, J., and Seal, J. (1996). Forming, losing, renewing, and replacing friendships: Applying temporal parameters to the assessment of children's friendship experiences. *Child Development*, 67, 2248–68.

Patterson, C. J., Griesler, P. C., Vaden, N. A., and Kupersmidt, J. B. (1992). Family economic circumstances, life transitions, and children's peer relations. In R. D. Parke and G. W. Ladd (eds.), *Family–Peer Relationships: Modes of Linkage* (pp. 385–424). Hillsdale, NJ: Erlbaum.

Perner, J. (1991). *Understanding the representational mind*. Cambridge, MA: MIT Press.

Perry, D. G., Perry, L. C., and Kennedy, E. (1992). Conflict and the development of antisocial behavior. In C. U. Shantz and W. W. Hartup (ed.), *Conflict in child and adolescent development* (pp. 301–29). New York: Cambridge University Press.

Peterson, C. C., and Siegal, M. (2000). Insights into theory of mind from deafness and autism. *Mind and Language*, 15, 123–45.

Piaget, J. (1932/1965). *The moral judgment of the child*. New York: Academic Press.

Pike, A., and Atzaba-Poria, N. (2003). Do sibling and friend relationships share the same temperamental origins? A twin study. *Journal of Child Psychology and Psychiatry*, 44, 598–611.

Plomin, R., and Neiderhiser, J. M. (1992). Genetics and experience. *Current Directions in Psychological Science*, 1, 160–3.

Renshaw, P. D., and Brown, P. J. (1993). Loneliness in middle childhood: Concurrent and longitudinal predictors. *Child Development*, 64, 271–84.

Renshaw, P. D., and Parke, R. D. (1992). Family and peer relationships in historical perspective. In R. D. Parke and G. W. Ladd (eds.), *Family–peer relationships: Modes of linkage* (pp. 35–74). Hillsdale, NJ: Erlbaum.

Rigby, K. (2002). Bullying in childhood. In P. K. Smith and C. Hart (eds.), *Blackwell handbook of childhood social development* (pp. 549–68). Oxford: Blackwell.

Ronald, A., Happé, F., Hughes, C., and Plomin, R. (forthcoming). The nature and nurture of nice and nasty theory of mind. *Social Development*.

Ross, H. S. (1982). The establishment of social games amongst toddlers. *Developmental Psychology*, 18, 509–18.

Ross, H. S., and Conant, C. L. (1992). The social structure of early conflict. Interaction, relationships, and alliances. In C. U. Shantz and W. W. Hartup (eds.), *Conflict in child and adolescent development* (pp. 153–85). Cambridge: Cambridge University Press.

Ross, H. S., Conant, C. L., Cheyne, J. A., and Alevizos, E. (1992). Relationships and alliances in the social interaction of kibbutz toddlers. *Social development*, 1, 1–17.

Ross, H. S., and Lollis, S. P. (1989). A social relations analysis of toddler peer relationships. *Child Development*, 60, 1082–91.

Ross, H. S., Lollis, S. P., and Elliot, C. (1982). Toddler–peer communication. In K. H. Rubin and H. S. Ross (eds.), *Peer relationships and social skills in childhood*. New York: Springer-Verlag.

Rotenberg, K. J., and Hymel, S. (1999). *Loneliness in childhood and adolescence*. Cambridge: Cambridge University Press.

Rowe, D. C. (1989). Families and peers. In T. J. Berndt and G. W. Ladd (eds.), *Peer relationships in child development* (pp. 274–399). New York: Wiley.

Rubin, K. H., Both, L., Zahn-Waxler, C., Cummings, E. M., and Wilkinson, M. (1991). Dyadic play behaviors of well and depressed mothers. *Development and Psychopathology*, 3, 243–51.

Rubin, K. H., Bukowski, W., and Parker, J. G. (1998). Peer interactions, relationships and groups. In W. Damon and N. Eisenberg (eds.), *Handbook of child psychology* (vol. 3) (pp. 619–700). New York: Wiley.

Rubin, K. H., Burgess, K. B., and Coplan, R. J. (2002). Social withdrawal and shyness. In P. K. Smith and C. H. Hart (eds.), *Blackwell handbook of childhood social development* (pp. 329–52). Oxford: Blackwell.

Ruble, D., and Martin, C. L. (1998). Gender development, social, emotional and personality development. In W. Damon (ed.), *Handbook of child psychology* (vol. 3). New York: Wiley.

Rutter, M., and the English and Romanian Adoptees (ERA) Study Team. (1998). Developmental catch-up, and deficit, following adoption after severe global early privation. *Journal of Child Psychology and Psychiatry*, 39, 465–76.

Saarni, C., Mumme, D. L., and Campos, J. J. (1998). Emotional development: Action, communication and understanding. In W. Damon (ed.), *Handbook of child psychology* (vol. 3: Social, emotional, and personality development, pp. 237–309). New York: Wiley.

Schadler, M., and Ayers-Nachamkin, B. (1983). The development of excuse-making. In C. R. Snyder, R. L. Higgins, and R. J. Stucky (eds.), *Excuses: Masquerades in search of grace* (pp. 159–83). New York: Wiley.

Schneider, B. H., Atkinson, L., and Tardif, C. (2001). Child–parent attachment and children's peer relations: A quantitative review. *Developmental Psychology*, 37, 86–100.

Schofield, J. W. (1982). *Black and white in school*. New York: Praeger.

Sebanc, A. M. (2003). The friendship features of preschool children: Links with prosocial behavior and aggression. *Social Development*, 12, 249–67.

Serbin, L. A., Moller, L. C., J, G., Powlishta, K. K., and Colbourne, K. A. (1994). The emergence of sex segregation in toddler playgroups. *New Directions in Child Development*, 65, 7–17.

Serbin, L. A., Sprofkin, C., Elman, M., and Doyle, A. B. (1982). The early development of sex differentiated patterns of social influence. *Canadian Journal of Social Science*, 14, 350–63.

Shatz, M., and Gelman, R. (1973). The development of communication skills: Modifications in the speech of young children as a function of the listener. *Monographs of the Society for Research in Child Development*, 38.

Simpkins, S. D., and Parke, R. D. (2001). The relations between parental friendships and children's friendships: Self–report and observational analysis. *Child Development*, 72, 569–82.

Slomkowski, C. L., and Dunn, J. (1992). Arguments and relationships within the family: Differences in young children's disputes with mother and sibling. *Developmental Psychology*, 28, 919–24.

Slomkowski, C., and Dunn, J. (1996). Young children's understanding of other people's beliefs and feelings and their connected communication with friends. *Developmental Psychology*, 32, 442–7.

Slomkowski, C. L., and Killen, M. (1992). Young children's conceptions of transgressions with friends and nonfriends. *International Journal of Behavioral Development*, 15, 247–58.

Smith, P. K., Morita, J., Junger–Tas, D., Olweus, D., Catalalano, R., and Slee, P. T. (1999). *The nature of school bullying: A cross national perspective*. London: Routledge.

Smith, P. K., and Sharp, S. (eds.) (1994). *School bullying: Insights and perspectives*. London: Routledge.

Sodian, B., and Frith, U. (1992). Deception and sabotage in autistic, retarded and normal children. *Journal of Child Psychology and Psychiatry*, 33, 591–605.

Stewart, R. B. (1983). Sibling attachment relationships: Child–infant interaction in the Strange Situation. *Developmental Psychology*, 19, 192–9.

Stewart, R. B., and Marvin, R. S. (1984). Sibling relations: The role of conceptual perspective taking in the ontogeny of sibling caregiving. *Child Development*, 55, 1322–32.

Stewart, R. B, Mobley, L., Van Tuyl, S., and Salvador, M. (1987). The firstborn's adjustment to the birth of a sibling. *Child Development*, 58, 341–55.

Stocker, C., and Dunn, J. (1990). Sibling relationships in childhood: Links with friendships and peer relationships. *British Journal of Developmental Psychology*, 8, 227–44.

Stocker, C., and Mantz-Simmons, L. Children's friendships and peer status: Links with family relationships, temperament and social skills. Unpublished manuscript. University of Denver.

Sullivan, H. (1953). *The interpersonal theory of psychiatry*. New York: Norton.

Sutton, J., Smith, P. K. and Swettenham, J. (1999). Bullying and theory of mind: A critique of the 'social skills deficit' view of anti-social behaviour. *Social Development*, 8, 117–27.

Tamplin, A. (1989). A study of six-year-olds' friendships. Doctoral dissertation, University of Cambridge, Cambridge.

Tannen, D. (1990). *You just don't understand*. New York: Ballantine.

Taylor, M. (1999). *Imaginary companions and the children who create them.* Oxford: Oxford University Press.

Tesla, C., and Dunn, J. (1992). Getting along or getting your own way: The development of young children's use of argument in conflicts with mother and sibling. *Social Development,* 1, 107–21.

Teti, D. M., and Ablard, K. E. (1989). Security of attachment and infant–sibling relationships: A laboratory study. *Child Development,* 60, 1519–28.

Thompson, R. A. (1998). Early sociopersonality development. In W. Damon (ed.), *Handbook of child psychology* (vol. 3; Social, emotional and personality development, pp. 25–104). New York: Wiley.

Thompson, R. A. (1991). Emotion and self-regulation. Paper presented at the Socioemotional development. Nebraska symposium on motivation.

Thorne, B. (1993). *Gender play: Girls and boys in school.* New Brunswick, NJ: Rutgers University Press.

Trevarthen, C. (1989). Origins and directions for the concept of infant intersubjectivity. *SRCD Newsletter* (pp. 1–4). Chicago: University of Chicago Press.

Trevarthen, C., and Hubley, P. (1978). Secondary intersubjectivity: Confidence, confiding and acts of meaning in the first year, *Action, gesture and symbol: The emergence of language* (pp. 183–229). London: Academic Press.

Trollope, A. (1999). *An Autobiography.* Oxford: Oxford's World Classics.

Twain, M. (1966). *The autobiography of Mark Twain.* New York: Harper and Row Perennial.

Updike, J. (1965). The dogwood tree: A boyhood. In J. Updike, *Assorted prose* (pp. 77–8). Harmondsworth: Penguin Books.

Vandell, D. L. (1987). Baby sister, baby brother: Reactions to the birth of a sibling and patterns of early sibling relations. *Journal of Children in Contemporary society,* 19, 13–37.

Ward, M. J., Vaughn, B. E., and Robb, M. D. (1988). Socio-emotional adaptation and infant–mother attachment in siblings: Role of the mother in cross-sibling consistency. *Child Development,* 59, 643–51.

Wallerstein, J. S., and Kelly, J. B. (1980). *Surviving the breakup: How children and parents cope with divorce.* New York: Basic Books.

Wasserstein, S. B., and LaGreca, A. M. (1996). Can peer support buffer against behavioural consequences of parental discord? *Journal of Clinical Child Psychology,* 25, 177–82.

Weiss, R. S. (1974). The provisions of social relationships, *Doing unto others.* Englewood, NJ: Prentice Hall.

Wellman, H. M. (1990). *The child's theory of mind.* Cambridge, MA: MIT Press.

Wellman, H. M., Cross, D., and Watson, J. (2001). Meta-analysis of theory of mind development: The truth about false belief. *Child Development,* 72, 655–84.

Wellman, H. M., Harris, P., Banerjee, M., and Sinclair, A. (1995). Early understanding of emotion: Evidence from natural language. *Cognition and Emotion,* 9, 117–49.

Whiting, B. B., and Edwards, C. P. (1988). *Children of different worlds*. Cambridge, MA: Harvard University Press.

Wolf, E. R. (1966). Kinship, friendship, and patron–client relations in complex societies. In M. Benton (ed.), *The social anthropology of complex societies* (pp. 11–22). London: Tavistock.

Wolke, D., Woods, S., Bloomfield, L., and Karstadt, L. (2000). The association between direct and relational bullying and behaviour problems among primary school children. *Journal of Child Psychology and Psychiatry*, 41, 989–1002.

Wulff, H. (1988). *Twenty girls: Growing up, ethnicity, and excitement in a south London microculture*. Stockholm: University of Stockholm Press.

Youngblade, L. M., and Belsky, J. (1992). Child–parent antecedents of five-year-olds' close friendships: A longitudinal analysis. *Developmental Psychology*, 28, 700–13.

Youngblade, L. M., and Dunn, J. (1995a). Individual differences in young children's pretend play with mother and sibling: Links to relationships and understanding of other people's feelings and beliefs. *Child Development*, 66, 1472–92.

Youngblade, L. M., and Dunn, J. (1995b). Social pretend with mother and sibling: Individual differences and social understanding. In A. Pellegrini (ed.), *The future of play theory: Essays in honor of Brian Sutton-Smith* (pp. 221–40). New York: SUNY Press.

Youngblade, L. M., Park, K. A., and Belsky, J. (1993). Measurement of young children's close friendship: A comparison of two independent assessment systems and their association with attachment security. *International Journal of Behavioral Development*, 16, 563–88.

Zahn-Waxler, C., Cummings, E. M., McKnew, D. H., and Radke-Yarrow, M. (1984). Altruism, aggression, and social interactions in young children with a manic-depressive parent. *Child Development*, 55, 112–22.

Zerwas, S. C., and Brownell, C. A. (2003, April). Partners in pretend play. Paper presented at the Society for Research in Child Development, Tampa, FL.

Name Index

Subject Index